COOKING MY WAY BACK HOME

Cooking
MY WAY
BACK HOME

Recipes from San Francisco's
TOWN HALL, ANCHOR & HOPE,
and SALT HOUSE

MITCHELL ROSENTHAL

with Jon Pult

Foreword by Wolfgang Puck

Photography by PAIGE GREEN

TEN SPEED PRESS
Berkeley

CONTENTS

FOREWORD

By Wolfgang Puck

IN 1989, I GOT A CALL FROM MY OLD FRIEND SEPPI RENGGLI, the legendary executive chef of The Four Seasons in New York. He told me he knew a very talented young guy who had cooked under him, and thought that maybe this budding chef could bloom in California, especially with his love of new ingredients and cuisines from around the world.

That's how I first heard of Mitch Rosenthal. The moment I met him, I was impressed not only by his talent and his enthusiasm for cooking good food but also by how much he knew—especially for someone who was basically self-taught, having risen from a New Jersey deli to apprentice in some of the finest kitchens in the country.

Mitch's mind was wide open to new experiences, a quality I love to see not only in cooks but in people in general. I liked him immediately.

I hired Mitch as a sous-chef on the opening kitchen team in my new San Francisco restaurant, Postrio. A year later, he left us to soak up even more culinary experiences, traveling in Asia and Europe. I was sorry to see him go, so when he returned to the United States I immediately offered him a job at my seafood restaurant Granita in Malibu, where the guests enjoyed so many of his exciting new dishes inspired by Mitch's travels.

In 1994, I offered Mitch and his brother, Steve, the opportunity to take over the kitchen of Postrio as its executive chefs. Even though he is someone so in love with travel and new experiences, Mitch stayed for eight years. Maybe that was because, though both brothers are great cooks, Steve took care of the management side of things, leaving Mitch to keep experimenting and trying new things at the stove.

What amazed me most about Mitch in his years at Postrio was what a positive influence he was on all the cooks around him. He was a good motivator, getting his young crew excited and always on the lookout for the best ingredients. Mitch has that rare ability to make other people feel the same passion he feels for good food.

I think Mitch's ability to share his passion in the kitchen is what makes his book, *Cooking My Way Back Home*, such a rare and wonderful experience for home cooks.

Mitch is a man who likes big flavors and sharp contrasts of taste and texture in the food he cooks, and he understands the best ways to combine and cook great ingredients to get such bold effects. After all, this is a guy who once served Cajun food in a Jewish deli!

Mitch has traveled the world, and he brings its influences back to his kitchen. He has a very good touch with seasonings, introducing a wide spectrum of flavors to his food. There's never a boring moment in Mitch's cooking; it's always exciting and full of discovery. That sense of excitement and discovery is why so many people love his restaurants. And that is why you will enjoy this book.

Looking through its pages, I find so many dishes I would love to eat right now, because I already know how good they taste. You don't have to be Jewish to enjoy his Grandma's Chopped Chicken Liver. His interpretation of Chicken and Andouille Sausage Gumbo is as good as anything you could find in Louisiana. As for his Bacon-Wrapped Stuffed Quail with Clams, I remember thinking when he first made that dish for me that it would be a strange combination; but I ended up eating two orders, marveling at how it reminded me of something you might find along the coast of Portugal or the Mediterranean, a perfect dish for San Francisco. And his Chocolate Butterscotch Pot de Crème from Town Hall is what every dessert should measure up to: Chocolaty, creamy, and rich with caramel, it has all of my favorite sweet flavors combined in one spectacular yet simple recipe.

It all tastes so good, and the recipes are so well written that you will get great results. It's nothing less than I would expect from Mitch Rosenthal. He has every reason to be satisfied with what he has accomplished. And yet, as he always has, Mitch just keeps on looking for new tastes, continues to experiment, always coming up with exciting new dishes for us all to try.

INTRODUCTION

A little about me

I GREW UP IN RESTAURANT KITCHENS. Honestly. From the time I was fifteen and washing dishes in a Jewish deli in Jersey until today, my entire life has been spent wearing kitchen whites. My chosen trade has allowed me opportunities I never thought possible. I've worked in some of the best restaurants in the country, and now, with my partners, Doug Washington and my brother, Steven Rosenthal, I own three restaurants in San Francisco and one in Portland, Oregon. Cooking has taken me places I never dreamed of. I've eaten food at roadside stands in Thailand and grand brasseries in Paris, sampled world-class smoked pork in rural Kansas and Iberian pork fat on the Catalan coast of Spain. But there's one place cooking never took me, and that's home.

I've survived much of the last thirty-five years on staff meals. The last thing I wanted to do after a double shift on the hot line was to go home and cook. But more recently things have changed. After establishing Town Hall, getting Salt House off the ground, and laying the groundwork for Anchor & Hope, I realized I was becoming a restaurateur. With each project, I was moving a little bit further away from the visceral pleasures of the kitchen. The less I cooked at work, the more I missed the simple act of cooking, of using a set of skills to create something memorable and delicious.

I offer this background by way of explanation for what I'm about to say: I had never really cooked at home until recently. Sure, I would whip up an omelet every once in a while, and knock out a turkey at Thanksgiving. But the experience of cooking for a few familiar faces around the kitchen table is new to me. It was only when testing the recipes in this book for the home cook that I actually cooked, really cooked, in my home kitchen. You see, I'm old school. I came up when kitchens still functioned on the apprentice system. I learned through the shared knowledge of the cook and a list of ingredients. Someone took you under his or her wing, showed you the proverbial ropes, and it was trial by smoke and fire. Those ingredient lists were just that: no amounts, just a list. I learned to cook by instinct, by feel. The idea of measuring a tablespoon of, say, black pepper, well, I just wasn't used to it. This produced some tense moments in the kitchen when my wife, Mary, and I first began testing these recipes at home. She's also a cook, and a good one, so when, by reflex, I would toss a couple of healthy pinches of salt into a pot of pozole, there would be a sharp, "Mitch, what are you doing? Did you write it down?"

M Y LIFE IN RESTAURANTS STARTED IN 1975, when I got a job washing dishes in the kitchen of a small Jewish joint in Edison, New Jersey, called Jack Cooper's Celebrity Delicatessen. It was run by Tom Plaganis, a big Greek guy who was passionate about food. After a few years of scrubbing pots and rinsing plates, he began to let me cover the breaks for the short-order cooks. Tom taught me not only how to handle a sauté pan, but also how to handle myself in a restaurant kitchen, how to understand the hierarchy, how to view the kitchen as a kind of machine. He taught me to focus on making sure my part of that machine operated smoothly. I fell in love with the whole idea and with its processes. Using all of my senses to create something tangible for someone appealed to me. But satisfying the customers wasn't the only thing that I appreciated. I was also interested in the relationship of the chef to his crew. That early apprenticeship gave me a thrilling sense of being part of a long story, part of the elemental passing on of knowledge and technique.

When I was a kid, at vacation time, the whole family would pile into the car and drive south—to Virginia, the Carolinas, Georgia. I was immediately taken by the world below the Mason-Dixon Line: the pace, the people, the hospitality of the South made a real impression on me. So did the food. There was nothing shy or genteel about southern flavors. And I liked its social function, how food brought people together.

As I became more confident (and competent) in the kitchen, Tom allowed me to start putting some of my own dishes on the menu at the deli. This was right around the time that a friend gave me the landmark cookbook *Chef Paul Prudhomme's Louisiana Kitchen*. If I had been impressed by the up-front flavors of the Piedmont South, imagine my reaction to the strength of flavor and seasonings that Prudhomme put into play. I immediately started adding dishes from the book to the menu at the deli. Looking back, there was something funny about serving New Orleans–style Cajun food in a Jewish-style delicatessen. Fortunately for me, Tom didn't care. The disconnect is apparent now, but at the time, nothing seemed strange about putting kishke, knishes, and corned beef sandwiches alongside jambalaya, blackened chicken, and gumbo.

This was in the mid-1980s, when Prudhomme was taking his restaurant, K-Paul's, on the road. When he came to Manhattan, I knew that I had to eat his food. I grabbed a buddy of mine, drove up to New York, stood in line for three hours, and, at long last, was given the chance to eat chef Paul's food. I was blown away. After the meal, Prudhomme graciously spent time with me, speaking at length about the techniques that made his approach unique. It was a heady experience, a kid from Jersey who cooked Cajun out of a Jewish deli in Edison talking to chef Paul Prudhomme, the king of New Orleans kitchens, about his philosophy on cooking.

K-Paul's was in town for six weeks. Of course, I went back. The line was long, but my patience was rewarded with another incredible meal. Prudhomme was the talk of New York, and I had heard that he occasionally let cooks train at K-Paul's, so when he made the inevitable visit to our table, I asked him about his "stage," a culinary internship program. Paul told me that they weren't bringing anyone on just then, but to call him on Friday and he would let me know. At noon on that Friday, and every other Friday for months, I would go into the office at the deli and call Paul Prudhomme. Finally, after nearly six months, I called one Friday and Paul said, "Come on down to New Orleans and cook."

During my two months at K-Paul's on Chartres Street in the French Quarter, I experienced a professional kitchen and the camaraderie that exists among chefs for the first time. Every single cook in that kitchen shared an enthusiasm, passion, and respect for food.

I felt as if I had received years' worth of experience in that short New Orleans stay (you need only look at the contents of this book to see how Prudhomme's influence has carried me forward). When my stage ended, I took that new knowledge and headed back north to cook at the Four Seasons in Manhattan. That's where I met Executive Chef Seppi Renggli, one of my most important mentors. Seppi taught me that it was okay to be unconventional, and that a chef did not need to stick to a single cuisine. On the same menu, he would offer an Indonesian curry alongside veal

Pozharsky—and it worked. Some of my most interesting ideas about food, as well as my basic kitchen philosophy of being open and adventurous, of not being bound by a single cuisine, of letting varied styles intermingle on the menu, come from my days working with Seppi at the Four Seasons.

After the Four Seasons, I began an unsettled period in my career, moving from kitchen to kitchen, my peregrinations landing me in such places as Le Cirque, and Coco Pazzo in Manhattan, Gitane in New Jersey, finally ending up at a resort on the island of Saint Lucia in the West Indies. After six months, the authorities found out I didn't have my work papers and kicked me off the island. Before I left I made a phone call. In my waning days at the Four Seasons, Seppi had told me that if I got the chance I should really cook with Wolfgang Puck. So before my unceremonious deportation, I rang up Wolfgang and asked him for a job.

My first of three tours in the Postrio kitchen was in 1989, the year it opened and took the San Francisco restaurant scene by storm. It's sort of amazing to think that Wolfgang has now been at the forefront of American cooking for 40 years, but I learned why during my first stint at Postrio. Like Seppi, Wolfgang had a sense of adventure and whimsy, but where Seppi's adventurousness appeared on the plate, Wolfgang's was not only on the plate, but also the table and the chair and the walls . . . he changed the paradigm of what fine dining could be. It wasn't just the food, it was the whole atmosphere and experience. Wolfgang also taught Doug, Steven, and me that focusing on the customer will always pay off. I'll never forget walking through the lobby of the Prescott Hotel (where Postrio was housed) with Wolfgang one Saturday night. There was an older couple from Texas at the concierge desk lamenting the fact that Postrio was the one place they just had to eat at in San Francisco, and they couldn't get a reservation. It was a Saturday night and there were over 400 on the books, yet Wolfgang walked up to the couple and said, "You want to eat at Postrio, come with me." He marched them right over to the Host Station and said, "Find this couple a table." I was just as surprised as those Texans.

The Postrio kitchen, with its emphasis on premium ingredients, opened up a new world of possibilities to me, a world populated with local farmers and purveyors, all with a deep dedication to their craft. Unlike New York, where ingredients would arrive to the belly of the restaurant in crates, or New Orleans, where food was often flown in from other parts of the country, at Postrio, fresh vegetables and meats were delivered by the people who grew them, the people who raised them. I had never experienced that kind of attention to ingredients.

Postrio didn't only open culinary possibilities. It was also the first restaurant where Doug, my brother Steven, and I worked together. Steven and I started in the kitchen at Postrio as line cooks and quickly moved up the ranks, finally being named coexecutive chefs in 1993. Doug ran the front of the house. Each night after the restaurant closed, we would talk for hours about the kind of restaurant that we might open together. We imagined a place that we would want to visit again and again, one that was comfortable and served straightforward dishes—a place that didn't take itself too seriously, but was still focused on great service and great food. We envisioned Town Hall.

A little about our restaurants

Walking into Town Hall for the first time is like arriving at a party that's in full swing and you don't know many people but still feel welcome. It's loud and boisterous; everyone is clearly enjoying themselves. With the low candles, the lamps and chandeliers, the restaurant has a celebratory glow. On the walls is a mix of old and new, fine art and anonymous nineteenth-century portraiture, and an assortment of old family photographs and flea market finds. The large alcove to the right of the entrance is dominated by a long communal table that seats sixteen, but is more often ringed by a couple dozen people There's a similar bustle at the bar, where drinks might be raised in celebration of, say, a rainy Tuesday night in San Francisco. That spirit even carries over into the dining room, where tables and chairs are set a little closer together than in most restaurants. That's how it is at Town Hall now and has been since we opened in the fall of 2003. It is a different kind of casual fine dining, one that is

completely contemporary, but with the feel and attitude of an old-time neighborhood joint.

Town Hall occupies the first two floors of a three-story corner brick building, one of the first structures built after the 1906 San Francisco earthquake. In a neighborhood of historic architecture, the building would not stand out, but because it's surrounded by glass-covered modern and post-modern facades, this relic from an earlier era has a vivid presence: a turn-of-the-twentieth-century meeting hall in the middle of a bustling twenty-first-century city. The building plays a part in the mood and personality of the restaurant.

Like Town Hall, the spaces our other restaurants inhabit set the tone for the dining experience. Salt House, a few blocks away on Mission Street, is in a building that housed one of the city's first postquake printing presses. Because of its brick walls and exposed steel I beams, the restaurant has a more industrial, edgy feel than Town Hall. The bare-bulb fixtures and artist Freya Prowe's oversized Don Quixote mural on the back wall remind you that you are sitting in a previously industrial neighborhood that has moved into the twenty-first century. The food, too, playing off the design, takes a more contemporary approach.

Just around the corner at 83 Minna is Anchor & Hope, our most recent addition to the neighborhood. For years, I often paused outside this building, wishing that someone would open the doors so I could steal a glimpse inside. Finally, one cold, rainy fall day, the garage doors started to open as I was passing by. What struck me initially was the thirty-foot trestle ceiling with its massive skylights flooding the space with light (I wasn't surprised when I later learned that the space had served as the studio of noted sculptor Beniamino Bufano). When the only things I saw inside were three parked cars and one car leaving, my mind began wandering to the architecture of coastal Maine. Doug, Steven, and I had been talking about opening a fish house, and this space, which had a weathered, faintly nautical look even before we draped knotty marine rope from the trestles, seemed tailor-made for the transformation. When a For Lease sign went up on the building three weeks later, we wasted no time in taking it over.

From Town Hall, on Howard Street, it's just a few short blocks to Salt House at 545 Mission Street, and less than six hundred feet from Salt House to the front door of Anchor & Hope. We had no idea when we struck out on our own and signed the lease on Town Hall that this once-quiet part of the new Financial District south of Market Street would become one of the city's liveliest neighborhoods: that the tallest building on the West Coast would start rising right next door to Anchor & Hope, that the empty lots nearby would soon become high-rent high-rises, or that the parking lot and bus station in the few hundred yards between Salt House and Anchor & Hope would be the future home of the largest development in the history of San Francisco, the Transbay Terminal and Urban Park, a massive hub for every train, bus, commuter rail, and rapid transit system in the entire Bay Area. At the same time this massive commercial enterprise has been undertaken, the area has been energized by the huge residential towers that have gone up nearby. So in the shadows of the cranes and pile drivers, there is a thriving neighborhood, a kind of small town that brings to each of the restaurants a clutch of regulars that know all of the staff by name and add a rich, welcoming atmosphere.

A little about this book

Writing a cookbook is a source of excitement, too. Every chef has dreams of seeing his or her book on the kitchen shelf, its pages dog-eared and favorite recipes splattered and smudged. I'm no exception. To get this book off your shelf and onto your countertop, I've brought together some of the favorite, most popular recipes from our restaurants. They represent a distillation of my thirty-five years working in professional kitchens. You'll see how my experiences in those kitchens have influenced what I do in my own, how the veal Pozharsky I learned at the Four Seasons became the classic meatball dish we serve at Town Hall, or how an Italian technique I learned for preparing squab at Coco Pazzo is used at Anchor & Hope to quick smoke the all-American rainbow trout. I even reveal a few secrets from that delicatessen in Jersey (lemon chicken, anyone?).

The dishes here reflect the spirited mix of styles present in our restaurants: the southern flair of Town Hall, the cleaner, more contemporary approach of Salt House, and the focus on fresh seafood of Anchor & Hope. I have even included a few nods to the restaurant we opened while putting this book together, Irving Street Kitchen in Portland, Oregon, which puts the spotlight on the bounty of the Pacific-Northwest. Drawing from four restaurants has allowed us to showcase certain ingredients in dissimilar ways, to celebrate versatility. Here, you can fry shrimp for a sandwich, stuff shrimp into a lobster, or grab a sauté pan and whip up a New Orleans–style BBQ shrimp. If you like duck, you can smoke a breast on the stove top and pair it with a nectarine salad, or stuff it with a rich mixture of vegetables and duck fat and confit it from the inside out.

Although I encourage you to use locally grown and raised produce and meats whenever possible, which both supports local growers and ensures the dishes taste their best, the majority of the ingredients called for in the recipes can also be found in most local supermarkets. Admittedly, some may require a bit of sleuthing on your part to secure, (the sea urchin for example, or the Peppadew peppers), but finding them will be well worth your efforts. You'll also notice that many recipes highlight the use of seasonal products. In other words, you want to make that tomato tart in summer, when tomatoes are at their peak of flavor.

Even though the recipes come from the four restaurants, they are aimed squarely at you, the home cook. All of our restaurants have small kitchens, so when we create our menus, we are forced to pare down the recipes to the fewest number of steps, so we can execute them for hundreds of guests in an evening. That means that relatively few changes were necessary to adapt them for this collection. Sometimes no shortcuts are possible, however, so some recipes are necessarily more involved than others, and while they might be daunting a first blush, they are still comparatively straightforward. These are what I call long-term relationship recipes. They take more time to prepare because you are layering flavors, introducing them at different points during the cooking process. For example, it requires time and patience to combine properly the caramelized vegetables, the Cajun spices, and the flavorful simmered meats for our jambalaya. But in the end, the work pays off in a jambalaya with incredible complexity and depth of flavor. It might be a challenge the first time, but a challenge never hurt, right?

Some of the dishes are presented as "sets," taken directly from the menus at the restaurants. I did this to highlight the choices we make in creating a dish and the interlocking quality of the ingredients we use. Seared Tuna with Gigante Beans, Chard, and Italian Sausage (page 191) is a prime example of this idea. It is presented here exactly as you have it in the restaurant. On the other extreme, say, smoking a prime rib, the focus is on the basic technique, and you are free to build a meal around that familiar centerpiece.

In these pages, I have tried to instill a sense of adventure and curiosity about cooking at home. That's because to articulate the proper way to cook, say, a steak is impossible. Sure, I can tell you to how to build a hot fire and grill a rib-eye for three minutes on each side, but that's inexact. In the end, cooking that steak is your experience, not mine. You should think of cooking that steak, or the clam chowder, or the pulled pork, as just that, an experience. I want you to have as much fun cooking the food as you do eating it.

While we often give approximate cooking times and cues, (your stove's medium heat might not be my stove's medium heat), these are not necessarily precise. So when you're cooking, I want you to use all your senses constantly. I want you to taste, smell, touch, look, and, yes, even listen to your food. Listen to the rhythm of a stock. It should be, as Louis Armstrong once commanded his band, "Not too slow, not too fast, just half-fast." Cooking should be sensuous, so open up that smoker and get your hands on that pork.

Although it took a while, I finally got the hang of measuring ingredients. I tested all of the recipes at home, to be sure that the dishes tasted like they do in the restaurants and to find the easiest path for you to arrive at the same flavors. In doing so, I hope I've been able to bring a little something from each of the kitchens I've been fortunate enough to work in these past thirty-five years.

DOUG WASHINGTON'S DINNER PARTY NOTES

WHEN WE WERE CONCEIVING TOWN HALL, many conversations focused on how we could make our restaurant feel more like a great dinner party. These discussions had nothing to do with food or recipes. They were about all the subtle, sometimes unconscious ways that we could use to make people feel more at ease, more relaxed and comfortable. After all, food is not the only reason you have a great time at dinner. It's a lot about how you feel and how these feelings can be altered in subtle and small ways. Here are some ideas to help you throw a great dinner party that people will remember.

1. Let dirty plates sit on the table for a few minutes too long. This is by far the best part of the meal, so don't kill it. People have eaten, had a glass (or two) of wine, and the mess makes them feel comfortable with one another.

2. Pack your guests in tight at the table. You don't want too much room between place settings. Think of it as a wall of guests and any space between them is space for all of the energy to bleed away. Never leave the ends of a rectangular table empty; always cap them. If someone doesn't show, remove the empty place setting right away.

3. Never move your guests. If they are all congregating in the kitchen or the front foyer or the hallway, leave them there. They are all there because (probably unconsciously) it's the place they all feel the most comfortable. If you had a vision of hors d'oeuvres and Prosecco in the living room, let it go.

4. Avoid a lot of speeches and toasts. They break up the conversations that are just beginning to get going.

5. Leave formality to fine-dining restaurants. It's okay if your silverware and/or plates are mismatched. Sometimes a table that is too "precious" creates an uptight feeling among the guests.

6. If little kids are present, always take care of them first. Forget about the food-magazine dinner party picture you have in your head. Feed them before they destroy your gathering.

7. Focus the lighting and candles (lots of small, low ones) on the table and avoid bright lights.

At Town Hall, we've seen it fifty times: A group buys out the whole restaurant and 150 people show up. All 150 crowd into a tight, little space at the bar and communal area and the entire dining room sits empty. People want to be crowded in with one another! They want to connect. Make it easier for them to do so.

CHAPTER ONE *Small* BITES

chapter **SMALL BITES** one

Fresh Chickpea Hummus with Grilled Flat Bread 14

Pickled Vegetables with Coriander and Celery Salt 16

Marinated Olives with Mint and Chiles 19

Angels on Horseback with Rémoulade 20

Hamachi Tartare with Melon and Cucumber 23

Bienville Stuffed Mushrooms 24

Grandma's Chopped Chicken Liver 28

Potato Croquettes with Peas and Ham 29

Hot Mixed Nuts with Truffle Honey and Maldon Salt 30

Medjool Dates Stuffed with Peanuts and Tasso 31

Like most chefs, I LIKE TO EAT WITH MY FINGERS. The variety of "small bites" here offers a touch of that chef's penchant for "kitchen tasting," the grabbing of a little something off a sheet pan while passing through on the way into the dining room. At our restaurants, guests will order snacks like these with a cocktail at the bar, or while looking over the menu trying to decide what to eat.

BY PACKING COMPLEX AND SOPHISTICATED FLAVORS into a small bite, these finger foods will get your guests' attention and put them in the right mood for the rest of the meal. That's because whether in a restaurant or your home, small dishes like these are the first contact with the kitchen, and serve as a harbinger for what is to come. The recipes in this chapter embody many of the flavors and textures that you'll see again and again throughout the book, here presented in miniature. All of them result in snacks that are intensely flavored, combining the sweet, the salty, and the aromatic. The stuffed dates (page 31) are a perfect example. The combination of the potency of the *tasso*, the crunch of the peanuts, and the creaminess of the dates combine to create a savory with a strangely candy-like experience. Similarly, the simplicity of the angels on horseback (page 20), which is just an oyster wrapped in bacon and fried, is made larger than the sum of its parts with the addition of the sharp mustard rémoulade.

SOME OF THESE RECIPES are perfect for dinner parties. They'll stimulate the appetite and invite guests to share in the dining experience from the beginning. Others are great to have around the house and can make a late-night trip to the refrigerator rewarding.

~Fresh~
CHICKPEA HUMMUS
with GRILLED FLAT BREAD

Hummus, a mixture of mashed chickpeas, tahini, olive oil, and garlic, is a classic of the Middle Eastern table. In recent years, it has developed staple status in the States. This recipe uses fresh chickpeas. They are available for only a few months during the summer, and not widely, but if you are lucky enough to find them, buy some. Admittedly, fresh hummus is a bit more labor-intensive, since you need to pluck the chickpeas from their pods. But it's worth it for the light, airy texture and bright, fresh green (for lack of a better term) flavor. Because fresh chickpeas are hard to find, directions for using dried chickpeas are also included. And although you can pick up a package of pita at most markets, you should grill homemade flat bread, the perfect warm, crispy accompaniment to the hummus.

SERVES 6 TO 3

HUMMUS

2 cups shelled fresh chickpeas or
1 cup dried chickpeas, picked over, soaked overnight
in water to cover, and drained

Salt

4 tablespoons extra-virgin olive oil

1/4 cup tahini

Juice of 2 lemons

2 cloves garlic, smashed and then roughly chopped

1 1/2 teaspoons salt

1 teaspoon ground cumin

1/2 teaspoon ground coriander

FLAT BREAD

1 tablespoon active dry yeast

1 tablespoon sugar

3/4 cup warm water (about 110°F)

1 1/4 cups all-purpose flour, plus more for dusting

1 tablespoon salt

Extra-virgin olive oil for drizzling

Smoked paprika, for dusting

To make the hummus, in a small pot, combine the chickpeas with water to cover by about an inch and bring to a simmer, and then begin to cook over medium-low heat, skimming off any foam that rises to the top. Add 1 tablespoon salt and 2 tablespoons of the olive oil and simmer the chickpeas, uncovered, for 20 to 25 minutes for fresh and 45 minutes to an hour for dried, or until they are tender. Drain, reserving 1 tablespoon of the cooking liquid.

Put the cooked chickpeas and the 1 tablespoon reserved cooking liquid in a food processor and add the remaining 2 tablespoons olive oil, tahini, lemon juice, garlic, cumin, coriander, and 1 1/2 teaspoons salt and process until smooth. Taste and adjust the seasoning. If you prefer your hummus more acidic, add a bit more lemon juice. Cover and refrigerate until serving. It will keep for up to 3 days.

To make the flat bread, in a bowl, sprinkle the yeast and sugar over the warm water and let stand until frothy. This should take about 5 minutes. Add the flour and salt and mix well with a wooden spoon until a dough forms. Transfer the dough to a lightly floured work surface and knead for 7 to 10 minutes, or until smooth and shiny. (You can also mix and knead using a stand mixer fitted with the dough hook attachment on medium speed for 7 to 10 minutes.) Transfer the dough to a lightly oiled bowl, cover with a towel and let rest for 1 hour.

Preheat the oven to 350°F. Prepare a hot fire in a charcoal or gas grill.

Divide the dough into 6 equal balls; each will weigh about 2 ounces. On a lightly floured work surface, roll out each ball into an oval, making it as thin as possible. It should be about 10 inches in diameter.

Place the rounds on the grill, and cook, turning once with tongs, until they begin to brown and crisp on both sides. This should take about 2 minutes on each side. Transfer the flat breads to a large rimmed baking sheet and slip into the oven for about 5 minutes, or until just crisp.

Transfer the hummus to a serving bowl. Drizzle with olive oil and dust with smoked paprika. Serve right away, with the warm flat bread on the side.

Pickled Vegetables

with CORIANDER

and CELERY SALT

At Salt House, we stay away from long-cured dill pickles, instead opting to pickle a variety of vegetables for just a day or two before serving them. This recipe, with its classic use of coriander, mustard seed, and celery salt, is a boon for lovers of tart pickles. I count myself in that number, but if you prefer them on the sweeter side, just boost the amount of sugar slightly. You can use different vegetables according to the season or what you prefer. A batch of these pickles is great for a party or for keeping in the fridge for snacking.

✦ YIELDS 2 QUART JARS ✦

BRINE

2 cups cider vinegar

2 cups distilled white vinegar

2 cups water

1 cup sugar

2 tablespoons salt

12 cardamom pods, crushed

1/3 cup coriander seeds

2 tablespoons mustard seeds

1 teaspoon celery seeds

1 cucumber, cut into 1/4-inch-thick slices

1 handful green beans, trimmed

1 bunch baby carrots, leafy tops discarded

6 pearl onions, blanched for 2 minutes and peeled

1 red bell pepper, halved lengthwise, seeded, and cut into 1/2-inch-wide slices

1/2 head cauliflower, cut into small florets

Celery salt to taste

To MAKE THE BRINE, in a saucepan, combine all of the ingredients and bring to a boil over high heat, stirring until the sugar dissolves. Lower the heat to medium and simmer for 3 minutes.

Meanwhile, blanch the vegetables. Bring a saucepan filled with lightly salted water to a boil over high heat. Add the cucumber, green beans, carrots, onions, pepper, and cauliflower and blanch for 2 to 3 minutes, or until their color brightens and they have just begun to soften. Drain the vegetables and transfer them to a widemouthed heatproof glass or plastic container. Pour in in hot brine and rest a plate on top of the vegetables to keep them submerged. Place the container in the refrigerator to cool the contents.

The pickles are ready to eat the next day. They will keep for up to 1 month. To serve, garnish with a sprinkling of celery salt.

Marinated
OLIVES *with* MINT
AND CHILES

Over the past thirty-five years, I've learned as much about food through my travels as I have cooking in restaurants. The first time my wife and I walked through the Marais district of Paris, we stumbled on an unusual market brimming with all sorts of spices and other specialties from around the world. Huge wooden barrels filled with different types of olives and other delights stood at the front of the shop. We explored each barrel, taking in the heady aromas. Our favorite was the barrel of olives flavored with mint, chiles, and orange peel. The simple addition of the aromatics gives another layer of flavor to each type of olive, rather than overpowering them, so while the marinade comes through, each olive's individual characteristics remain.

MAKES 4 CUPS

4 cups mixed olives, preferably 4 varieties that vary in color and size (I always include niçoise and picholine)

1 cup olive oil

2 cloves garlic, each sliced lengthwise into 4 pieces

Zest of 1 orange, removed in strips with a vegetable peeler

Leaves from 2 mint sprigs, torn

Leaves from 1 rosemary sprig

½ teaspoon dried chile flakes

PLACE the olives in a bowl. Add the oil, garlic, orange zest, mint, rosemary, and chile flakes and toss well. Transfer to a jar, cover tightly, and refrigerate for at least 3 days before serving. The olives will keep in the refrigerator for up to 1 month.

Angels
ON HORSEBACK
WITH RÉMOULADE

This dish has roots in Britain, where oysters are typically wrapped in bacon, broiled, and served on toast. But in the States, it is seen as a sort of upscale version of the familiar pastry-wrapped frank known as pigs in a blanket, except, well, the pig is the blanket. These angels are the most popular appetizer on the menu at Anchor & Hope. Unlike the Brits, we deep-fry the bacon-wrapped oyster, which not only cooks the bacon quickly but also makes it exceptionally crispy. The pronounced mustard flavor in the rémoulade works beautifully with the smokiness of the bacon. This rémoulade recipe is a good one to have in your arsenal. It's perfect for shrimp cocktail or as a dipping sauce for deep-fried seafood.

MAKES 24 PIECES; SERVES 3 TO 12

RÉMOULADE

2 large egg yolks, room temperature

1/3 cup canola oil

1/2 cup chopped celery

1/4 cup chopped fresh flat-leaf parsley

1/4 cup chopped fresh tarragon

Juice of 1/2 lemon

2 tablespoons ketchup

2 tablespoons Worcestershire sauce

1 tablespoon Dijon mustard

1 tablespoon whole grain mustard

1 tablespoon malt vinegar

1 tablespoon minced garlic

1 teaspoon sweet smoked paprika

1/2 teaspoon celery salt

1 tablespoon capers, rinsed

4 gherkins, chopped

Salt and freshly ground pepper

Canola oil, for deep-frying

24 oysters, shucked

12 thin slices bacon, halved crosswise

To make the rémoulade, place the egg yolks in a food processor and process for 1 minute. With the machine running, add the oil in a slow, steady stream, processing until emulsified. Then, with the machine still running, gradually add the celery, parsley, tarragon, lemon juice, ketchup, Worcestershire sauce, both mustards, vinegar, garlic, paprika, celery salt, capers, and gherkins and process until well incorporated and smooth. Taste and season with salt and pepper.

Pour the oil to a depth of about 3 inches into a deep fryer or deep, heavy-bottomed pot and heat to 375°F. While the oil is heating, wrap a half bacon slice around each oyster and secure with a toothpick.

When the oil is ready, working in batches to avoid crowding, add the wrapped oysters to the hot oil and fry for 2 to 3 minutes, or until the oysters are golden and the bacon is crispy. Using a slotted spoon, carefully transfer the oysters to paper towels, then keep them warm while you fry the remainder.

Arrange the oysters on a platter, drizzle with the rémoulade, and serve right away.

A Note on Deep-Frying

Angels on Horseback with Rémoulade (left) is the first of a number of recipes in the book that call for deep-frying. I swear that I'm not trying to raise your cholesterol. All I am trying to do is offer you some very tasty food. Remember, everything in moderation. With its high temperatures, spits, and spatters, deep-frying can seem a daunting prospect. When I was a kid, I thought my mom was going to burn

continued

down the house every time she decided to make French fries (that added fear made them extra delicious). So to lessen any worries of possible conflagration, I suggest that you buy a deep-fryer. You will find plenty on the market to choose from, including a number of which can be had at a decent price. That way, you'll not only be able to control the temperature of your oil with precision, but you'll also get the added benefit of a little peace of mind. Failing that, an eight quart cast-iron Dutch oven is your next best choice. It maintains a constant temperature and, paired with a deep-frying thermometer, will deliver perfectly fried foods . . . in moderation, of course.

Finally, in all of the frying recipes here we have called for canola oil. It's economical and easy to find (safflower oil is another good choice). At the restaurants, we use peanut oil which, though more expensive, has a higher smoking point. Use it if you can.

Hamachi

TARTARE *with*

MELON *and* CUCUMBER

You'll be hard-pressed to find a small bite with fresher flavors than this one. Melon, plum, cucumber—they are like summer on a plate. I first experimented with these flavors following a trip to Italy, where I sampled a slew of variations of prosciutto and melon. That trip coincided with a period when *crudo* was the culinary buzzword of the day. So I took prosciutto and melon, added raw *hamachi*, and served them all in a melon broth. This dish is Salt House chef Bob Leva's refined variation: he took out the prosciutto and replaced the melon broth with just the right amount of soy-lime dressing to enhance the fish without obscuring its buttery flavor. Make sure you put the two together just before serving. If you mix them too early, the vinegar and lime will start to "cook" the fish. I like to use the French Charentais melon, but you can use honeydew or even cantaloupe. Whichever type you choose, make sure it is the ripest, most aromatic melon you can find.

MAKES ABOUT 24; SERVES 6 TO 3

SOY-LIME DRESSING

3 tablespoons canola oil

1 tablespoon champagne vinegar

1 tablespoon freshly squeezed lime juice

$1/4$ teaspoon soy sauce

Salt and freshly ground pepper to taste

$1/3$ pound hamachi (sold as amberjack or yellowtail), finely diced

$1/4$ cup finely diced melon, preferably Charentais

1 radish, trimmed and finely diced

1 plum, peeled, halved, pitted, and finely diced (about $1/4$ cup)

1 tablespoon finely diced English cucumber, plus 1 whole cucumber, sliced $1/8$ inch thick (about 24 rounds)

1 tablespoon finely diced jalapeño chile

1 teaspoon chopped fresh mint

1 teaspoon chopped fresh lemon verbena

To make the dressing, in a small bowl, whisk together all of the ingredients. Taste and adjust the seasoning.

In a bowl, combine the *hamachi*, melon, radish, plum, diced cucumber, chile, mint, lemon verbena and toss gently to mix well. Drizzle with the dressing and toss again. Taste and season with salt and pepper as necessary.

Put about 2 teaspoons of the *hamachi* tartare on top of each cucumber slice. Arrange on a platter and serve right away.

Bienville
STUFFED
MUSHROOMS

Bienville stuffing is a New Orleans French Quarter classic, invented, depending on who you talk to, at either Antoine's or Arnaud's, where it's most commonly found sitting atop an oyster. Here, it's paired with mushrooms. Later in the book, you'll find a recipe for stuffed lobster. When we decided to stuff a lobster—which, you'll agree, is a pretty good idea—we weren't sure what to stuff it with. A number of ideas were in the running, including the Bienville. When we finished testing the Bienville, we had some leftover stuffing, and we also had some mushrooms. Well, as they say, if life gives you mushrooms and Bienville stuffing, make Bienville Stuffed Mushrooms.

I was first exposed to this superrich stuffing at K-Paul's, where it was tucked inside a flounder. But no matter how it's used, it's a great expression of the flavors and ingredients of New Orleans. It calls for both shrimp and oysters, as well as what's known in Louisiana cooking as the Holy Trinity—celery, onions, and bell peppers—a combination that forms the basis for a number of New Orleans specialties.

MAKES 24 STUFFED MUSHROOMS; SERVES 3 TO 12

BREAD CRUMBS
4 thick slices coarse country bread such as pain levain

Few drops of olive oil

Salt and freshly ground pepper

BIENVILLE STUFFING
1 tablespoon canola oil

3 slices thick-cut bacon, diced

1 large yellow onion, diced

1 celery stalk, diced

1 large red bell pepper, seeded and diced

3 crimini mushrooms, diced

2 tablespoons Town Hall Spice Mixture (page 253)

6 ounces shrimp, peeled, deveined, and diced

2 oysters, shucked, with their liquor reserved

1 1/2 teaspoons chopped garlic

2 tablespoons unsalted butter

1 tablespoon all-purpose flour

2 cups Chicken Stock (page 250) or Shrimp Stock (page 250)

1 bay leaf

1 teaspoon firmly packed golden brown sugar

Salt and freshly ground pepper

24 crimini mushrooms, each about 1 to 1 1/2 inches in diameter

To make the bread crumbs, cut off and discard the crusts from the bread slices, then cut the slices into cubes. Place the cubes in a food processor and pulse until fine crumbs form. Transfer to a bowl, add the oil, and season with salt and pepper, then toss to mix. You should have about 1 cup. Set aside.

To make the stuffing, in large frying pan heat the oil over medium-low heat. Add the bacon and fry for 7 to 8 minutes, or until crispy and all of the fat has been rendered. Raise the heat to high, add the onion, celery, and bell pepper, and cook, stirring occasionally, for about 10 minutes, or until the vegetables start to caramelize. Add the mushrooms and spice mixture and cook for 1 minute, all the while scraping the bottom of the pan. Add the shrimp, oysters and their liquor, and garlic and stir well, continuing to scrape the bottom of the pan. Add the butter and flour and stir to combine. Pour in the stock, add the bay leaf and brown sugar, stir well, and bring to a simmer over medium-low heat. Let cook, stirring occasionally, for about 15 minutes, or until most of the liquid is reduced and the stuffing has a nice thick consistency.

Remove from the heat, remove and discard the bay leaf, and let cool slightly. Transfer the stuffing mixture to the food processor and process until it is thick and a bit chunky. Season with salt and pepper. You should have about 2 cups.

Preheat the oven to 375°F. Pull the stems off of the mushrooms. Spoon a generous amount of the stuffing (about 4 teaspoons) into the stem side of each mushroom and top with some of the bread crumbs (about 2 teaspoons). Arrange the stuffed mushrooms on a sheet pan.

Bake for 20 to 25 minutes, or until the mushrooms are cooked through and the bread crumbs are toasted. Transfer to a platter and serve immediately.

Grandma's
CHOPPED CHICKEN
LIVER

What do you think this recipe is, chopped liver? Yes, that's exactly what it is. It is not, however, a delicate liver pâté or mousse that you might dab onto a crostino. No, this is *chopped* liver, deli style, to be smeared on a chunk of fresh rye. You'll know what I mean when you take the first bite. It has *texture*. You see, Steven and I don't come from a long line of cooks (that's why there are so few family recipes in this book). Our paternal grandmother, Helen, was the exception, however. She could cook, and one of her specialties was chopped liver. What sets this recipe, *her recipe*, apart is its sweetness, which is achieved by caramelizing both the livers and the onion, steps that also provide the dish with a nice balance. This chopped liver was on Town Hall's opening menu, and Stevie always makes plenty of it around the holidays to share with the staff. Although Grandma's original notes call for using *schmaltz* (rendered chicken fat), we use canola oil, which makes our chopped liver a little more heart healthy. As I mentioned, we like to spread this chopped liver on rye bread, but you can also serve it with crostini or crackers.

❧ MAKES 2 CUPS ❧

Pictured on pages 26–27.

¹⁄₃ cup plus 2 tablespoons canola oil

1¹⁄₄ pound (about 2 cups) chicken livers, cleaned of any fat and sinew, rinsed, and patted dry

1 large yellow onion, cut into 8 pieces

1 large egg, hard boiled and peeled

Salt and freshly ground pepper

IN A FRYING PAN, heat 2 tablespoons of the oil over high heat. Add the livers and sauté for about 5 minutes, or until well caramelized and cooked through. Transfer to a bowl and place in the refrigerator.

Now, heat the remaining ¹⁄₃ cup oil in a 1-quart saucepan over medium-high heat. Add the onion pieces and cook, stirring often, for about 15 minutes, or until golden brown. If the pieces begin to get too dark, lower the heat. Transfer the onion pieces and oil to the bowl holding the livers, and return the bowl to the refrigerator until both the livers and the onion pieces are well chilled.

Pass the chilled livers, onion and oil, and hard-boiled egg through a meat grinder fitted with the medium disk or the food grinder attachment of a stand mixer fitted with the coarse blade into a bowl. If you don't have a meat grinder, you can chop the ingredients by hand, preferably with a crescent knife (curved blade with a handle on either end). Mix the ground ingredients together well, season with salt and pepper, and serve.

Potato
CROQUETTES
with PEAS AND HAM

The use of fresh peas and ham makes these croquettes an appealing expression of early spring. Two important things ensure a great potato croquette: first, it needs to be well seasoned; and second, it has to have the proper consistency. Too little binder and it will explode when it hits the hot oil; too much and the texture will be grainy. The trick is to use as little of the egg yolk and flour binder as possible. Freezing the croquettes before you fry them will help them hold together, too, which also means you can make them a few days ahead. Serve these croquettes as a small bite to get a party started. And although potato croquette sounds fanciful and French, remember it is just another name for that lunchroom staple the Tater Tot.

MAKES 36 TO 40 CROQUETTES

2 large russet potatoes, about 1½ pounds total, peeled

½ cup fresh or frozen shelled English peas

4 tablespoons unsalted butter

¼ pound cooked ham, finely chopped

1 cup grated Gruyère cheese

½ cup grated Parmesan cheese

1 teaspoon salt

Freshly ground pepper

2 large egg yolks, beaten

2 tablespoons all-purpose flour

⅔ cup all-purpose flour, plus more for dusting

3 large whole eggs, lightly beaten

2 cups panko bread crumbs

Canola oil for deep-frying

IN A SAUCEPAN, combine the potatoes with salted water to cover generously, bring to a boil, and boil for about 20 minutes, or until tender when pierced with a fork. Drain the potatoes, then pass them through a food mill or ricer into a large bowl (or mash them in the bowl with a potato masher). Set aside.

If using fresh peas, bring a small saucepan filled with water to a boil, add the peas, and blanch for 2 minutes, then drain well. In a small frying pan, melt the butter over medium heat. Add the peas and cook, stirring occasionally, for 2 to 3 minutes, or until tender. Add the peas to the potatoes along with the ham, both cheeses, salt, and a few grinds of pepper. Mix well and taste for seasoning. Adjust as necessary and then add the egg yolks and 2 tablespoons flour, and mix well. Let cool completely.

Lightly dust a clean work surface with flour. Scoop up a handful of the cooled potato mixture and roll it gently on the floured surface to form a log about 1 inch (2.5 cm) in diameter. Repeat the process with the rest of the mixture, flouring the surface as needed. Cut the logs into pieces about 1½ inches long.

Place the flour in a small, shallow bowl. Put the whole eggs in a second small, shallow bowl, and the *panko* in a third bowl. One at a time, roll the croquettes in the flour, then dip them in the eggs, and finally roll them in the *panko*, shaking off the excess after each pass and making sure they are coated completely. As the croquettes are coated, put them on a sheet pan. Refrigerate the croquettes for at least 20 minutes or freeze for up to one week before frying.

When you are ready to cook the croquettes, pour the oil to a depth of about 3 inches into a deep fryer or deep, heavy-bottomed pot and heat to 375°F. Working in batches to avoid crowding, add the croquettes to the hot oil and fry for 3 to 4 minutes, or until golden brown. Using a slotted spoon, transfer the croquettes to paper towels to drain, then keep them warm while you fry the remainder. Serve hot.

HOT MIXED NUTS

with Truffle Honey

AND MALDON SALT

1 cup peanuts

1 cup almonds

1 cup walnuts

1 cup pistachios

1 tablespoon canola oil

2 tablespoons clover honey

2 tablespoons truffle oil

1 tablespoon Maldon salt

At Salt House, we cook these nuts to order and serve them right away. But while testing the recipe for this book, I realized that the nuts may sit around for a while—perhaps at a party or other get-together—before they are eaten. If you can't serve them right out of the oven, after you toss them with the honey and salt, spread them out on a tray and allow them to cool and dry a bit so they are not so sticky. The truffle oil brings an earthy sophistication to this recipe, and the soft, flaky Maldon sea salt, a specialty from England, nicely balances the honey. Feel free to experiment with different mixtures of nuts, flavors of honey, and types of salt.

PREHEAT the oven to 350°F. In a large bowl, toss all of the nuts with the canola oil. Spread the nuts in a single layer on a sheet pan.

Place the pan in the oven and toast the nuts, shaking the pan once halfway through cooking, for 10 to 12 minutes, or until they appear toasted and are fragrant. Meanwhile, in a small bowl, stir together the honey and truffle oil.

When the nuts are ready, transfer them to a bowl, drizzle with the honey mixture, and toss to coat evenly. Crush the salt gently between your fingers, then sprinkle it over the nuts, toss to coat evenly, and serve warm.

❈ MAKES 4 CUPS ❈

MEDJOOL DATES
Stuffed with
PEANUTS *and* TASSO

You might find a dish similar to this one on a Spanish tapas menu: a date stuffed with chorizo, wrapped in bacon, and served warm from the oven. At Town Hall, we take that idea and give it some southern flair. We use *tasso*, a spicy Cajun-style pork (which we cure for three days, cover with a spicy rub, and then smoke), instead of chorizo. And then we add peanuts, which provide a nice crunchy contrast to the creaminess of the dates. We bake the stuffed dates, but you can also grab a half dozen skewers, put four dates on each one, and grill them until the bacon is crispy. Whichever method you use, it's better to eat the dates hot because the dates themselves become incredibly creamy, and that texture is just as important as the burst of flavor from the filling.

MAKES 24; SERVES 6 TO 3

24 dates, pitted

12 thin slices bacon, halved crosswise

FILLING

1/2 cup skinned roasted peanuts

3 ounces tasso or pastrami, roughly chopped

2 tablespoons unsalted butter

1 1/2 teaspoons Worcestershire sauce

2 teaspoons maple syrup

2 teaspoons Town Hall Spice Mixture (page 253)

1 teaspoon salt

PREHEAT the oven to 375°F.

TO MAKE THE FILLING: place the peanuts in a food processor and pulse a few times to chop coarsely. Add the ham, butter, Worcestershire sauce, maple syrup, spice mixture, and salt and pulse until finely chopped and well combined. Taste and adjust the seasoning.

Using your fingers, fill each date with about 1/2 teaspoon of the peanut mixture, wrap with a half slice of bacon, and secure with a toothpick. Arrange the dates on a sheet pan.

Bake, turning once halfway through cooking, for about 15 minutes, or until the bacon is browned and crispy and the dates are hot. Transfer to a platter and serve immediately.

CHAPTER TWO

Big BITES

Cooking, PROFESSIONAL OR OTHERWISE, is by its very nature a shared, communal experience. It is a collaboration on every level, from the farm to the flame. Cooking also reflects the importance of tradition. To be a cook is to be part of a historical line of styles and techniques grounded in tradition yet ripe for innovation. This chapter, perhaps more than any other, illustrates my journey, and the dishes are a good representation of my years working as a cook. You'll find a little bit here from almost every kitchen I have ever worked in, from my experience at K-Paul's in New Orleans, where I learned to cook Cajun from the master, to my years working alongside Seppi Renggli in one of the great New York restaurants, the Four Seasons.

THIS CHAPTER IS CALLED BIG BITES because even though these dishes are included in the appetizer section of the restaurants' menus, diners often point a finger toward them when they order their entrees: "You know what, I think I'll have the BBQ shrimp as my main course." In other words, don't be afraid to serve the oyster salad for dinner.

SAVE FOR ONE OR TWO ITEMS, these recipes use basic ingredients, but they use them in interesting ways. Throughout the chapter, you'll find a constant play and tension between the familiarity of the food and the way that food is presented. Why do the meatballs seem so exciting? Because instead of the tomato sauce with which they are typically associated, they are served with mashed potatoes and a green peppercorn sauce, accompaniments usually found with a big, thick steak, that's why.

THE LATKE RECIPE is a good example of how tradition and innovation coexist in the kitchen. Although it is tied to my earliest cooking experience—the deli in Edison, New Jersey—here it is offered with a salmon prepared using a curing technique developed by the chef at Anchor & Hope. Putting the two together also reminds me why I love working in kitchens, where people are constantly bringing fresh ideas to the pantry, to the stove, and to the table.

Butter
LETTUCE SALAD
with ASIAN PEARS and
BUTTERMILK–BLUE CHEESE DRESSING

When we were starting to talk about the menu for Town Hall, Steven and I recalled the times when we were kids, out for family dinners in Jersey. Everyone at the table would order the classic wedge of iceberg lettuce drenched with Thousand Island dressing. (Now *that* was eating.) We wanted something as simple and satisfying as a wedge of iceberg on our opening menu. This is what we came up with. Here, the butter lettuce stands in for the iceberg, and the blue cheese dressing is a bit more up-to-date, but we still lay it on just as thick. People have responded. It's still on the menu today.

At Town Hall, we use Farmstead Cheese Company's Point Reyes Original Blue. The cheese, which is made in Tomales Bay, just forty-five minutes up the coast from San Francisco, has a creamy texture and briny character. That brininess is due to the cows grazing on the coastal grasses that thrive in the salt air of the Pacific. If you can't get your hands on Point Reyes Original Blue, you can try Maytag Blue, which will impart a sharp and classic tang to the dish, or use a blue of your choice.

SERVES 6

CANDIED WALNUTS

Canola oil, for deep-frying

$1/2$ cup powdered sugar

1 cup walnut halves

DRESSING

$1/2$ cup Mayonnaise (page 251)

$1/4$ pound blue cheese, crumbled

$1/4$ cup buttermilk

2 tablespoons heavy cream

1 tablespoon freshly squeezed lemon juice

Salt and freshly cracked pepper

2 heads butter lettuce, leaves separated

1 Asian pear, halved, cored, and thinly sliced

6 radishes, trimmed and thinly sliced

3 ounces blue cheese, crumbled

To MAKE THE CANDIED WALNUTS, pour the oil to a depth of $1^1/2$ inches into a deep, heavy-bottomed pot and heat to 350°F. While the oil is heating, line a sheet pan with parchment paper, put the sugar in a bowl, and bring a saucepan filled with water to a boil.

Add the nuts to the boiling water and blanch for 1 minute. Using a wire skimmer or a strainer, scoop out the nuts, shake off the excess water, and add the nuts to the sugar. Toss the nuts to coat them completely with the sugar. The sugar should form a light paste. Then, working in batches to avoid crowding, carefully spoon the nuts into the hot oil, spreading them out so they don't stick together. Fry for about 2 minutes, or until golden brown. Using a slotted spoon, transfer the nuts to the prepared sheet pan, spreading them in a single layer, and let cool completely. (The nuts can be prepared up to a week in advance; store in an airtight container at room temperature.)

TO MAKE THE DRESSING, combine the mayonnaise, cheese, buttermilk, cream, and lemon juice and stir together until well blended. Season with salt and pepper.

Place the lettuce, pears, and radishes in a large bowl. Add the dressing and toss to coat well. Divide the salad among individual plates. Garnish each serving with 3 to 6 candied walnut halves, the sliced radishes, and the crumbled cheese, dividing it evenly. Serve right away.

Summer
HEIRLOOM TOMATO
WITH OLIVES, FETA,
and TOMATO TOAST

This refreshing salad is especially welcome in the summer months when tomatoes are at their peak of flavor. We use those ripe, flavorful tomatoes two ways: we pair a Greek-inspired tomato salad, thick with feta cheese and kalamata olives, with a garlicky tomato toast, a Catalan classic.

❧ SERVES 6 ❧

CUCUMBERS

3 lemon cucumbers peeled, halved and cut into ¼ inch slices

¼ cup olive oil

1 teaspoon Dijon mustard

Juice of one lemon

TOMATO JAM

1 pound Roma tomatoes, blanched, peeled and chopped

2 cloves garlic

¼ cup olive oil

6 slices levain bread, ¼ inch thick

VINAIGRETTE

½ cup olive oil

2 tablespoons sherry vinegar

SALAD

3 pounds heirloom tomatoes (or the ripest tomato of your choice), quartered

½ cup kalamata olives, pitted and quartered

1 cup of feta cheese, cut into ¼-inch cubes

Salt and pepper to taste

2 tablespoons fresh oregano leaves

2 tablespoons thinly sliced green onion (green parts only)

FIRST, place the bread loaf in the freezer, it will be easier to get even ¼-inch slices with the bread chilled.

TO MAKE THE CUCUMBERS, mix the olive oil, mustard and lemon juice together and pour over the cucumbers. Stir to coat and set aside.

Next, make the tomato jam for the toast. Place the peeled and chopped tomatoes, garlic, olive oil, and a bit of salt and pepper in a blender. Pulse until the tomatoes are reduced to very small chunks. (If your tomatoes are watery, strain out some of the liquid) Transfer to a small bowl and set aside.

Preheat oven to 375 degrees. Take the bread from the freezer and cut into ¼-inch slices. Brush both sides of each slice bread with olive oil and place on a sheet pan. Place in oven and bake for 7 minutes.

In a small bowl, prepare the vinaigrette by mixing together the olive oil and sherry vinegar. Place the tomatoes in a large bowl, pour over the vinaigrette and mix to coat. Season with salt and pepper.

On six plates, evenly divide each of the following in this order: tomatoes, cucumbers, olives, feta cheese, oregano and green onions. Then, spread about 2 tablespoons of the tomato jam on each piece of toast and place one on each plate. Serve.

AUTUMN SALAD
with CIDER VINAIGRETTE
and Candied
HAZELNUTS

This salad is a pretty good representation of the approach Salt House chef Bob Leva takes to cooking: classic, simple, elegant. Here you'll find all of the elements of a great dish. The bitterness of the greens is offset by the sweetness of the fruit. Notice, too, the many textures put into play: the creaminess of the goat cheese combined with the crunch of the candied hazelnuts and pomegranate seeds.

❧ SERVES 6 ❧

CANDIED HAZELNUTS

Canola oil, for deep-frying

$^1\!/_2$ cup powdered sugar

1 cup hazelnuts

VINAIGRETTE

2 tablespoons cider vinegar

$1^1\!/_2$ tablespoons sherry vinegar

$1^1\!/_2$ teaspoons whole grain mustard

1 teaspoon Dijon mustard

$^1\!/_2$ teaspoon salt

$^1\!/_4$ cup canola oil

$^1\!/_4$ cup extra-virgin olive oil

2 tablespoons walnut oil

Freshly ground pepper

1 pound mixed bitter greens such as Treviso radicchio, Chioggia radicchio, dandelion greens , frisée, arugula, mizuna, and watercress

2 Fuyu persimmons

1 sweet-tart apple such as Crispin or Pink Pearl

$^1\!/_2$ cup pomegranate seeds

$^1\!/_4$ pound fresh goat cheese, crumbled

Salt and freshly ground pepper

TO MAKE THE CANDIED HAZELNUTS, pour the oil to a depth of $1^1\!/_2$ inches into a heavy-bottomed saucepan and heat to 350°F. While the oil is heating, line a sheet pan with parchment paper, put the sugar in a bowl, and bring a saucepan filled with water to a boil.

Add the nuts to the boiling water and blanch for 1 minute. Using a wire skimmer or a strainer, scoop out the nuts, shake off the excess water, and add the nuts to the sugar. Toss the nuts to coat them completely with the sugar. The sugar should form a light paste. Then, working in batches to avoid crowding, carefully spoon the nuts into the hot oil, spreading them out so they don't stick together. Fry for about 2 minutes, or until golden brown. Using a slotted spoon, transfer the nuts to the prepared sheet pan, spreading them in a single layer, and let cool completely, then coarsely chop and set aside. (The nuts can be prepared up to a week in advance; store in an airtight container at room temperature.)

TO MAKE THE VINAIGRETTE, in a small, wide bowl whisk together both vinegars, both mustards, and the salt. Pour in the oils in a slow, steady stream while whisking constantly, continuing to whisk until emulsified. Season with a few grinds of pepper, then taste and adjust the seasoning. Set aside.

If using Treviso radicchio, core and cut crosswise into 1-inch-wide strips. If using Chioggia radicchio, core and slice thinly crosswise. If using dandelion greens, discard tough stems and tear into bite-sized pieces. Remove any tough stems from the smaller greens. Cut off the crown and a thin slice from the bottom of each persimmon, then peel them, being careful not to cut into the flesh. Cut into quarters through the stem end, cut away the core from each quarter, and then cut each quarter lengthwise into ¼-inch-thick slices. Quarter the apple, leaving the skin on, and cut away the core. Cut each quarter lengthwise into ⅛-inch-thick slices.

In a large bowl, combine the greens, fruits, nuts, and goat cheese. Drizzle the vinaigrette over the top and toss to coat evenly. Season with a pinch of salt and some pepper and toss again. Mound on individual plates, making sure to distribute the fruits and nuts evenly. Serve right away.

FRIED OYSTERS
with SPINACH SALAD
and HERBSAINT DRESSING

When you fry an oyster, you want the outside nice and crispy without losing the creamy texture of the flesh. So for this recipe, you'll want to use an oyster with some heft. Oysters from the Gulf of Mexico are ideal, but any medium or large oysters will work fine. Herbsaint is an anise-flavored liqueur, and just like a fat Gulf oyster, it is a New Orleans classic. It was introduced as an absinthe substitute in 1934, and it remains the basis for many New Orleans cocktails. We use it in the kitchen for its rich licorice flavor. This salad features one of my favorite combinations: hot and cold. You'll know what I mean when you bite into the just-fried oyster and it plays against the cold spinach. Also, the salad includes bacon, which makes it that much tastier.

An interesting thing happened when I tested this dish at home. I used the recipe from Town Hall, a staple on our menu for more than five years. When I made it in my own kitchen, the dressing seemed a little flat: some of the Herbsaint's anise flavor was lost. I decided to throw in a couple of tablespoons of Herbsaint straight from the bottle. The result had a rounder, fuller flavor. The next day I changed the recipe at the restaurant. Believe it, old dogs can learn new tricks.

SERVES 6 AS FIRST COURSE OR 4 AS A MAIN COURSE

DRESSING
1 cup plus 2 tablespoons Herbsaint or Pernod

2 tablespoons finely diced shallot

2 tablespoons champagne vinegar

1/2 cup Mayonnaise (page 251)

1/2 cup buttermilk

1/4 cup heavy cream

2 tablespoons chopped fresh tarragon

SALAD
1 tablespoon canola oil

1/2 pound thick-cut bacon slices, cut into 1/4-inch cubes

3/4 pound baby spinach

1 red onion, thinly sliced

Salt and freshly ground pepper

OYSTERS
18 medium to large oysters, preferably from the Gulf of Mexico

1 cup buttermilk

1 cup all-purpose flour

1 cup cornmeal

Salt and freshly ground pepper

Canola oil, for deep-frying

To make the dressing, pour the 1 cup Herbsaint into a small saucepan, place over medium heat, and simmer until reduced to 1 tablespoon. This will take about 10 minutes. Set aside to cool.

In a bowl, combine the shallot and vinegar and let stand for 5 minutes. Then add the mayonnaise, buttermilk, cream, and both the reduced Herbsaint and the 2 tablespoons Herbsaint straight from the bottle and mix well to combine. Finally, stir in the tarragon. Cover and chill before serving.

To make the salad, heat sauté pan over medium heat. Add the bacon and cook, stirring occasionally, for about 7 minutes, or until just crispy. Using a slotted spoon, transfer to paper towels to drain.

Put the spinach in a large bowl. Scatter the bacon and onion over the top and set aside to finish after you cook the oysters.

To cook the oysters, put the buttermilk in a small, shallow bowl. In a second small, shallow bowl, stir together the flour and cornmeal and season with salt and pepper. Pour the oil to a depth of 2 inches into a deep fryer or deep, heavy-bottomed pot and heat to 375°F.

While the oil is heating, one at a time, coat the oysters with the buttermilk, allowing the excess to drip away, and then roll them in the flour-cornmeal mixture, coating them completely and shaking off the excess. As the oysters are coated, put them on a large platter or sheet pan.

When the oil is ready, working in batches to avoid crowding, add the oysters and fry for about 2 minutes, or until golden brown. Using a slotted spoon, transfer to paper towels to drain.

TO FINISH THE SALAD, drizzle the dressing over the top and toss to coat evenly. Season with a pinch of salt and some pepper and toss again. Mound on individual plates, top each salad with 3 fried oysters, and drizzle each oyster with a little of the dressing. Serve right away.

HARICOTS VERTS

with **HARISSA VINAIGRETTE**

Serrano Ham,
and SPICED ALMONDS

Here's another example of playing with texture and flavor. In this recipe, we bring our version of the spicy North African condiment *harissa*, which we use as the basis for a spicy vinaigrette, to bear on a salad of snappy green beans. We call for the elegant haricot vert, but any variety, such as wax or Blue Lake, will also work beautifully. You can serve this salad on individual plates or throw the whole thing in the middle of the table and have at it. Just make sure everybody gets some almonds, because they tend to sneak to the bottom of the bowl.

❧ SERVES 6 ❧

SPICED ALMONDS

½ teaspoon coriander seeds

½ teaspoon cumin seeds

½ teaspoon fennel seeds

1 cup whole natural almonds

1 tablespoon olive oil

1 teaspoon salt

1 pound haricots verts, trimmed

5 ounces spicy, small-leaved greens such mizuna or arugula

1 bunch chervil, stems removed

1 bunch tarragon, stems removed

1 bunch mint, stems removed

3 ounces thinly sliced serrano ham or prosciutto, each slice torn into 2 or 3 pieces

Salt and freshly ground pepper

Harissa Vinaigrette (page 251)

TO PREPARE THE ALMONDS, preheat the oven to 375°F. In a small, dry frying pan, toast the coriander, cumin, and fennel seeds over medium heat, shaking the pan often to avoid scorching, for about a minute, or until fragrant and just turning color. Let cool completely, then grind in a spice grinder or in a mortar with a pestle to a medium-fine grind.

Put the almonds in a bowl, drizzle with the oil and salt, and toss to coat evenly. Add the spice mixture and toss again to distribute evenly. Spread the nuts in a single layer on a sheet pan.

Place the pan in the oven and toast the nuts, shaking the pan once at the halfway point, for 7 to 10 minutes, or until they appear toasted and are fragrant. Let cool completely, then coarsely chop and set aside.

TO READY THE HARICOTS VERTS, first prepare an ice bath. Then bring a large pot filled with water to a rolling boil. (If you don't have a large pot, you will need to cook the haricots verts in batches.) Add the haricots verts and cook for about 4 minutes, or until just tender. They should still have a slight crunch. Drain the beans and immediately submerge them in the ice bath for a minute or two to halt the cooking. Drain well again and spread on a kitchen towel to dry. Refrigerate until needed.

TO ASSEMBLE THE SALAD, in a large salad bowl, place the haricots verts, greens, all of the herbs, the ham, and the almonds. Drizzle the vinaigrette over the top and toss to coat evenly. Season with salt and pepper and toss again. Serve right away.

Anchor & Hope
CLAM CHOWDER
WITH HORSERADISH
AND TABASCO

Anchor & Hope is our nod to the classic New England fish house, so we always have chowder on the menu. Our version, developed by chef Sara Schafer, has an interesting twist. The addition of fresh horseradish and Tabasco at the end gives this soup an unexpected kick.

If you're pressed for time, you can use bottled clam juice for the stock and canned chopped clams. But it's better to avoid these shortcuts. Not only will making stock from fresh cherrystones (they are called "chowder clams" for good reason) result in a better-tasting chowder, but you will also have the satisfaction of knowing you made the chowder from scratch.

❧ SERVES 6 ❧

CLAM STOCK

1 tablespoon canola oil

½ yellow onion, sliced

1 Fresno chile, (or other medium hot chile, such as jalapeño or serrano) sliced

2 cups water

1 cup dry white wine

5 pounds cherrystone clams

1 tablespoon canola oil

3 slices thick-cut bacon

2 cups diced celery

2 cups diced yellow onion

3 thyme sprigs

1 bay leaf

2 cups peeled and cubed potatoes

4 tablespoons unsalted butter

¼ cup all-purpose flour

2 cups heavy cream

1 cup whole milk

1 cup half-and-half

2 teaspoons salt

2 tablespoons grated fresh horseradish

2 teaspoons Tabasco sauce

Freshly ground pepper

To make the stock, in a large, wide pot, heat the oil over medium heat. Add the onion and chile and sweat, stirring occasionally with a wooden spoon, for 5 to 7 minutes, or until beginning to soften. Do not allow them to color. Add the water, wine, and clams, stir well, cover, raise the heat to high, and cook, shaking the pot occasionally, for 10 to 12 minutes, or until the clams open.

Remove from the heat. Remove the clams from the pot, discarding any that failed to open. Strain the stock through a cheesecloth-lined strainer into a large measuring pitcher or bowl. You should have 4 cups. Pick the clams from the shells and discard the shells. Chop the clam meats. You should have about 1½ cups. Set the stock and clams aside separately for the chowder.

To make the chowder, in a large pot, heat the oil over medium-low heat. Add the bacon and sweat, stirring occasionally, for 7 to 9 minutes, or until soft and translucent. Do not allow the bacon to brown. Add the celery, onion, thyme, and bay leaf, reduce the heat to low, cover, and cook, stirring occasionally, for about 10 minutes, or until the vegetables are soft.

Add the potatoes, stir, and cook for about 5 minutes, then add the butter. When butter has melted, add the flour, stir to mix well, and then cook, stirring, for about 2 minutes to rid the flour of its raw flavor. Slowly pour in the 4 cups stock while stirring constantly. Raise the heat to medium and bring the mixture to a simmer and cook, stirring constantly, for 2 or 3 minutes, until it starts to thicken. Add the cream, milk, half-and-half, and salt and stir well. Bring to a simmer and cook, stirring occasionally, for about 15 minutes, or until potatoes are tender.

Add the $1^1/_2$ cups clams, the horseradish, and the Tabasco sauce, mix well, and then cook at a very low simmer for 5 minutes, or until the clams are heated through and flavors have blended.

Remove the thyme and bay leaf and discard. Season with pepper and stir well. Ladle into bowls and top each serving with a grind of pepper. Serve immediately.

Smoky
CHICKEN-HOCK GUMBO
with **ANDOUILLE SAUSAGE** and GREEN ONION

Down in New Orleans, everyone claims to have a gumbo recipe that's "the best ever." Well, I've got mine, too. Here it is. I learned the technique for making this gumbo twenty-five years ago, while working at K-Paul's in the French Quarter. The addition of the ham hock is something I came up with when we opened Town Hall. It adds body, richness, and a slightly smoky flavor. (If you can't find a ham hock, just double the amount of andouille sausage.) Making gumbo is an example of what I call a long-term relationship recipe. Not only do you have to find your way with it over time, but, let's face it, making gumbo takes a while. So think of this dish as an opportunity to cook for a group of your friends and get everyone involved. Simply put, gumbo is the perfect party dish. If you are on your own, gumbo, like most soups and stews, matures with time, so preparing it early in the morning or even a day in advance will only make it better.

A good gumbo demands a good roux, and making a good roux is an art. First, it helps to have the right tools. For the amount of roux this recipe requires, you need a cast-iron pan 8 to 10 inches in diameter. That's the perfect size for the amount of flour and oil you are going to use. Also, let's be honest here: When you make a roux, you need to be careful. If it gets on your skin, it is going to burn. They don't call it Cajun napalm for nothing.

SERVES 6

CHICKEN-HOCK STOCK

$2\frac{1}{2}$ pounds chicken bones (such as wings, necks, and backs)

1 ham hock

4 quarts water

1 carrot, sliced

1 celery stalk, sliced

1 yellow onion, sliced

1 bay leaf

1 teaspoon peppercorns

CHICKEN

1 whole chicken, or 6 pieces, such as 3 thighs and 3 breast halves, totaling $3\frac{1}{2}$ to 4 pounds

Oil, for frying

Salt

1 cup all-purpose flour

2 tablespoons Town Hall Spice Mixture (page 253)

ROUX

$\frac{3}{4}$ cup oil reserved from frying chicken (or fresh canola oil, if you prefer)

$\frac{3}{4}$ cup all-purpose flour

$\frac{1}{2}$ cup diced yellow onion

$\frac{1}{4}$ cup diced celery

$\frac{1}{4}$ cup diced green bell pepper

1 tablespoon Worcestershire sauce

1 teaspoon chopped garlic

1 teaspoon Town Hall Spice Mixture (page 253)

2 tablespoons oil reserved from frying chicken (or fresh canola oil, if you prefer)

4 cups diced yellow onion

$\frac{1}{4}$ pound andouille sausage, diced

3 tablespoons Town Hall Spice Mixture (page 253)

$2\frac{1}{2}$ cups diced green bell pepper

$1\frac{1}{2}$ cups diced celery

1 heaping teaspoon chopped garlic

1 heaping teaspoon diced jalapeño chile

1 teaspoon salt

2 quarts chicken-hock stock (above)

Freshly ground pepper

About 3 cups cooked white rice

2 green onions, green part only, thinly sliced on the diagonal

To MAKE THE STOCK, preheat the oven to 375°F. Place the chicken bones and ham hock on a sheet pan and roast, turning once, for about 45 minutes, or until golden brown.

Transfer the browned bones and hock to a large stockpot. With a spatula, scrape up any browned bits stuck to the sheet pan and add to the pot, then pour in the 4 quarts water. Bring to a boil over high heat, then lower the heat to a simmer and skim off any fat and foam that has accumulated on the surface. Add the carrot, celery, onion, bay leaf, and peppercorns and stir well. Simmer uncovered, stirring occasionally, for 1 hour.

Remove the pot from the heat. Lift out the ham hock, let cool, pull off the meat, and set aside. Strain the stock through a fine-mesh sieve, discarding the solids. Measure out 2 quarts of the stock for the gumbo, cover, and refrigerate. Reserve the remaining stock for another use. It will keep in the refrigerator for up to 3 to 4 days or in the freezer for up to 2 months.

To COOK THE CHICKEN, pour the oil to a depth of $1^{1}/_{2}$ inches into a large, deep frying pan and heat to 375°F. Meanwhile, season the chicken with a little salt. In a large zippered plastic bag, combine the flour and spice mixture, seal closed, and shake to mix. Then, add the chicken pieces to the flour mixture one at a time and shake to coat evenly.

Shake off the excess flour from each chicken piece, place in the hot oil skin side down, and fry, turning once, for about 7 minutes on each side, or until the pieces are a deep golden brown and cooked through. (If the pan is not large enough to fry the chicken without crowding, cook the pieces in batches, always allowing the oil to return to 375°F before adding a new batch.) Using a slotted spoon, transfer the pieces to a plate.

When the chicken pieces are cool enough to handle, pull the meat off the bones, discard the bones, and set the meat aside. Let the oil cool to room temperature, then strain through a fine-mesh strainer into a clean container and set aside.

To MAKE THE ROUX, have a sheet pan ready for cooling it. Heat the oil in a cast-iron pan over a high flame until the surface of the oil just starts to ripple. Add the flour and whisk continuously. When it starts to brown lightly, turn down the heat to medium-low and continue whisking for about 5 minutes, or until the roux becomes a deep reddish brown. Take the pan off the heat, stir in the onion, celery, and bell pepper, and continue to stir for 1 minute. Transfer the mixture to the sheet pan, spread it out, and let it cool for 2 to 3 minutes. Drizzle the Worcestershire sauce evenly over the top, then scatter the garlic and spice mixture evenly over the top. Stir to combine and set aside.

To FINISH THE GUMBO, in a large pot, heat the oil over medium-high heat. Add the onions and cook, stirring occasionally, for about 5 minutes, or until they start to brown. Lower the heat to medium, add the sausage and 1 tablespoon of the spice mixture, and stir and scrape for about 1 minute, or until the spice mixture is lightly toasted and fragrant. Lower the heat to medium-low and cook for 2 more minutes, continuing to stir and scrape and doing your best to prevent anything from sticking to the bottom of the pot.

Add the bell pepper and celery and stir well. Add the garlic, jalapeño, the remaining 2 tablespoons of the spice mixture, and the salt and cook, stirring and scraping occasionally, for about 10 minutes.

Skim off and discard any fat from the surface of the 2 quarts stock, then add the stock to the pot and stir well, making sure you scrape the bottom and sides of the pot. Bring to a boil over high heat, then lower the heat to a simmer and skim off any fat from the surface. Begin adding the roux, 1 tablespoon at a time, stirring to incorporate each addition completely before adding the next tablespoon. When all of the roux has been incorporated, stir well and simmer for 45 minutes, stirring occasionally.

Finally, fold in the reserved chicken and ham hock meat and heat through. Season with the pepper, then taste and adjust the seasoning.

To SERVE, place a heaping spoonful of rice into each individual bowl and ladle the gumbo over the top. Garnish with the green onions and serve right away.

TUNA TARTARE

with TABASCO VINAIGRETTE

and Fried Green TOMATOES

I love southern flavors. I also love tuna tartare. At first glance, that seems like an odd pair, but the Tabasco adds a vinegary heat that brightens the flavor of the tuna. We serve the tartare with fried green tomatoes (and it doesn't get more southern than that). The tomatoes can also go solo as a first course. Drizzle them with the aioli included here, with the chile-lime dipping sauce that accompanies the shrimp fritters on page 53, or with a few dashes of Harissa Vinaigrette (page 251).

❋ SERVES 6 ❋

GARLIC OIL

$\frac{1}{2}$ cup canola oil

2 cloves garlic, halved

VINAIGRETTE

$\frac{1}{2}$ cup garlic oil (above)

2 tablespoons champagne vinegar

1 tablespoon Tabasco sauce

2 tablespoons finely diced shallot

$1\frac{1}{2}$ tablespoons green onions, green part only, thinly sliced

$\frac{1}{2}$ teaspoon salt

Freshly ground pepper

RED PEPPER AIOLI

1 red bell pepper

1 large egg yolk, at room temperature

1 clove garlic, chopped

$\frac{1}{4}$ cup extra-virgin olive oil

$\frac{1}{4}$ cup canola oil

1 tablespoon freshly squeezed lemon juice

$\frac{1}{8}$ teaspoon cayenne pepper

Salt and freshly ground black pepper

TARTARE

1 pound sushi-grade yellowfin (ahi) tuna, finely diced

1 tablespoon thinly sliced fresh chives

$\frac{3}{4}$ cup vinaigrette (above)

1 tablespoon Tabasco sauce

Salt and freshly ground pepper

FRIED GREEN TOMATOES

Canola oil, for frying

2 cups buttermilk

$\frac{1}{2}$ cup all-purpose flour

$\frac{1}{2}$ cup fine ground yellow cornmeal

Salt and freshly ground pepper

3 green tomatoes

To make the garlic oil, in a small saucepan, combine the oil and garlic over low heat and bring to a simmer, taking care not to let the garlic brown. Simmer for 5 minutes, then remove from the heat and let stand for 3 hours. Strain through a fine-mesh sieve and reserve to use for the vinaigrette.

To make the vinaigrette, whisk together the garlic oil, vinegar, and Tabasco sauce. Then whisk in the shallot, green onion, salt, and a few grinds of pepper. Set aside.

To make the aioli, using tongs, hold the bell pepper over the flame of a gas burner, turning as needed, until blackened and blistered on all sides. Or, blacken and blister the pepper under a preheated broiler, watching carefully to

continued

avoid burning the flesh. Transfer the blackened pepper to a bowl, cover with plastic wrap, and let stand for 10 minutes.

Remove from the bowl and let cool to room temperature. Peel the pepper, cut in half, and discard the seeds. Coarsely chop half of the pepper. Reserve the other half for another use.

In a blender, combine the egg yolk and garlic and blend until smooth. With the blender running, add the olive oil and then the canola oil in a slow, steady stream, processing until emulsified. Add the roasted bell pepper and process until smooth. Finally, add the lemon juice and cayenne pepper, season with salt and black pepper, and process to mix. Cover and refrigerate until serving.

TO MAKE THE TARTARE, in a bowl, combine the tuna, chives, and vinaigrette. Season with the Tabasco and with salt and pepper and stir gently with a fork, taking care not to overmix. Cover and refrigerate until serving.

TO FRY THE GREEN TOMATOES, pour the oil to a depth of 1 inch into a cast-iron frying pan and heat to 350°F (to test, place a tomato in the pan, it should sizzle rapidly). While the oil is heating, pour the buttermilk into a shallow bowl. In a second shallow bowl, stir together the flour and cornmeal and season with salt and pepper. Slice the tomatoes into $^{1}/_{4}$-inch-thick rounds, then cut each slice in half.

One at a time, coat the tomato slices with the buttermilk, allowing the excess to drip away, and then coat with the flour-cornmeal mixture, coating completely and shaking off the excess. As the tomatoes are coated, put them on a large platter or sheet pan.

When the oil is ready, working in batches, add the tomatoes to the hot oil and fry, turning once, for about 2 or 3 minutes on each side, or until golden brown. Using a slotted spatula, transfer the slices to paper towels to drain. Season the hot slices with salt.

To serve, place a small mound of tartare on each plate. Fan the tomato slices around the tartare, and drizzle with the aioli.

SHRIMP FRITTERS

with CHILE-LIME

Dipping Sauce

People love shrimp. So it makes sense that people love these shrimp fritters. We use seltzer in the batter, something Sarah Schafer picked up from a friend's mom who uses it when making matzo balls. The carbonation in the seltzer makes the fritters fluffier. Remember, a good fritter is golden brown on the outside and light and fluffy on the inside. With that in mind, I can't emphasize enough testing a single fritter. If it comes out too dark, turn down the oil; too dense, thin out the batter. Like in all things, you have to find the right balance.

MAKES 24 FRITTERS; SERVES 6

CHILE-LIME DIPPING SAUCE

3 red Fresno, or jalapeño chiles

1 red bell pepper

1 tablespoon firmly packed brown sugar

1 tablespoon champagne vinegar

3/4 teaspoon salt

Freshly ground pepper

1 cup canola oil

Juice of 1 lime

FRITTERS

Canola oil, for deep-frying

1 1/2 pounds peeled and deveined shrimp, chopped

1 small yellow onion, finely minced

1 large red bell pepper, seeded and finely minced

1/4 cup chopped fresh cilantro

2 large eggs

5 tablespoons seltzer

5 tablespoons freshly squeezed lime juice

1 tablespoon salt

Freshly ground pepper

1 1/2 cups pastry flour

To make the dipping sauce, place the chiles and the bell pepper in a dry cast-iron frying pan over high heat. Cook, turning as needed, for about 15 minutes, or until the skin is blackened and blistered on all sides. Or, blacken and blister the chiles and pepper under a preheated broiler, watching carefully to avoid burning the flesh. Transfer the blackened chiles and pepper to a bowl, cover with plastic wrap, and let stand for 10 minutes. Remove from the bowl and let cool to room temperature. Peel the bell pepper, cut in half, and discard the seeds. Reserve half of the pepper for another use. Peel the chiles but do not seed. Chop the chiles and pepper coarsely.

In a blender, combine chopped chiles and pepper, sugar, vinegar, salt, and a few grinds of pepper and process until smooth. With the blender running, add the oil slowly, about 1 tablespoon at a time, and process until emulsified. Then add the lime juice and process until blended. Taste and adjust the seasoning.

To make the fritters, pour the oil to a depth of 3 to 3 1/2 inches into a deep fryer or deep, heavy-bottomed pot and heat to 375°F. While the oil is heating, in a bowl, combine the shrimp, onion, bell pepper, cilantro, eggs, seltzer, lime juice, salt, and a few grinds of pepper and stir until well combined. Add the flour and mix well.

When the oil is ready, work in batches, cooking 6 to 8 fritters at a time, to avoid crowding. To form each fritter, drop 1 tablespoon of the batter into the hot oil. Fry the fritters for 2 to 3 minutes, or until golden brown. Using a slotted spoon, transfer to paper towels to drain. Keep warm while you fry the remaining fritters.

Serve immediately on a platter or individual plates with the dipping sauce on the side.

Cured Salmon

with POTATO LATKES

and DILL CRÈME FRAÎCHE

My brother, Steven, is our go-to guy when it comes to making latkes. He learned this recipe more than thirty years ago from Tom Plaganis at the Jewish deli in New Jersey where we got our start. Even after he retired, Tom would come in every day to make what we called his "crazy pies." He'd bake all morning and then we'd drive him home in the afternoon for a nap. One day he never woke up. The owner, Jack Cooper, went to his widow and apologized: "I'm so sorry," he said, "I shouldn't have let him to continue to work." Mrs. Plaganis shot back, "Are you crazy, Jack? Tom was so happy doing what he loved to do. It was a perfect ending." Tom's recipe has served us well, not only in our restaurants, but also as a staple at just about every party we throw. Two things set these latkes apart: the high onion-to-potato ratio that gives them a lot more flavor, and the "shallow-fry" method of cooking. Make sure the oil is half as deep as the height of a latke, and your latkes will have crispy exteriors and creamy centers, just like Tom's. At the deli, we served these latkes with smoked salmon, which you can use if you don't have time to cure the salmon. They are also good enough to eat on their own with a spoonful of crème fraîche.

This cured salmon, also known as gravlax (literally, "salmon in the grave"), originated in Scandinavia. At Anchor & Hope, we tried a variety of curing mixtures before hitting on this recipe, which gives you a salmon that is highly aromatic, evenly cured, and wonderfully versatile. It reminds me of the salmon we used to serve at the Celebrity Deli, so it is paired here with latkes. At Anchor & Hope, it tops a salad. You can also spin it in a food processor with some butter to make a great spread, or chop some and add it to scrambled eggs. You will need to begin curing the salmon three days before you want to serve it.

❧ SERVES 6 ❧

1 skin-on center-cut salmon fillets, about 1½ pounds

CURING MIXTURE

1 cup sugar

1 cup sea salt

1 tablespoon ground allspice

1 tablespoon freshly ground pepper

1 tablespoon ground coriander

1 tablespoon ground fennel

1 tablespoon ground star anise

Grated zest of 1 lemon

Grated zest of 1 lime

Grated zest of 1 orange

½ fennel bulb, trimmed

DILL CRÈME FRAÎCHE

½ cup crème fraîche

½ cup sour cream

1 tablespoon chopped fresh dill

⅛ teaspoon salt

Grated zest of 1 lemon

LATKES

1 yellow onion

1 very large russet potato, about 1 pound, peeled

1 large egg

1 teaspoon salt

Freshly ground pepper

2 tablespoons all-purpose flour

¼ teaspoon baking powder

Canola oil, for frying

Caviar (optional)

continued

To prepare the salmon, using a sharp knife, cut 10 to 12 evenly spaced small slits in the skin of the salmon.

To make the curing mixture, in a bowl, stir together the sugar, salt, all of the spices, and all of the citrus zests, mixing well. Using a mandoline or a sharp knife, thinly shave the fennel bulb, then add it to the bowl and mix well.

Lay a long sheet of plastic wrap on a sheet pan, and spread half of the curing mixture on the plastic wrap, forming it into a rectangle about the size of the salmon fillet. Place the salmon, skin side down, on top of the mixture. Spread the remaining curing mixture on the flesh side of the salmon, then wrap the salmon tightly in the plastic wrap. Refrigerate the salmon on the tray for 3 days, turning the salmon over once a day.

When the salmon is ready, unwrap it, rinse it well, dry it well, and then rewrap. It will keep in the refrigerator for up to 1 week.

To prepare the crème fraîche, in a small bowl, stir together all of the ingredients, mixing well. Refrigerate until serving.

To prepare the latkes, place a fine-mesh strainer over a bowl. You will use the strainer to drain the grated onion and potato. Using the medium holes on a hand grater, grate the onion and place it in the strainer. Then grate the potato and add to the strainer. (Be sure to grate the onion first, as the potato will oxidize and discolor quickly.) Mix together the grated onion and potato well in the strainer, then press down gently to remove excess liquid. Transfer to a bowl.

Add the egg, salt, and a few grinds of pepper and stir to mix. When the ingredients are evenly combined, add the flour and baking powder and mix well.

Pour the oil to a depth of about ½ inch into a heavy frying pan (preferably cast-iron) and heat to 325°F. To form each latke, drop a heaping tablespoon of the potato mixture into the hot oil and fry, turning once, for about 4 to 6 minutes, or until brown and crispy on both sides. Be careful not to crowd the latkes in the pan. When they are ready, using a slotted spoon, transfer to a paper towels. You should have about 18 latkes.

To serve, thinly slice the salmon. Place three latkes on each of six plates (or serve on a platter), spoon a dollop of the crème fraîche on each hot latke, then lay a salmon slice on top.

BBQ SHRIMP

with Toasted

GARLIC BREAD

A few years ago, my brother-in-law Jonny and I took a road trip through Cajun country. The restaurant I had wanted to visit, in Lafayette, Louisiana, was closed. So we drove to the nearby town of Breaux Bridge and ended up at a place called Café Des Amis. We ordered a ton of food, including some BBQ shrimp. It was such an amazing dish that we ended up fighting over the last few bites. I won. When I got back to San Francisco, I immediately set to work trying to replicate those BBQ shrimp. It took a while to get the amounts right and to reduce the sauce to the correct consistency, but once I did, I was transported back to that small Cajun café and the memory of sopping up that incredible sauce. And the hard work paid off. BBQ shrimp is the most popular appetizer on the Town Hall menu.

You'll notice that while every other recipe in this chapter serves six, this recipe is for three. There's no way around it. To serve six, you'll have to make it twice. No "doubling" here. That's because to create the beautiful, silky sauce . . . well, it has to do with emulsification and ratios (it's science, just trust me here). If you decide to make the recipe twice, your labor will be worth the extra time. This sauce smothers the whole dish and is so intensely flavored that it makes the bread as much of a headliner as the shrimp.

❧ SERVES 3 ❧

Pictured on pages 60–61.

GARLIC BREAD

3 slices coarse country bread such as pain levain, about 1 inch thick

1 tablespoon olive oil

1 clove garlic, peeled but left whole

2 tablespoons chopped fresh flat-leaf parsley

BBQ SHRIMP

9 to 12 large tail-on shrimp, peeled, with tail segments intact, and deveined

Kosher salt

2 tablespoons canola oil

3/4 cup (6 ounces) plus 1 tablespoon unsalted butter

1 tablespoon chopped garlic

1 tablespoon Town Hall Spice Mixture (page 253)

1/2 cup Dixie Beer or your favorite lager such as Budweiser

1 cup Shrimp Stock (page 250)

2 tablespoons Worcestershire sauce

1 tablespoon freshly squeezed lemon juice

To MAKE THE GARLIC BREAD, preheat the oven to 350°F. Brush the bread slices on one side with the olive oil and place on a sheet pan. Toast in the oven, turning the slices over at the halfway point, for about 15 minutes, or until golden brown and very crisp. (The bread must be very crisp so that it can support the sauce.)

Remove from the oven, and rub each slice on one side with the garlic clove. Sprinkle evenly with the parsley and keep warm.

TO PREPARE THE SHRIMP, season them with salt. In a large sauté pan, heat the canola oil over medium-high heat. Add the shrimp and cook for about 2 minutes, or until they begin to turn pink. Lower the heat to medium, push the shrimp to one side of the pan, and add 1 tablespoon of the butter. Once it melts, add the garlic and spice mixture and cook for 1 minute, giving the pan a few shakes to distribute the garlic and seasoning. Add the beer and toss. With a pair of tongs, remove the shrimp from the pan, giving each one a little shake to drive off as much of the seasoning as possible, and set aside.

Turn the heat up to high and boil for 2 to 3 minutes, or until the beer mixture is reduced by half. Add the stock and Worcestershire sauce and continue to boil until the liquid is reduced by three-fourths.

Meanwhile, cut the remaining ¾ cup butter into 6 equal pieces. Lower the heat and whisk in the butter, one piece at a time, working each piece in completely before adding the next. When all of the butter has been incorporated, add the lemon juice and a pinch or two of salt, and stir well. Return the shrimp to the pan and stir until well coated.

Divide the garlic bread among individual plates and arrange the shrimp on top, dividing them evenly. Spoon a generous amount of the sauce over the shrimp and serve immediately.

Warm SEA URCHIN

with CRAB AND VERJUS BUTTER SAUCE

Sea urchin is scary. For most Americans, it is familiar as the uni they find on the menu at a Japanese restaurant or the round, spiky thing in the tide pool exhibit at the aquarium. Here it shares a bowl with crab and pureed potato, all slathered in a rich butter sauce, making for a tasty and approachable introduction to eating urchin and allowing its distinctive flavor to come through. This dish, which is served in a hollowed-out sea urchin shell at Anchor & Hope, has gotten more positive press than anything we've ever served. Look for the *verjus* (also known as verjuice; the juice of semiripe, unfermented wine grapes) in specialty-food stores and well-stocked supermarkets.

SERVES 6

POTATO PUREE

3 large or 5 medium russet potatoes, peeled and cut into 2-inch cubes

¹/₂ cup unsalted butter, at room temperature, cut into 4 or 5 pieces

1 cup heavy cream, warmed

Salt and freshly ground pepper

BUTTER SAUCE

¹/₄ cup verjus

¹/₄ cup dry white wine

¹/₄ cup champagne vinegar

1 shallot, sliced

10 ounces unsalted butter, cut into pieces

3 ounces freshly cooked lump crabmeat, picked over for shell and cartilage bits

4 plum tomatoes, peeled, seeded, and very finely diced (page 254)

2 tablespoons chopped fresh chervil

2 tablespoons chopped fresh flat-leaf parsley

2 tablespoons chopped fresh tarragon

2 tablespoons thinly sliced shallot

6 ounces sea urchin, about 9 "tongues," each tongue halved crosswise

TO MAKE THE POTATO PUREE, in a large pot, combine the potatoes with salted water to cover, place over medium-high heat, and bring to a boil. Lower the heat to a simmer and cook for about 20 minutes or until the potatoes are fork-tender.

Drain the potatoes, then return them to the pot and mash with a potato masher or pass them through a ricer or food mill back into the pot. Add the butter and cream and whisk or stir until well blended. Season with salt and pepper and keep warm.

TO MAKE THE BUTTER SAUCE, in a saucepan, combine the *verjus*, wine, vinegar, and shallot and bring to a boil over high heat. Lower the heat slightly and cook until reduced to about 1 tablespoon. Turn the heat to low and whisk in the butter, a few pieces at a time, making sure each addition is completely incorporated before adding more. When all of the butter has been added, strain the mixture through a fine-mesh strainer into a clean saucepan. Place over low heat and stir in the crabmeat, tomatoes, all of the herbs, and the shallot, mixing well. Cook for about 1 minute, then remove from the heat. Fold in the sea urchin to warm.

Divide the potato puree among individual plates, and spoon the urchin mixture on top. Serve right away.

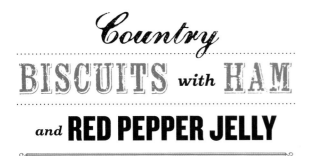

Country
BISCUITS *with* HAM
and RED PEPPER JELLY

A couple of months before Town Hall opened, an article about artisanal ham producers in the South appeared in the New York Times. It was good timing because we were looking for an interesting ham dish for the menu. We ordered hams from each company. They were all great, but when we tried the prosciutto-style from Johnston County Ham of Smithfield, North Carolina, we knew we had the one we wanted.

While testing this recipe, I found that the pepper jelly can be used in lots of ways, too. My wife and I found ourselves using it throughout the day, spreading it on an English muffin in the morning, pairing it with sausage in a sandwich at midday, and stirring it into a sauce for dinner. The biscuits and ham are also good with blackberry compote (following).

SERVES 6

RED PEPPER JELLY

2 red bell peppers

1 green bell pepper

3¼ cups sugar

¾ cup cider vinegar

1 teaspoon dried chile flakes

One 3-ounce packet liquid pectin

12 to 18 thin slices cured ham

Country Biscuits (page 252)

TO MAKE THE JELLY, halve all of the peppers lengthwise and remove and discard the stem, seeds, and membranes. Chop into 1-inch pieces. Working in batches, add the peppers to a food processor and pulse until finely chopped. Transfer the peppers to a heavy-bottomed pot and add the sugar, vinegar, and chile flakes.

Have ready a candy thermometer or place 2 or 3 small saucers in the freezer. Place the pot over high heat and bring to a boil, stirring to dissolve sugar. Lower the heat to medium-high, add the pectin, and cook, stirring occasionally, until the jelly registers 220°F on a candy thermometer (about 10 minutes). Alternatively, remove the pot from the heat and drop a small spoonful of the jelly onto a cold saucer, let stand for 1 minute, then push the edge of the jelly with a fingertip; if the top of the jelly wrinkles, it is ready. If it doesn't it, return the pot to the heat, cook for 2 to 3 more minutes, and test again.

Remove the jelly from the heat and let cool to room temperature before serving. The jelly can be covered and refrigerated for up to 1 month. Bring to room temperature before serving.

Arrange the ham slices on a platter and serve with warm biscuits and the pepper jelly alongside.

BLACKBERRY COMPOTE

4¼ cups fresh blackberries

½ cup granulated sugar

1½ tablespoons water

1½ tablespoons cornstarch

In a 2-quart saucepan, combine 2½ cups of the blackberries with the sugar over medium heat. Stir occasionally as the sugar melts and the berries release their juices. Meanwhile, in a small bowl, stir together the cornstarch and water to make a slurry. When the blackberry sugar mixture just starts to boil, whisk in the cornstarch slurry, then boil gently for a minute or two, or until slightly thickened. Remove from the heat, let cool slightly, and fold in the remaining berries. Let cool completely and serve at room temperature. The compote can be covered and refrigerated for up to a week. Bring to room temperature before serving.

Roasted
VEAL MEATBALLS
with GREEN PEPPERCORN
Sauce

These meatballs are the stuff of legend. This dish was reportedly invented when Czar Nicholas I ordered a veal cutlet and was served chicken disguised as veal instead. That dish, the Pozharsky cutlet, became a staple of Russian cuisine. I learned a variation of Pozharsky from legendary chef Seppi Renggli while working at the Four Seasons. It didn't occur to me at the time how funny it was to be grinding the finest veal in the world; mixing it with other ground meats, eggs, and white bread; molding the mixture into the shape of a veal chop; and attaching a bone for effect. My interpretation includes ricotta and Parmesan cheeses and is formed into bite-sized meatballs. But I've kept the classic green peppercorn sauce Seppi used, which surprises people because they are so used to having meatballs with tomato sauce. We served these meatballs as hors d'oeuvres on the opening night of Town Hall. Since that time, my wife, a great cook in her own right, has tried to take credit for putting them on the menu. The jury is still out on who deserves recognition for the idea, but one thing is known for sure: it was definitely a good idea because they are still on the menu.

SERVES 6

MEATBALLS

2 slices white bread, crusts removed, cubed, and soaked in ¹/₂ cup milk

1 pound ground veal

¹/₄ pound ground pork

¹/₄ pound ground beef

¹/₃ cup grated Parmesan cheese

¹/₄ cup fresh ricotta cheese

1 tablespoon chopped fresh flat-leaf parsley

4 teaspoons salt

Freshly ground pepper

Canola oil, for cooking

Potato Puree (see page 62)

GREEN PEPPERCORN SAUCE

1 tablespoon Canola oil

3 large shallots, thinly sliced

1 carrot, peeled and sliced

2 celery stalks, sliced

2 tablespoons Dijon mustard

¹/₂ cup sherry vinegar

¹/₂ cup brandy

2 tablespoons whole green peppercorns, plus 1 tablespoon crushed

2 cups dry red wine

1 cup port

2 cups veal demi-glace or Chicken Stock (page 250)

Freshly ground pepper

¹/₂ cup heavy cream

1 teaspoon salt

2 tablespoons unsalted butter, cut into pieces

Chopped fresh flat-leaf parsley, for garnish

To make the meatballs, gently squeeze out any excess milk from the bread. To mix the meat mixture in a stand mixer, fit the mixer with the paddle attachment and place the bread, all of the ground meats, both cheeses, the parsley, the salt, and a few grinds of pepper in the bowl and mix on low speed just until combined. Do not overmix. To mix the meat mixture by hand, put the ingredients in a large bowl and stir until just combined. Using your hands, shape the mixture into about 24 golf ball–sized balls (a generous 1 ounce each), and place them on a sheet pan. Refrigerate until you are ready to cook.

continued

TO MAKE THE SAUCE, heat the oil over medium heat in a sauté pan. Add the shallots, carrot, and celery and cook, stirring occasionally, until soft, about 10 minutes. Lower the heat, add the mustard, and stir well, then add the vinegar. Return the heat to medium and cook until the vinegar has evaporated. Add the brandy and the whole peppercorns, bring to a simmer, and simmer for 1 to 2 minutes. Add the red wine and port and simmer for about 10 minutes, or until reduced by one-fourth. Add the demi-glace and simmer for 15 minutes, or until reduced by half.

Remove from the heat and strain through a fine-mesh strainer into a clean saucepan. Season with a few grinds of pepper, place over medium heat, and whisk in the cream, the crushed peppercorns, and the salt. Bring the sauce to a simmer and simmer for a minute or two, then lower the heat and whisk in the butter, a few pieces at a time, whisking constantly. Remove from the heat and keep warm.

TO FINISH THE MEATBALLS, preheat the oven to 350°F. Pour the oil to a depth of $^1/_8$ inch into a large ovenproof frying pan and heat over medium-high heat. Add the meatballs and fry for about 3 to 5 minutes, or until browned on the underside. Transfer the pan to the oven and roast the meatballs for 7 to 8 minutes, or until nicely colored on top and cooked through.

To serve, place a small mound of the potatoes on each plate. Pile 4 meatballs on top of the potatoes and then ladle 4 tablespoons-or-so of the sauce over the top. Garnish with the parsley and serve right away.

CHAPTER THREE *The*

CHEESE

DEPARTMENT

What is it ABOUT CHEESY THINGS? They always seem to get people's attention. Maybe it's because you have a childhood memory of sitting at the kitchen table eating a grilled cheese sandwich. Or, perhaps it's the sheer ubiquity of cheese. After all, have you ever been to a party where there wasn't a cheese plate . . . which, of course, you were quick to graze? For some folks, it feels downright wicked to order something rich and decadent, like, say, cheese-rich *poutine* (page 92), in the middle of the meal, instead of reserving that sort of indulgence for the dessert course.

FOR REASONS OF FLAVOR AND VERSATILITY, most cultures around the world use cheese in their cuisines, and local cooks typically take great satisfaction in the quality and distinctiveness of their regional products. If you have ever had a cheese, any cheese, at perfect ripeness, you'll understand and appreciate the maker's pride. Cheese is something a friend of mine calls a "low-rent luxury." Unlike Champagne or caviar, a world-class artisanal cheese is not out of reach of most pocketbooks (well, yes, the five-hundred-dollar-a-pound Swedish moose milk cheese is, but that's the exception).

PART OF THE APPEAL OF CHEESE, part of the spell is that it is seemingly simple—milk, acid, enzyme—but can be had in an infinite number of variations to satisfy nearly everyone. And you can play with these variations, combine different types, and get interesting results. Faith's Warm Ham and Cheese Toast with Jalapeño Cream (page 90) is an example of mixing two types of cheese to bring a complex layered quality to otherwise simple ingredients, making it much more than that basic grilled cheese sandwich of your childhood.

Slow Roasted
TOMATO-BASIL TART
with ST. GEORGE CHEDDAR

This is another recipe inspired by a trip my wife and I took to Paris. We were there in the late summer and fell in love with a tomato and basil tart. When we got home, we went to the market, found the freshest heirloom tomatoes and basil available, and then made that tart. Although it was delicious, the tomatoes released too much of their liquid, which made the crust soggy. So we decided to slow roast the tomatoes to draw out their moisture and intensify their flavor before we added them to the tart shell. The smell and taste of the finished tart were so vivid that eating the tart was like taking a sensory vacation to Paris. If you have been to Paris, this tart will take you back. If you haven't been to Paris, it will give you a taste of what you will find when you do go.

I make a free-form tart shell using an Italian pastry dough known as *pasta frolla*, a shortbread-type dough that is more commonly used for fruit *crostate* (tarts), though I nix most of the sugar. St. George cheese—made in Northern California—is reminiscent of Cheddar but in the style of a traditional cheese of the Azorean island of Sao Jorge. What I like about this dish is that it can be used at any point during a meal. You can cut it up into small pieces for a great "small bite," serve it as an appetizer, or pair it with a salad for a satisfying main course.

❧ SERVES 3 ❧

SLOW-ROASTED TOMATOES

2 pounds plum tomatoes

¼ cup extra-virgin olive oil

1 tablespoon finely chopped fresh rosemary

Salt and freshly ground pepper

DOUGH

1 cup all-purpose flour, plus more for dusting

¼ teaspoon salt

6 tablespoons unsalted butter, cut into small pieces and chilled

5 tablespoons ice-cold water

2 tablespoons extra-virgin olive oil, plus more for drizzling

1 large yellow onion, thinly sliced

Salt and freshly ground pepper

½ pound St. George or medium-aged white Cheddar cheese, shredded

½ cup chiffonade-cut fresh basil (long, narrow strips)

2 tablespoons crème fraîche

1 large egg mixed with 1 tablespoon whole milk, for wash

To PREPARE THE TOMATOES, preheat the oven to 225°F. Cut each tomato in half crosswise and arrange, cut side up on a sheet pan. Drizzle the tomato halves evenly with the olive oil, then sprinkle with the rosemary. Season with salt and pepper.

Place in the oven and roast the tomatoes for 4 hours, or until the moisture is removed. Remove from the oven and let cool completely.

TO PREPARE THE DOUGH, in a bowl, whisk together the flour and salt. Scatter the butter over the flour mixture and, using your fingers, gently press the butter and flour together until it resembles a coarse meal. Drizzle the ice water over the top and, using a fork, gently stir and toss just until the dough comes together.

Gather the dough into a ball and place on a lightly floured work surface. Flatten the dough into a thick disk and wrap in plastic wrap. Refrigerate for at least 1 hour or up to two days.

TO FINISH THE TART, position a rack in the lower third of the oven and preheat to 375°F. In a sauté pan, heat the 2 tablespoons oil over low heat and stir in the onion. Cover and sweat over low heat for 10 to 15 minutes, or until the onion is soft and translucent. Do not allow the onion to color. Remove from the heat, season with salt and pepper, and let cool completely.

continued

Line a sheet pan with parchment paper. On a lightly floured work surface, roll out the dough into a round about 12 inches in diameter. Carefully transfer the round to the prepared sheet pan.

Layer half of the cheese on the dough round, leaving a 1-inch border uncovered around the edge. In a small bowl, combine the cooled onion, the basil, and the crème fraîche and mix well. Spread the onion mixture evenly over the cheese layer. Top with the roasted tomatoes, then cover with the remaining cheese. Season with salt and pepper and top with a drizzle of olive oil. Fold up the uncovered edge of the tart, folding it onto itself to form uniformly spaced pleats every few inches around the perimeter. Brush the upturned edge with the egg wash.

Bake the tart for about 50 minutes, or until the crust is a nice golden brown.. Remove from the oven, transfer to a wire rack and let cool. Slice and serve.

Creamy

STONE-GROUND GRITS
with VERMONT CHEDDAR

4 cups whole milk

4 cups water

2 cups stone-ground grits

1 cup grated sharp Vermont Cheddar or other sharp
Cheddar cheese

3/4 teaspoon salt

Freshly ground pepper

These grits, with the generous use of Cheddar cheese, are a southern classic. Perfectly cooked high-quality grits will have body and form and offer an easy-to-understand example of what I mean when I talk about mouthfeel. Put another way, this ain't polenta. At our restaurants, we use heirloom grits from Anson Mills in South Carolina (seek them out; the product is an American treasure) and prepare them in a double boiler. This method may take a little longer, but it ensures that your grits won't scorch.

❦ SERVES 6 ❦

IN A HEAVY-BOTTOMED PAN, combine the milk and water and bring to a simmer over medium heat. Slowly add the grits in a steady stream while whisking constantly. Continue whisking for about 8 minutes, or until the grits thicken.

Meanwhile, pour water into the bottom of a double boiler, place over medium-low heat, and bring to a simmer. When the grits are ready, transfer them to the top of the double boiler and place over (not touching) the simmering water. Cook, stirring occasionally, for about 35 minutes, or until creamy.

Add all but 1 tablespoon of the cheese, the salt, and a few grinds of pepper and stir until the cheese melts and is well combined. Just before the grits are ready, preheat the broiler.

Transfer the cheese grits to a flameproof gratin dish and sprinkle the reserved 1 tablespoon cheese evenly over the top. Broil until bubbly, then serve at once.

Crispy Stuffed

ZUCCHINI BLOSSOMS

with BASIL CREAM

On one level, this is a very delicate dish: a flower filled with a lovely combination of summer flavors—tomato, basil, a quartet of cheeses—then dipped into a light batter and gently fried in oil. On another level, using zucchini blossoms is a pretty great way to eat fried cheese.

❧ MAKES 12 STUFFED BLOSSOMS; SERVES 6 ❧

FOUR CHEESE FILLING

1 cup fresh ricotta cheese

1/2 cup grated Parmesan cheese

1/2 cup grated sharp white Cheddar cheese

1/4 cup crumbled fresh goat cheese

1 tablespoon chiffonade-cut fresh basil (long, narrow strips)

1/2 teaspoon salt

Freshly ground pepper

BATTER

1/2 cup plus 2 tablespoons all-purpose flour

1/2 cup plus 2 tablespoons rice flour

1 1/2 cups seltzer

1 large egg yolk

1/2 teaspoon salt

Freshly ground pepper

BASIL CREAM

2 cups loosely packed fresh basil leaves

1 cup loosely packed spinach leaves, tough stems removed

1/2 cup crème fraîche

1 tablespoon heavy cream

1/2 teaspoon salt

Canola oil, for deep-frying

12 zucchini blossoms

Salt

12 to 18 cherry tomatoes, sliced

To MAKE THE FILLING, scoop the ricotta into a fine-mesh strainer lined with cheesecloth, place over a bowl and let stand for at least 30 minutes.

In a bowl, combine the drained ricotta, the remaining cheeses, the basil, the salt, and a few grinds of pepper and mix well. Taste and adjust the seasoning.

TO MAKE THE BATTER, in a large bowl, combine all of the ingredients and mix well, until all the lumps are gone. Set aside to rest for at least 15 minutes.

TO MAKE THE BASIL CREAM, have ready an ice bath. Bring a saucepan filled with water to a boil. Add the basil and spinach and blanch for 30 seconds, then drain and immediately transfer to the ice bath to halt the cooking. Drain again, squeeze out as much water as possible, and place in a blender. Add the crème fraîche, cream and salt and process until smooth.

TO FILL AND FRY THE BLOSSOMS, pour the oil to a depth of 3 to 3 1/2 inches into a deep fryer or deep, heavy-bottomed pot and heat to 365°F. Meanwhile, take a squash blossom in your hand, open it up, and remove the stamen (this sounds vaguely naughty but is necessary). Spoon about 2 tablespoons of the filling into the blossom (the amount will vary depending on the size of the flower), then gently press the blossom together and softly twist the end closed. Repeat with the remaining blossoms.

Working in batches to avoid crowding, twirl each filled blossom in the batter, allowing the excess to drip off, and add to the hot oil. Fry for about 2 minutes, or until they are a light-golden brown. Using a slotted spoon, drain on paper towels and season with salt. Keep warm while you fry the remaining blossoms.

Put a few tablespoons of the basil sauce on each individual plate and top with 2 squash blossoms. Place 2 or 3 sliced cherry tomatoes on each pair of blossoms and serve.

CAESAR SALAD
with Croutons

At a restaurant, it is rare to be served a Caesar salad that's made just right. More often than not, the problem is one of balance: too much anchovy, too much garlic, too little lemon juice. This recipe avoids all of those pitfalls. This is a variation on the Caesar dressing that was served at Postrio, which was simply called garlic vinaigrette. But that recipe was designed for large quantities and required extra steps, such as coddling the eggs before emulsifying them. So I decided to coddle the home cook by using this recipe, which is not only easier, but also results in a fresher, brighter, and more direct preparation of the classic dressing.

SERVES 6

CROUTONS

4 thick slices coarse country bread such as pain levain, cut into ³/₄-inch cubes

¹/₄ cup extra-virgin olive oil

Salt and freshly ground pepper

DRESSING

1 large egg

1 tablespoon whole grain mustard

2 tablespoons freshly squeezed lemon juice

1 tablespoon sherry vinegar

1 tablespoon finely chopped garlic (about 4 cloves)

1 tablespoon finely chopped anchovy (about 4 fillets)

1 tablespoon capers, rinsed

¹/₂ cup extra-virgin olive oil

¹/₂ cup canola oil

¹/₄ cup grated Parmesan cheese

Salt and freshly ground pepper

3 to 4 heads of romaine lettuce, cut into 1-inch pieces

³/₄ cup grated Parmesan cheese

Freshly ground pepper

To make the croutons, preheat the oven to 350°F. Place the bread cubes in a bowl, drizzle with the olive oil, season with a few pinches each of salt and pepper, and toss to coat evenly. Spread the seasoned cubes on a sheet pan, place in the oven, and toast for 12 to 15 minutes, or until nicely browned. Remove from the oven and let cool completely.

To make the dressing, in a food processor, combine the egg, mustard, lemon juice, vinegar, garlic, anchovy, and capers and pulse for 45 to 60 seconds, or until well combined. With the processor running, add both oils in a slow, steady stream, processing until emulsified. Add the cheese and pulse for 4 or 5 seconds to combine. Season with salt and pepper.

Put the lettuce in a large bowl, drizzle with the dressing, and toss to coat evenly. Add the croutons and toss again. Divide the salad among individual plates and garnish with the Parmesan, dividing it evenly. Top each salad with a few grinds of pepper and serve immediately.

Cheesy Rösti
POTATO CAKE
with ROASTED GARLIC and Thyme

Working on this book has caused me to reflect on my life as a cook, mining the memories of more than a third of a century spent in the kitchen. In doing so, I realized that one of my constant companions over this time has been the potato cake. At the Jewish, deli I was frequently tasked with frying the latkes I introduced you to earlier, and in my early days at Postrio, I was often found preparing the delicate French gallete, which we served with smoked sturgeon. This version of the potato cake, beautifully crisp and loaded with roasted garlic and cheese, was one of the first things I was responsible for during my apprenticeship with Seppi Renggli at the Four Seasons. It was a popular side dish there, and Seppi was incredibly meticulous about its method of preparation. That meticulousness comes as no surprise when you consider that Seppi trained in Switzerland, where rösti is considered the national dish.

❧ SERVES 6 TO 3 ❧

2 heads garlic

1/3 cup plus 2 tablespoons olive oil

3 large russet potatoes

4 ounces fontina cheese, grated

1 ounce Parmesan cheese, grated

1 teaspoon chopped fresh thyme

Salt and pepper

PREHEAT oven to 350°F.

TO ROAST THE GARLIC, cut the top off of each head of garlic, about 1/8 of an inch to expose the cloves. Put in a shallow pan and drizzle a tablespoon of the olive oil over each, season with salt and pepper. Cover the pan with foil and roast in the oven until cloves are soft and creamy, about 45 minutes to an hour. When done, and cool enough to handle, squeeze the cloves from their papery skin and set aside.

TO STEAM THE POTATOES, place a collapsible metal vegetable steamer basket in a large heavy-bottomed pot with an inch of water. Bring the water to a boil, add the whole, unpeeled potatoes and steam for 16 minutes. Set the potatoes aside to cool.

It is important that the potatoes are completely cool before continuing. When they are, peel the potatoes and grate on the largest hole of a box grater and season with salt and pepper.

In a bowl, toss together the grated fontina and Parmesan and set aside.

TO MAKE THE RÖSTI, heat one-half of the oil in a heavy-bottomed frying pan over medium heat. Add half of the grated potatoes and distribute them evenly, pushing them down with the spatula and shaping them to the form of the pan. Next layer the roasted garlic cloves evenly on top of the potatoes. Then, layer the grated cheese over the garlic and potatoes in an even circle, leaving about 1/4 inch from the edge of the pan. Pack the cheese down with the spatula, and then sprinkle with the chopped thyme, and cover with the remaining half of the grated potatoes, making sure to cover the garlic and cheese completely and evenly. Pack it down and cook for 5 to 7 minutes, or until the potatoes are crispy and golden brown. When ready, turn the rösti over. This can be accomplished using either a spatula, a quick flick of the wrist, or by turning it out onto a plate, and then back into the pan. After it has been flipped, cook for 5 more minutes, then slip the pan into the oven for another 5 minutes. Slice and serve immediately.

PENNE PASTA
QUATTRO FORMAGGI
with BUTTERNUT SQUASH *and Sage*

A national cooking magazine once named my wife's version of macaroni and cheese the creamiest in the country. That was some accolade. Although that happened a few years ago, she still deserves the recognition, as evidenced by this dish. Here, we add the classic winter pairing of roasted butternut squash and sage to the pasta and quartet of rich cheeses, which makes a lovely combination—and is a deliciously sneaky way to get kids to eat their vegetables.

SERVES 6

Pictured on pages 82–83.

1-pound piece butternut squash, peeled and cut into large batons

3 tablespoons olive oil, divided

1 tablespoon chopped fresh sage

Salt and freshly ground pepper

1 pound penne pasta

1 tablespoon olive oil

CHEESE SAUCE

3 tablespoons unsalted butter

3 tablespoons all-purpose flour

2 cups whole milk

2 cups heavy cream

1⅓ cups grated fontina cheese

¾ cup crumbled Point Reyes Original Blue, Maytag Blue, or other good-quality blue cheese

½ cup grated Pecorino Romano cheese

¾ cup grated Parmesean cheese

Salt and freshly ground pepper

TOPPING

4 thick slices coarse country bread such as pain levain

Few drops of olive oil

Salt and freshly ground pepper

½ cup grated Parmesan

1 tablespoon chopped fresh sage

2 tablespoons unsalted butter, melted

PREHEAT THE OVEN to 375°F. Place the squash in a bowl, drizzle with the 2 tablespoons of oil, sprinkle with the sage, and toss to coat evenly. Season with salt and pepper and toss again. Spread in a single layer on a sheet pan, place in the oven, and roast for 15 to 20 minutes, or until tender. Remove from the oven and set aside.

Bring a large pot filled with salted water to a boil. Add the penne, stir, and cook until al dente, according to package directions. Drain into a colander and hold under cold running water to stop the cooking. Transfer to a large bowl, drizzle with the remaining tablespoon of oil, and toss to coat.

TO MAKE THE CHEESE SAUCE, in a saucepan, melt the butter over low heat. Whisk in the flour, then whisk constantly for 3 to 4 minutes to cook away the raw flour taste. Slowly add the milk and cream, whisking constantly to prevent lumps from forming. Raise the heat to medium and simmer, stirring occasionally, for about 15 minutes, or until reduced by a third. Remove from the heat, add all of the cheeses, and stir until melted. Season with salt and pepper and set aside.

TO MAKE THE TOPPING, cut off and discard the crusts from the bread slices, then cut the slices into cubes. Place the cubes in a food processor and pulse until fine crumbs form. Transfer to a bowl, add the oil, and season with salt and pepper, then toss to mix. Add the Parmesan and the sage, and stir to mix.

Preheat the oven to 400°F. Add the cheese sauce and squash to the pasta and stir to mix well. Transfer the mixture to a 9 by -13-inch baking dish and scatter the topping evenly over the surface.

Bake for 10 to 12 minutes, or until heated through, the topping is lightly browned, and the cheese sauce is bubbly. Serve immediately.

Sweet Onion
AND FUNKY CHEESE
FONDUE

Paris again. This fondue was inspired by a visit my wife and I made to a restaurant in the Marais district called Au Bourguignon du Marais which serves, as the name implies, Burgundian wine and food. After we had eaten there a few times, the owner befriended us. When he found out I was a chef, he wanted to treat us to something special. He served us one of the most delicious cheese preparations I have ever eaten: warmed Époisses on a sweet onion–vermouth sauce. I immediately asked if he would take me into the kitchen and teach me how to make it. Years later, when thinking about fondues, I thought if I added a funky cheese, such as the locally produced Cowgirl Creamery's triple-cream, rind-washed Red Hawk, to an onion-vermouth sauce it would make a great combination. And it did.

❧ SERVES 6 TO 3 ❧

3 tablespoons unsalted butter

1 large yellow onion, sliced (about 3 cups)

1 tablespoon salt

3 tablespoons all-purpose flour

2¹⁄₂ cups dry vermouth

2 cups heavy cream

6 ounces Red Hawk, Époisses, or other ripe triple-cream cheese, rind removed and sliced into ¹⁄₈-thick pieces

3 ounces Gruyère cheese, grated

Freshly ground pepper

1 medium-sized loaf coarse county bread such as pain levain, cubed

In a heavy-bottomed saucepan, melt the butter over low heat and stir in the onion and 1¹⁄₂ teaspoons of the salt. Cover and sweat the onion for about 15 minutes, or until soft and translucent. Do not allow the onion to color.

Stir in the flour and cook, stirring constantly, for a few minutes to cook away the raw flour taste. Pour in 2 cups of the vermouth, stir, and raise the heat to medium-high. Bring to a simmer and cook for 2 minutes. Pour in the cream and continue to simmer, stirring occasionally, for about 15 minutes, or until reduced to 3 cups. Add the remaining ¹⁄₂ cup vermouth and cook for 5 more minutes.

Remove from the heat and let cool slightly, then transfer the mixture to a blender and process until smooth. Return the puree to the pan, place over low heat, add both cheeses, and stir until smooth. Season with the remaining 1¹⁄₂ teaspoons salt and a few grinds of pepper, then taste and adjust the seasoning.

Pour the fondue into a fondue pot placed over a warmer (or similar setup). Serve immediately with the bread for dipping.

ASPARAGUS FONDUE
with Truffle Oil

In California, asparagus season starts in late February and, with luck, lasts until early June. At Town Hall, we serve this seasonal asparagus cheese fondue during those months. We know that you can find a bunch of asparagus in your produce aisle year-round, but we recommend that you make this fondue when asparagus is in season in your area, when the spears are at their most tender. Although a poached egg is a classic accompaniment to asparagus, it's not absolutely necessary here. That said, we recommend it highly.

❧ SERVES 6 TO 8 ❧

ASPARAGUS PUREE

1 tablespoon olive oil

1 shallot, thinly sliced

1 pound asparagus, tough ends discarded and cut into $1/2$-inch pieces

$3/4$ teaspoon salt

$1/2$ cup water or Chicken Stock (see page 250)

FONDUE

3 tablespoons unsalted butter

3 tablespoons all-purpose flour

3 cups whole milk

1 cup dry white wine

1 teaspoon salt

$1^1/2$ cups asparagus puree (above)

2 cups grated Gruyère cheese

1 cup grated Emmentaler cheese

2 teaspoons black truffle oil

$1/4$ teaspoon freshly ground pepper

1 medium-sized loaf of coarse county bread such as pain levain, cubed

To MAKE THE ASPARAGUS PUREE, in a sauté pan, heat the oil over low heat, add the shallot, and cook, stirring occasionally, until for about 5 to 7 minutes, or until soft and translucent. Add the asparagus, cover, and sweat for about 15 minutes, or until the asparagus is tender. Uncover, add the salt and water (or stock), stir well, and simmer for about 4 to 6 minutes, or until the liquid is reduced by half.

Remove from the heat and let cool slightly. Transfer to a blender and process until smooth. You will need $1^1/2$ cups puree for the fondue

TO MAKE THE FONDUE, in a saucepan, melt the butter over low heat. Whisk in the flour, then whisk constantly for 2 to 3 minutes to cook away the raw flour taste. Slowly add the milk, whisking constantly to prevent lumps from forming. Raise the heat and bring to a simmer, stirring occasionally, for about 8 to 10 minutes, or until thickened and reduced to about 2 cups.

Add the wine and salt and simmer over low heat for 5 minutes. Add the asparagus puree and stir well. Add both cheeses and whisk until melted. Add the truffle oil and pepper, stir well, and then taste and adjust the seasoning.

Pour the fondue into a fondue pot placed over a warmer (or similar setup). Serve immediately with the bread for dipping, and if you choose, a poached egg.

Soft Scrambled

EGGS *with* LOBSTER

AND MASCARPONE

I'm going to dispense with humility for a moment and just say it: I'm the Egg King. It's true, I've got a way with them. I must also admit that I find eggs the most difficult thing to cook for people. That's because how people like their eggs is often tied to their earliest food memories. If, for example, your early egg memories are of hard-cooked eggs, you may want to turn the page. That's because the soft, loose texture of these eggs is one of the two things that make this dish great. The other, of course, is lobster. Combined with some mascarpone and a little seasoning, it is a dish fit for, well, royalty. To ensure the eggs have the right consistency, you must cook them over very, very low heat and stir and scramble constantly. Your attention to these matters will pay off. And for those of you who might consider turning the page, let me say that sometimes you can get past old habits: I'm a Jersey boy, which means I love ketchup. I especially like ketchup on my eggs. This is the only egg dish where I don't use it.

❧ SERVES 3 ❧

9 large eggs

1¹/₂ teaspoons of salt

Freshly ground pepper

1 tablespoon unsalted butter

6 ounces fresh-cooked lobster meat, cut into small pieces (see note)

¹/₃ cup mascarpone cheese

1¹/₂ teaspoons finely chopped fresh chives

Buttered coarse country toast, for serving

IN A BOWL, beat together the eggs until blended. Season with the salt and a bit of pepper and stir to mix.

In a nonstick frying pan, melt the butter over medium-low heat. Add the eggs and, using a rubber spatula, stir gently until they just begin to set. Add the lobster meat and continue to stir until it is warmed, about 30 seconds.

When eggs are ready, pull the pan from the heat, add the mascarpone and chives, and fold them gently into the eggs. Be careful not to overmix. You should still see streaks of the cheese running through the eggs. Season with salt and pepper.

Transfer to a plate and serve immediately with buttered toast.

NOTE: A lobster weighing 1¹/₂ pounds will yield about 6 ounces cooked lobster meat.

Faith's Warm
HAM and CHEESE TOAST
with JALAPEÑO CREAM

This dish sprang from a conversation I had with our friend (and then-publicist) Faith Wheeler about the menu for the Town Hall opening night. Faith believed that every menu should include something cheesy, gooey, and hot. She was also convinced that eggs were the next big trend in cooking. Believe it or not, we met all of her "requirements" with a single dish. We use country ham and St. George cheese, a locally made Cheddar-like cheese, but any medium-aged white Cheddar will do. We press the sandwich, then place a poached egg on top and drench the entire thing in a spicy jalapeño sauce. This knife-and-fork-required sandwich is our answer to the croque-madame. It has been on the menu since the beginning.

SERVES 6

JALAPEÑO CREAM

4 cups heavy cream

4 jalapeño chiles, split lengthwise

1/2 cup grated Parmesan cheese

1/2 cup grated St. George or medium-aged white Cheddar cheese

1 teaspoon salt

Freshly ground pepper

12 slices sourdough bread, each 1/2 inch thick

1/2 cup grated St. George or medium-aged white Cheddar cheese

1/4 cup grated parmesan

6 slices Smithfield ham or prosciutto

6 tablespoons unsalted butter, at room temperature

6 poached eggs, warm

To MAKE THE JALAPEÑO CREAM, in a saucepan, combine the cream and chiles over medium heat, bring to a simmer, and simmer, stirring occasionally to prevent scorching, for 10 to 15 minutes, or until the cream coats the back of a wooden spoon and takes on the flavor of the chiles. Remove and discard the chiles. Add both cheeses and continue to simmer, stirring occasionally, until the cheeses are completely melted. Add the salt and season with a few grinds of pepper. Set aside and keep warm.

Place 6 bread slices on a work surface, and top each slice with 1 ham slice. Top the remaining 6 bread slices evenly with both cheeses. Turn the ham-topped bread slices, ham side down, on the cheese-topped slices, creating 6 sandwiches. Using 1 tablespoon of the butter for each sandwich, brush both sides of the sandwich. Place the sandwiches in a panini press and grill until golden brown, according to the manufacturer's directions (see note).

To serve, preheat the broiler. Place each sandwich on a flameproof plate or sheet pan and top with a poached egg. Ladle the jalapeño cream over the egg and sandwich. In a small bowl, stir together the Parmesan and St. George cheeses, then sprinkle evenly over the sandwiches. Place under the broiler until the cheese is lightly browned. Serve immediately.

NOTE: If you do not have a panini press, place the sandwiches, one or two at a time, in a hot, lightly oiled sauté pan over medium heat. Place a second sauté pan slightly smaller than the first on top of the sandwich(es) and place a heavy object, such as a brick, in the top pan to weight it down. After a few minutes, flip the sandwich over and heat for a few minutes until golden brown on the second side, or until both sides are golden brown and the cheese is melted.

POUTINE

When you open a restaurant, you never really know what will become the "signature dish," the menu item that creates a buzz and gets people talking. That's because it's not something you can force. You can't tell customers what the signature dish is. Instead, they tell you. At Town Hall, they chose the BBQ shrimp (page 58) and at Anchor & Hope, angels on horseback (page 20). At Salt House, the people also spoke, and what they had to say did not make Doug Washington happy. They have (and loudly) made this poutine with fontina and short-rib gravy that special dish that everyone has to try. I'll be honest, I put poutine on the Salt House opening menu as a kind of joke. You see, Doug is Canadian, and poutine is too (Quebecois to be exact). It's a staple dish of greasy spoons and ubiquitous Ontario chip wagons. Let's just say there's a bit of a stigma associated with the decadent combination of fries, fresh cheese curd, and gravy. In fact, one recent history of the dish includes a section titled "The Embarrassment of Poutine."

For Doug's sake, we've done our best to take poutine out of the diner by double frying thick-cut Kennebec potatoes (yes, they're fried twice, first a "blanch" in oil heated to only 300°F, and then finished at 375°F), replacing the curd with fontina, and topping it all with a rich short-rib gravy. It's a decadent combination that is meant to be shared, but it is so addictive that some people don't quite understand that communal idea. More than once I've seen a table of four order one plate of poutine . . . each.

After the poutine sits around for a while, the fries and cheese and gravy coalesce into a single, delicious mass. That's when I love it best (and Doug hates it most). Sorry, Doug. As I said, the people have spoken.

❧ SERVES 6 ❧

SHORT-RIB GRAVY

2 pounds bone-in beef short ribs

3 cups dry red wine

2 cloves garlic, sliced

2 bay leaves

1 small carrot, peeled and sliced

1 celery stalk, sliced

1 small yellow onion, sliced

6 thyme sprigs

1 tablespoon Canola oil

2 tablespoons tomato paste

4 cups Chicken Stock (see page 250)

CHEESE SAUCE

1 tablespoon unsalted butter

1 tablespoon all-purpose flour

1 cup whole milk

1/2 cup grated fontina cheese

FRENCH FRIES

Canola oil, for deep-frying

2 pounds Kennebec, or Russett potatoes

To PREPARE THE GRAVY, place the short ribs in a baking dish just large enough to accommodate them. Add the wine, garlic, bay leaves, carrot, celery, onion, and thyme, cover, and marinate overnight in the refrigerator.

The next day, preheat the oven to 375°F. Remove the ribs from the marinade and pat dry. Reserve the marinade. In an ovenproof frying pan, heat the oil over medium heat. When the oil is hot, working in batches to avoid crowding, sear the ribs, turning as needed, for 4 to 5 minutes on each side, or until browned and caramelized on all sides. As the ribs are ready, transfer them to a plate.

When all of the ribs are browned, pour off the excess oil from the pan, return the pan to medium heat and add the tomato paste. Using a wooden spoon, spread the tomato paste around for a moment, then add all of the liquid and vegetables from the marinade. Raise the heat to high and cook, stirring occasionally, for 5 minutes. Add the stock and lower the heat to medium. When the stock is simmering, return the ribs, meat side down, to the pan and transfer to the oven. Cook for about 2 hours, or until very tender.

Remove from the oven and let cool for about 30 minutes. Remove the short ribs to a plate and refrigerate for 2 hours. Strain the cooking liquid through a fine-mesh strainer into a saucepan, place over medium heat, bring to a simmer, and cook until reduced by half and is a gravy consistency. Remove from the heat and set aside.

Remove the ribs from the refrigerator, then remove and discard the bones, connective membranes, and any fat. Cut the meat lengthwise into strips $1/2$ inch wide, and then cut crosswise into $1/2$-inch cubes.

Just before serving, return the gravy to medium heat and bring to a simmer. Stir in the meat cubes, heat through, and remove from the heat.

TO MAKE THE CHEESE SAUCE, in a saucepan, melt the butter over low heat. Whisk in the flour, then whisk constantly for 2 to 3 minutes to cook away the raw flour taste. Slowly add the milk, whisking constantly to prevent lumps from forming. Raise the heat to medium and simmer, stirring

occasionally, until reduced by one-third. Add the fontina and stir until melted. Remove from the heat and keep warm.

While the cheese sauce is simmering, begin making the French fries. Pour the oil to a depth of 3 to $3^{1}/2$ inches into a deep fryer or deep, heavy-bottomed pot and heat to 300°F. Have ready a large bowl of cold water. Cut the unpeeled potatoes lengthwise into large, flat, thick or wedge-shaped fries (like steak fries). As the pieces are cut, add them to the water.

When all of the potatoes are cut, drain them well and pat dry. Add the potatoes to the hot oil and blanch for 8 to 10 minutes, or until the potatoes begin to soften. Using a wire skimmer, transfer to paper towels to drain.

Raise the heat to bring the oil to 375°F. Fry the potatoes a second time for 8 to 10 minutes, or until golden brown. Using the wire skimmer, transfer to paper towels to drain.

Pile the French fries on a large plate, spoon the cheese sauce over the fries, and then ladle the short-rib gravy over the top. Serve immediately.

Pssst: I realize the next chapter is all sandwiches, and you'll find a few in the Smoke and Fire chapter, too, but in New Orleans there's something called a potato po'boy. It's fries and roast-beef-debris gravy on airy French bread. At the very least, this *poutine* on French is a middle-class boy.

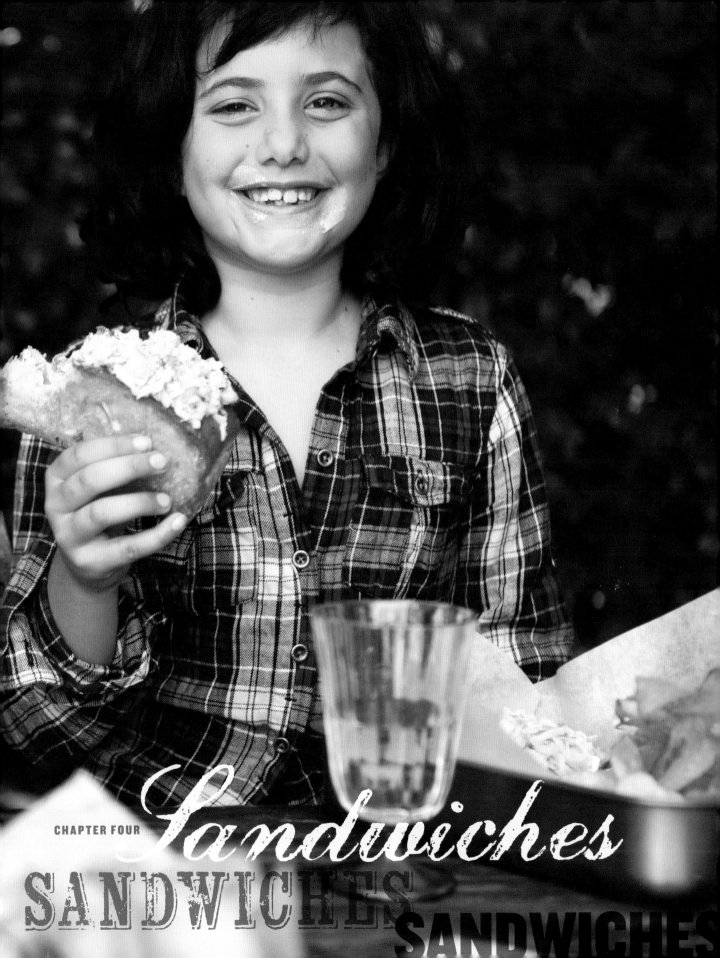

SANDWICHES

SANDWICHES

When YOU'RE IN MY BUSINESS, the question you always get is "What kind of restaurant is it?" Some places afford a straightforward answer. Anchor & Hope, for example, can be easily described as a fish house. But a restaurant like Town Hall, which takes its culinary cues from a variety of sources, is more difficult. Probably the best description of its menu is regional American. And nothing fits that tag better than a sandwich.

SANDWICHES, maybe more than any other dishes, evoke a certain place, region, or even era. A lobster roll is the essence of New England, a fried chicken sandwich is the South, and a tuna salad sandwich evokes a midcentury, suburban idyll. They can be more specific representations of place, too. In New Orleans, I don't feel as if I've really arrived, am not really there, until I've grabbed a roast beef po'boy at Domilise's (or one from Magazine Street Po Boy, an unheralded gem) or a muffaletta at the Central Grocery. Not only are some sandwiches emblematic of entire cities (cheesesteak anyone? beef on weck?), but sandwiches also reveal the tastes and flavors of a region's ethnic enclaves. Falafel in pita is available in a city's Middle Eastern district, Cubanos are everywhere in the Latin neighborhoods of urban Florida, and isn't the taco just an open-faced sandwich with a fold? In other words, you can learn a lot about a place by checking out what it stuffs between two slices of bread.

THIS CHAPTER will take you to places in the kitchen that perhaps you've never gone. Here you'll find a recipe to grind and case your own sausage, and after you poach tuna in olive oil, you might never buy canned again. Sorry, Charlie.

STEVEN AND I started our careers in a delicatessen. Those years taught us what makes a sandwich great. One thing I learned is that a sandwich is the sum of its parts, so always try to get the best-quality ingredients, especially bread. That shouldn't surprise you. After all, what makes a sandwich a sandwich but its infrastructure?

The Israeli Guy's

FALAFEL

SANDWICH

One of my and Steven's coworkers at the Celebrity Deli was from Israel. For the life of me, I can't remember his name. What I do remember is that he made great falafel. I was talking with Steven one day, going over what to put in this chapter, and I said, "Remember that Israeli guy at the deli? I want to put his falafel in the book." Steven replied, "Why don't you?" I told him I didn't have the recipe. But he did. An hour later I received this recipe by email. We dress the falafel with a bright Turkish salad, tahini sauce, and a spicy harissa. That last flourish is an homage to L'As du Fallafel, a favorite spot in the Marais.

❧ MAKES 6 SANDWICHES ❧

Pictured on pages 98–99.

FALAFEL

1 rounded cup (1/2 pound) dried chickpeas, picked over, soaked overnight, and drained

1 bunch cilantro, stems removed

1 bunch flat-leaf parsley, stems removed

1 tablespoon ground coriander

1 tablespoon ground cumin

1 yellow onion, coarsely chopped

2 cloves garlic, coarsely chopped

1 large egg

1/4 cup chickpea flour

1 tablespoon salt, plus more for seasoning

1 teaspoon baking soda

Canola oil, for deep-frying

TAHINI SAUCE

2 cloves garlic

Salt and freshly ground pepper

3 tablespoons tahini

Juice of 1 lemon

4 tablespoons water

TURKISH SALAD

1 red bell pepper, seeded and diced

1 cucumber, trimmed and diced

1/2 red onion, diced

24 cherry tomatoes, halved

1/4 cup extra-virgin olive oil

Juice of 1 lemon

2 tablespoons chopped fresh cilantro

2 pinches of salt

4 pita breads, halved

Harissa Vinaigrette (page 251)

To MAKE THE FALAFEL, place the drained chickpeas in a food processor and process until smooth. Add the cilantro, parsley, coriander, cumin, yellow onion, and garlic and process until the mixture forms a smooth paste. Transfer the paste to a large bowl, add the egg, chickpea flour, salt, and baking soda, and mix well. Let rest for at least an hour or up to a day.

TO PREPARE THE TAHINI SAUCE, place the garlic cloves in a mortar with a pinch of salt and pound with a pestle until a paste forms. Transfer the garlic paste to a small bowl and stir in the tahini, lemon juice, and water. Season with salt and pepper and set aside.

TO MAKE THE SALAD, in a bowl, combine the bell pepper, cucumber, red onion, and tomatoes and toss to mix. Add the oil, lemon juice, cilantro, and salt and stir well to combine.

TO FRY THE FALAFEL, pour the oil to a depth of 3 1/2 inches into a deep fryer or deep, heavy-bottomed pot and heat to 350°F. While the oil is heating, using your hands, form the falafel mixture into 24 walnut-sized pieces then flatten into patties.

Working in batches to avoid crowding, add the falafel to the hot oil and fry for 3 to 4 minutes, or until they are a deep, dark brown. Using a slotted spoon, transfer the falafel to paper towels and season with salt. Keep warm while you fry the remaining falafel.

To serve, place 3 or 4 hot falafel in a halved pita, add a few spoonfuls of the salad, and top with the tahini sauce and the vinaigrette. Serve immediately.

TUNA NIÇOISE
Sandwich with
ARUGULA *and* FRISÉE

You want a tuna sandwich? This is a tuna sandwich. No fooling with canned tuna here. Instead, this calls for fresh tuna marinated in olive oil, garlic, and thyme, and then poached in more olive oil. Your tuna confit is then all done up as a salad in the niçoise manner. And then, if your feeling extra fancy and decadent, go ahead and top that beautiful tuna niçoise with, yes, more tuna, this time seared. Of course, that final flourish is not necessary, but it does take the sandwich to another realm, so I've included the directions if you want to give it a try (take one look at the accompanying photograph and you are going to want to do it). And for good measure, the whole thing is topped with a hard-boiled egg. Yes, this is a tuna sandwich.

You can prepare the tuna confit a day ahead, and if you have any of the tuna salad left over, it's also delicious stuffed into a tomato or bell pepper.

❦ MAKES 6 SANDWICHES ❦

TUNA CONFIT
1 pound albacore tuna fillet cut into walnut-sized pieces

2 tarragon sprigs

2 thyme sprigs

1 shallot, sliced

2 cloves garlic, peeled but left whole

About 1½ cups extra-virgin olive oil

TAPENADE
¼ cup niçoise olives, pitted and chopped

Grated zest of 1 lemon

1 clove garlic, minced

1 tablespoon extra-virgin olive oil

TUNA SALAD
Tuna confit (above)

¼ cup tapenade (above)

1 tablespoon red wine vinegar

1 tablespoon whole grain mustard

¼ cup extra-virgin olive oil

¼ cup Mayonnaise (page 251)

Juice of 1½ lemons (about ¼ cup)

2 tablespoons chopped fresh tarragon

2 tablespoons chopped flat-leaf parsley

2 tablespoons chopped chervil

2 tablespoons chopped chives

Salt and freshly ground pepper

SEARED TUNA (OPTIONAL)
¾ pound yellowfin tuna (ahi) loin

Ground coriander

Salt and freshly ground pepper

Canola oil, for cooking

2 cups arugula

2 cups frisée

3 tablespoons lemon oil or 3 tablespoons extra-virgin olive oil mixed with a few healthy squeezes of lemon juice

Salt and freshly ground pepper

2 baguettes, each cut crosswise into thirds, then each third split horizontally

3 large eggs, hard boiled, peeled, and quartered lengthwise

To PREPARE THE TUNA CONFIT, arrange the tuna pieces in a sauté pan just large enough to hold them in a single layer. Add the tarragon and thyme sprigs, shallot, and garlic. Pour in the olive oil just to cover. Place the pan over very low heat and cook for 15 to 20 minutes, or until just cooked through. Remove from the heat and let the tuna cool completely in the oil. Remove the cooled tuna from the oil and set aside to use in the salad.

continued

TO MAKE THE TAPENADE, in a small bowl, stir together all of the ingredients until well mixed.

TO MAKE THE TUNA SALAD, in a bowl, combine the tuna confit, tapenade, vinegar, mustard, oil, mayonnaise, lemon juice, and herbs and stir to combine. Season with salt and pepper, then set aside.

If you have decided to include the extra-special variation, season the tuna loin liberally with coriander, salt, and pepper. Pour the oil to a depth of about $\frac{1}{8}$ inch into a sauté pan over high heat. When the oil shimmers, add the tuna and sear for about 1 minute on each side. Transfer the tuna to a cutting board and cut against the grain into $\frac{1}{4}$-inch-thick slices.

TO ASSEMBLE THE SANDWICHES, in a bowl, combine the arugula and frisée, drizzle with the lemon oil, and toss to coat evenly. Season with salt and pepper and toss again. Place the bottom halves of the baguette sections, cut side up, on a work surface. Spread them evenly with the tuna salad. If using the seared tuna, divide the slices evenly among the baguette pieces, arranging them on top of the salad. Divide the arugula-frisée mixture among the sandwiches, piling it on top, then place 2 egg quarters on each sandwich. Season the egg with salt and pepper. Close the sandwiches with the baguette tops and serve.

Pressed
VEGETARIAN
MUFFALETTA
on Focaccia

Much like the battle between proponents of the Dungeness crab and those who favor the blue, the muffaletta is one of those things that prompts people to take sides. In this case, it's a question of hot versus cold. Again, I take the generous view: I appreciate the toasted airy bread, barely melted cheese, warmed olive salad, and Italian meats (just releasing their fat) served on a light brown melamine plate at the Napoleon House. I am equally admiring of the thick, butcher paper–swaddled disk handed over by one of the stoics behind the counter at Central Grocery that, when opened, reveals a soft dense bread, pungent olive salad, and layers of cold meats and cheeses. They are both New Orleans classics. Here I take out the meat and opt for hot. A meatless muffaletta may seem an odd choice. But when we opened Town Hall, we wanted a vegetarian sandwich, and since the olive salad sets the muffaletta apart (as does the bread, though focaccia is a worthy stand-in), I think you'll be pleased with the results. And if you're feeling carnivorous, go ahead. You know what to do.

MAKES 6 SANDWICHES

OLIVE SALAD

2 cups pitted green Spanish olives, coarsely chopped

1 cup pitted green Greek olives, preferably garlic stuffed, or kalamata olives, coarsely chopped

7 peperoncini, coarsely chopped

2 cloves garlic, finely chopped

2 tablespoons capers, rinsed and lightly chopped

1¼ cups Pickled Vegetables with Coriander and Celery Salt (page 16) or jarred pickled Italian vegetables (giardiniera), roughly chopped, plus 1 tablespoon of the pickling liquid

1 teaspoon dried oregano

¼ cup red wine vinegar

1¼ cups olive oil

½ lemon

1 teaspoon salt

2 large red bell peppers

6 pieces focaccia, each 4 inches square, split horizontally, or 3 muffaletta loaves, each halved crosswise and then split horizontally

12 slices provolone cheese

Unsalted butter, at room temperature, or olive oil

To make the olive salad, in a large bowl, combine all of the ingredients and mix well. Let stand for at least 1 to 2 hours, or preferably overnight.

Using tongs, one at a time, hold the bell peppers over the flame of a gas burner, turning as needed, until blackened and blistered on all sides. Or, blacken and blister the peppers under a preheated broiler, watching carefully to avoid burning the flesh. Transfer the blackened peppers to a bowl, cover with plastic wrap, and let stand for 10 minutes. Remove from the bowl and let cool to room temperature. Peel the peppers, cut in half, and discard the seeds, then cut lengthwise ½-inch-wide slices. Set aside.

Preheat the oven to 400°F. Arrange the bottom halves of the split focaccia squares on a work surface. Spoon a few heaping tablespoons of the olive salad on each square and spread evenly. Top the olive salad with 2 cheese slices and a few slices of roasted pepper, and then with the tops of the squares.

Smear the top and bottom of each sandwich with the butter (or brush with the olive oil). Heat a large nonstick frying pan over medium heat. Add as many sandwiches as will fit comfortably and heat for 3 to 4 minutes, or until browned on the first side. Carefully flip the sandwiches over and place a sandwich press (or a brick covered with aluminum foil) on top of the sandwiches. Cook for 1 minute, then transfer to a sheet pan. Repeat with the remaining sandwiches.

When all of the sandwiches have been browned, put the sheet pan in the oven for about 6 minutes, or until the sandwiches hot throughout. Serve at once.

LOBSTER ROLL
with Old Bay
AND CELERY

This lobster roll, lightly dressed on a buttery center-sliced bun, is directly tied to the founding of Anchor & Hope. A few years back, on a family vacation in Maine, we were waiting for some friends at a ferry landing for a trip to Little Cranberry Island. They arrived a touch late, carrying a large box that they offered in apology for the delay. The box was filled with lobster rolls from the local "pound." We tore into its contents right after we boarded. This was my introduction to Maine. The first bite told me that I liked Maine, and I was immediately committed to trying every lobster roll I could get my hands on (I'm all hands). Some were dressed with just clarified butter, and others used mayonnaise. Either way, I was taken by the flavor and the play of the cool lobster against the warm, toasty roll.

Fast-forward a few months and I'm walking past a small building being used as parking lot on Minna Street, right around the corner from Salt House. The wide garage door was open, and when I peeked inside, its wood floors and airy, weathered appearance reminded me of the structures on the coast of Maine. Doug was keen on a fish house. This was it.

I'll emphasize it again: lightly dressed. You want to enhance the flavor of the lobster, not overwhelm it. As Wolfgang Puck once said, while instructing a young cook who oversauced a plate of lobster, "Why would you cover gold?"

MAKES 6 SANDWICHES

1½ pounds fresh-cooked lobster meat, chopped and chilled (see How to Cook and Clean a Lobster, page 255)

1 celery stalk, finely diced

1 tablespoon freshly squeezed lemon juice

2 teaspoons finely chopped fresh tarragon

½ teaspoon Old Bay Seasoning

1 or 2 pinches of salt

½ cup Mayonnaise (page 251), chilled

Unsalted butter, at room temperature, for spreading

6 top-loading hot dog buns (see note)

6 lemon slices

PLACE a dry cast-iron frying pan in the oven and preheat the oven (as well as the pan) to 375°F.

Meanwhile, in a bowl, combine the lobster, celery, lemon juice, tarragon, Old Bay, salt, and mayonnaise and stir and toss gently to distribute all of the ingredients evenly. Make sure all of the lobster chunks are lightly coated with mayonnaise. Set aside.

Spread a liberal amount of the butter on the exposed outer sides of each bun. Then, working in batches to avoid crowding, put the buns in the hot frying pan and cook, turning once, for about 3 minutes on each side, or until golden brown.

Spoon the lobster mixture into the hot buns, dividing it evenly. Serve the lobster rolls immediately with a slice of lemon.

NOTE: Ideally, you want to use a top-loading hot dog bun. That's because the outer crust is removed from the sides of the bun, exposing the soft inside, making it perfect to slather with butter and cook to a crispy golden brown. If you cannot find the buns, look for an uncut roll of similar size. With a bread knife, cut a thin portion off each side of the roll, then slice down the center of the top, stopping just short of cutting all of the way through.

FISH TACOS with

Avocado Crème and

SPICY CHIPOTLE SALSA

This chapter is emphatically titled Sandwiches, Sandwiches, Sandwiches. Is a taco a sandwich? Who am I to say? So let's dispense with semantics and admit that, whatever the category, the taco is classic hand food. Here, a warmed tortilla is folded over a perfectly grilled chunk of fish and, instead of an avocado slice, a dollop of avocado crème is added, which contributes a welcome lightness and contrasts nicely with the spicy salsa. Because of their size, it is best to grill the fish pieces in a basket or on a screen, which makes them easier to turn. If you're not comfortable grilling, you can always cook the fish in a pan on the stove top (see note). And if you're not comfortable calling a taco a sandwich, just take a pen and add "and a Taco" to the title of this chapter.

❧ MAKES 12 TACOS; SERVES 6 ❧

CHIPOTLE SALSA

6 dried chipotle chiles

$1/2$ pound tomatillos, papery skins removed

$1/2$ pound tomatoes

2 jalapeño chiles, split lengthwise and seeded

8 cloves garlic, peeled and roughly chopped

$1/2$ yellow onion, sliced

$1^1/2$ teaspoons salt

$1/4$ cup canola oil

$1/4$ cup water

2 teaspoons cider vinegar

AVOCADO CRÈME

1 avocado, halved, pitted, and peeled

$3/4$ cup crème fraîche

Juice of 1 lime

1 tablespoon chopped fresh cilantro

1 teaspoon salt

$1^1/2$ pounds firm-fleshed white fish fillets such as grouper, tilapia, or bass

$1/3$ cup extra-virgin olive oil

Juice of 1 lime

$1/4$ teaspoon pure chili powder

Pinch of salt

12 corn tortillas, about 6 inches in diameter

$1/2$ head green cabbage, cored and thinly sliced

To prepare the salsa, bring a small pot of water to a boil. Meanwhile, in a dry frying pan, lightly toast the chipotle chiles over medium heat for a few minutes, or until fragrant. Transfer the chiles to a heatproof bowl, pour the boiling water over the top to cover, and set aside.

Place the tomatillos, tomatoes, jalapeño chiles, garlic cloves, and onion slices in a large, ridged stove-top grill pan or cast-iron frying pan over medium heat. Roast the vegetables, turning often, for 10 to 15 minutes, until they are nicely charred. Remove from the heat and then let cool for 5 to 10 minutes.

While the vegetables are cooling, remove the chipotles from the water. Chop off the stems and scrape out the seeds.

Remove the skin from the tomatoes only, and then place the tomatoes in a food processor or blender. Add the remaining roasted vegetables, the seeded chipotles, the salt, oil, water, and vinegar and process until smooth. Transfer to a bowl and set aside.

To prepare the avocado crème, place the avocado in a bowl and mash it into small chunks with a fork. Transfer the avocado to the food processor, add the crème fraîche,

continued

lime juice, cilantro, and salt, and process until smooth. Transfer to a bowl and set aside.

Prepare a medium-hot fire for direct-heat grilling in a charcoal or gas grill. While the grill is heating, cut the fish into 12 equal portions (about 2 ounces each). In a bowl, whisk together the oil, lime juice, chili powder, and salt. Add the fish and toss well.

Grill the fish, turning once, for 3 to 4 minutes on each side (depending on the thickness), or until just opaque at the center. At the same time, place the tortillas around the edge of the grill rack and heat for 30 to 45 seconds on each side.

TO ASSEMBLE THE TACOS, place a piece of fish in the center each tortilla, add a spoonful of salsa, some sliced cabbage, and a dollop of the avocado crème fraîche. Serve 2 tacos to each diner.

NOTE: I prefer grilling, but you can also cook the fish in a frying pan. In a large frying pan, heat a tablespoon or two of olive oil over medium-high heat. Working in batches to avoid crowding, add the fish and cook, turning once, for $1^{1}/_{2}$ to 2 minutes on each side (depending on thickness), or until just opaque at the center. Heat the tortillas in cast-iron frying pan over medium heat at the same time.

Smoked

SHRIMP BLT

This sandwich has been with me for a long time, and with good reason. It originated at Postrio, moved on to Anchor & Hope, and now is a popular staple on the lunch and brunch menu at the Irving Street Kitchen in Portland. Make sure you use thick-cut apple-smoked bacon, and take care to pat the shrimp *very dry* before cooking. The less moisture there is, the better the smoke adheres to the shrimp, and the more smoke adheres to the shrimp, the more that is picked up by the sauce. You get the idea. Like any good sandwich, this one is messy, but what a mess. And if you're feeling extravagant, go ahead and smoke some lobster.

MAKES 6 SANDWICHES

12 slices thick-cut apple-smoked bacon

36 large shrimp (about 1½ pounds), peeled and deveined

12 slices coarse country bread such as pain levain, cut as thinly
as possible on the diagonal

Olive oil, for brushing

Salt

BUTTER LEMON SAUCE

½ cup water

2 tablespoons freshly squeezed lemon juice

½ cup (¼ pound) unsalted butter, chilled, cut into
8 tablespoons

Salt

¾ cup Mayonnaise (page 251)

2 large tomatoes, each cut into 6 thin slices

4 cups mixed salad greens

PREPARE an offset smoker or a grill for smoking as directed on page 126. You want it to be at about 225°F.

Meanwhile, preheat the oven to 375°F. Lay the bacon on a sheet pan and bake for 10 to 15 minutes, or until crisp. Transfer to paper towels to drain. Turn the oven to broil.

Pat the shrimp dry with a kitchen towel to rid them of as much moisture as possible (the smoke flavor will adhere better to dry skin). Arrange the shrimp on the grill rack and smoke over very low for about 8 minutes, or until medium-rare (half cooked).

While the shrimp are cooking, toast the bread and make the sauce. Arrange the bread slices on a sheet pan. Brush the top side of each slice with oil and then season with a pinch of salt. Place under the broiler for a few minutes, or until nicely toasted. Set aside.

TO MAKE THE SAUCE, in a sauté pan, combine the water and lemon juice over medium-high heat and simmer until reduced by half. Turn down the heat to low and add the cold butter, 1 tablespoon at a time, whisking constantly after each addition until incorporated. Season with a few pinches of salt.

When the shrimp are ready, add them to the sauce for 1 minute or so, to finish cooking and warm through.

TO ASSEMBLE THE SANDWICHES, spread 1 tablespoon of the mayonnaise on the oiled side of each bread slice. Place 6 shrimp, side by side, on 6 of the bread slices, then top the shrimp with 2 tomato slices followed by 2 bacon slices. Arrange a handful of greens on top, then a second slice of bread, mayonnaise side down. Cut each sandwich in half on the diagonal and serve.

The PEACEMAKER

Food in New Orleans causes lots of arguments. Like when you are on line at the neighborhood po'boy shop and arguing whether to go with the fried oyster loaf or the fried shrimp. This argument is internal, and results in a series of interior negotiations and deliberations until compromise is reached: half oyster, half shrimp. One sandwich, both cravings assuaged. That's why this is called The Peacemaker: it helps you make peace with yourself.

Use medium-sized oysters and large shrimp for the best result. The key here is to make sure the crispy coating on the shrimp and oysters is neither coarse nor mealy. Corn flour does the trick beautifully. Finally, I like to use Crystal hot sauce, but as this sandwich is called The Peacemaker, I'd rather not argue. Use any hot sauce you'd like.

MAKES 6 SANDWICHES

1 cup Mayonnaise (page 251)

2 tablespoons Crystal hot sauce

Canola oil, for deep-frying

2 cups corn flour

2 cups all-purpose flour

2 teaspoons cayenne pepper

2 teaspoons salt

Freshly ground black pepper

2 cups buttermilk

1 pound large shrimp, peeled and deveined

1 pound freshly shucked medium-sized oysters
(sold in a jar or tub)

1 head romaine lettuce, thinly sliced crosswise

2 tomatoes, thinly sliced

2 loaves French bread, each cut crosswise into thirds
(about 6 inches long), then each third
split horizontally

IN A SMALL BOWL, stir together the mayonnaise and hot sauce, mixing well. Set aside.

Pour the oil to a depth of about 3 inches into a deep fryer or deep cast-iron frying pan and heat to 375°F. While the oil is heating, line a sheet pan with waxed paper. In a large bowl, stir together both flours, the cayenne pepper, the salt, and a few grinds of pepper. Pour the buttermilk into a second bowl, add the shrimp, toss to coat, and let soak for a minute or two. Then, working in batches, scoop the shrimp out of the buttermilk, allowing the excess liquid to drip back into the bowl, and add to the flour mixture. Toss to coat evenly, then shake off the excess and place on the prepared sheet pan. When all of the shrimp are coated, repeat the process with the oysters. (It is important that you soak the shrimp in the buttermilk first, as the oysters tend to, for lack of a better term, and because this is a New Orleans specialty, make the buttermilk funky).

Again working in batches to avoid crowding, add the shrimp to the hot oil and fry for about 1½ minutes, or until golden brown. Using a wire skimmer or slotted spoon, transfer to paper towels to drain. Keep warm. Repeat with the oysters, frying each batch for about 2 minutes, or until golden brown, then drain on paper towels.

Smear a liberal amount of the mayonnaise–hot sauce mixture on the bottom of each bread piece, then place 3 or 4 each of the hot fried shrimp and oysters on top. (If you want a little more spice, hit the shrimp and oysters with a few dashes of hot sauce, straight from the bottle.) Top with the lettuce and tomato slices and then the bread tops and serve.

Curried
CHICKEN SANDWICH
WITH CASHEWS
AND CURRANTS

This sandwich is a mystery to me. For one thing, I don't remember how or why it came on the menu. I mean, it really is outside of what we usually do at Town Hall, but whenever we run this Curried Chicken sandwich for the noon-time crowd, it is super-popular. One theory I have for this sandwich making its way to the Bill of Fare is that while curry is an important element here, by Town Hall standards, this sandwich is pretty mild. It harkens to a British tea sandwich, but bigger, you know, for Americans. It would be easy to make the flavors more aggressive, but this sandwich is subtle, making for an easy lunch. Feel free, though, to take out any aggression you might have and spice this one up with a fruit chutney or some pickled mango.

✤ MAKES 6 SANDWICHES ✤

POACHED CHICKEN
½ yellow onion, sliced

1 teaspoon dried chile flakes

3 cardamom pods

½ cinnamon stick

1 bay leaf

Salt

2 quarts water

2 pounds boneless chicken breasts

⅓ cup dried currants

½ cup roasted cashews, roughly chopped

½ cup diced apple

⅓ cup diced fennel

⅓ cup diced celery

½ cup Mayonnaise (page 251)

1½ tablespoons curry powder

2 tablespoons freshly squeezed lemon juice

Salt and freshly ground pepper

4 cups mixed salad greens

8 fresh basil leaves, torn

8 fresh mint leaves, torn

6 soft rolls, split horizontally

To POACH THE CHICKEN, in a wide saucepan, combine the onion, chile flakes, cardamom, cinnamon, bay leaf, 1 teaspoon salt, and water, bring to a boil, and boil for about 10 minutes. Lower the heat so the water is barely simmering, add the chicken breasts, and cook gently for 15 to 20 minutes, or until the chicken is opaque throughout.

Remove the chicken breasts from the poaching liquid and discard the liquid. Pat the chicken breasts dry, season with a little salt, and let cool completely.

Meanwhile, in a small bowl, soak the currants in luke-warm water to cover for 10 minutes to plump them. Drain well and set aside.

When the chicken is cool, shred it into a large bowl. Add the currants, cashews, apple, fennel, celery, mayonnaise, curry powder, and lemon juice and mix well to combine. Season with salt and pepper.

TO ASSEMBLE THE SANDWICHES, in a bowl, toss together the salad greens, basil, and mint. Lay the bottom halves of the rolls, cut side up, on a work surface. Divide the chicken salad equally among them, then top the salad with a handful of greens. Close with the roll tops, cut in half, and serve.

Fried
CHICKEN SANDWICH
with **BUTTERMILK-JICAMA** *Slaw*

Think about a picnic: a checkered tablecloth, a basket filled with fried chicken and coleslaw, a bottle of wine. Now think about it between two slices of bread. Not the basket and the tablecloth but the chicken and the slaw (wine is always best in a glass). That's what this sandwich is like.

Although the chicken is soaked in buttermilk and dredged in flour like the fried chicken in Chapter 7, these boneless breasts are cooked at a higher temperature, resulting in an incredibly moist, beautifully colored piece of meat. Make sure you drain the spicy slaw well so you don't drench the wonderful crisp exterior of the chicken.

At Town Hall's lunch service, we sell 150 of these pocket picnics daily, so they are, by necessity, served at room temperature.

✣ MAKES 6 SANDWICHES ✣

BUTTERMILK-JICAMA SLAW
½ **head green cabbage, cored and thinly sliced crosswise**
½ **small jicama, peeled and julienned**
2 **shallots, thinly sliced**
¼ **cup fresh cilantro leaves, chopped**
2 **jalapeño chiles, seeded and thinly sliced**
Grated zest of 1 lime
1 **cup buttermilk**
½ **cup crème fraîche**
1 **tablespoon cider vinegar**
Juice of 1 lime
1 **teaspoon salt**
Freshly ground pepper

FRIED CHICKEN
6 **boneless, skinless chicken breasts**
Salt and freshly ground pepper
1 **cup buttermilk**
Canola oil, for deep-frying
2 **cups all-purpose flour**
¼ **cup Town Hall Spice Mixture (page 253)**

½ **cup Mayonnaise (page 251)**
6 **ciabatta rolls, split horizontally**

To MAKE THE SLAW, combine the cabbage, jicama, shallots, cilantro, chiles, and lime zest and toss to mix. In a small bowl, whisk together the buttermilk, crème fraîche, vinegar, lime juice, salt, and a few grinds of pepper. Pour the dressing over the vegetables and toss to coat evenly. Let stand for at least 30 minutes before serving or refrigerate for up to 2 days.

One at a time, place the chicken breasts between 2 sheets of plastic wrap. Using a meat mallet or a rolling pin, pound gently until flattened to a uniform ½ inch thick. Season on both sides with salt and pepper.

Pour the buttermilk into a bowl. Add the chicken breasts, turn to coat, and let soak for about 15 minutes.

TO FRY THE CHICKEN, pour the oil to a depth of 3½ inches into a deep fryer or a deep, heavy-bottomed pot and heat to 375°F. In a bowl, stir together the flour, spice mixture, and 1 teaspoon salt. Line a sheet pan with waxed paper. One at a time, remove the chicken breasts from the buttermilk, allowing the excess liquid to drip back into the bowl, and add to the flour mixture. Toss to coat evenly, then shake off the excess and place on the prepared sheet pan.

Add the chicken breasts to the hot oil and cook for 4 to 5 minutes, or until golden brown. Transfer to paper towels to drain.

TO ASSEMBLE THE SANDWICHES, spread a generous tablespoon of mayonnaise on the bottom of each roll. Lay a fried chicken breast on the bottom half and top with a few heaping spoonfuls of the slaw. Place the other half of the roll on top, slice in half, and serve hot or cold.

Hot Fried
CHICKEN SANDWICH
with *Biscuits* and
COFFEE-LACED GRAVY

Here is another way to use the fried chicken breast on page 116, this time for an open-faced, knife-and-a-fork sandwich. The country-style gravy, generously flecked with bits of sausage and bacon, uses a shot of strong coffee for a variation on red-eye gravy, a southern favorite.

✥ 6 SANDWICHES ✥

1 teaspoon canola oil

3 slices thick-cut bacon, cubed

3 ounces breakfast pork sausage links, casings removed

$^1/_2$ yellow onion, sliced

2 tablespoons unsalted butter

$^1/_4$ cup all-purpose flour

3 tablespoons brewed espresso or other strong coffee

3 cups Chicken Stock, warmed (page 250)

Salt and freshly ground pepper to taste

$^1/_2$ cup heavy cream

1 teaspoon chopped fresh sage

6 Country Biscuits (page 252)

6 fried chicken breasts,

(see Fried Chicken Sandwich with Buttermilk-Jicama Slaw, page 116)

IN A FRYING PAN, heat the oil over medium heat. Add the bacon and cook, stirring occasionally, for about 3 minutes, or until some of the fat is rendered. Add the pork sausage meat and cook, breaking up the meat with a wooden spoon or spatula, for 3 minutes more, or until it just starts to brown. Add the onion. Continue cooking, stirring occasionally, for about 5 minutes, or until the onion is soft.

Add the butter and stir until melted. Lower the heat to medium-low. Stir in the flour and cook, stirring constantly, for 2 to 3 minutes to cook away the raw flour taste. Pour in the espresso and stock and stir well, making sure to scrape the bottom of the pan to dislodge any browned bits. Raise the heat to medium and simmer for about 10 minutes, or until reduced by half.

Add the cream and cook, stirring occasionally, for about 10 minutes, or until the mixture has a nice gravy consistency. Finally, stir in the sage, then taste and correct the seasoning.

Split each biscuit in half horizontally and lay the halves, cut side up and side by side, on a plate. Top with a hot fried chicken breast, ladle the hot sauce on top, and serve immediately.

BOB'S CUBANO

with Gruyère

AND DILL PICKLE

The roots of this sandwich are as controversial as any, but while Miami and Key West attempt to lay claim to the original, my research finds that the famous Cubano was introduced by cigar workers in Tampa's Ybor City neighborhood, who used a tailor's iron to press and heat sandwiches of ham, pork, and pickle. I am not entirely sure it is true (though I do like the detail of the tailor's iron), but whoever invented the Cubano, well, good for him or her and for the rest of us. At Salt House, we use roasted pork tenderloin dusted with cumin and coriander, *serrano* ham (you can use prosciutto or *speck*) and Gruyere cheese. If you have a sandwich press, great. If not, you can press it in the pan. And if you're a tailor . . .

❧ MAKES 6 SANDWICHES ❧

ROASTED PORK

2 cups freshly squeezed orange juice

1 jalapeño chile, sliced

1 small bunch cilantro, chopped

2 pounds pork tenderloin

1 teaspoon coriander seeds

1 teaspoon cumin seeds

Salt and freshly ground pepper

2 tablespoons olive oil

6 torpedo rolls, split horizontally

Mayonnaise (page 251)

Dijon mustard

12 slices serrano ham, prosciutto, or speck

12 slices Gruyère cheese

1 large dill pickle, sliced

4 pickled jalapeño chiles, sliced

Unsalted butter, at room temperature

TO MAKE THE MARINADE for the roasted pork, in a small bowl, stir together the orange juice, chile, and cilantro. Place the pork in a baking dish, pour the marinade over the top, and turn the pork to coat evenly. Cover and refrigerate overnight, turning once.

When ready to cook, preheat the oven to 400°F. Place a rack in a roasting pan just large enough to accommodate the pork.

Meanwhile, in a small, dry frying pan, toast the coriander and cumin over medium heat, shaking the pan often to avoid scorching, for about a minute, or until fragrant and just turning color. Let cool completely, then grind finely in a spice grinder or in a mortar with a pestle.

Remove the pork from the marinade and pat dry. Season liberally with salt, pepper, and the ground cumin and coriander. In a large sauté pan, heat the oil over high heat. When the oil shimmers, add the pork and sear, turning as needed, for about 1½ minutes on each side, or until lightly browned. Transfer the pork to the rack in the roasting pan and roast for 30 to 40 minutes, or until an instant-read thermometer inserted into the thickest part of the pork registers 150°F. Remove from the oven and let cool completely.

TO ASSEMBLE THE SANDWICHES, slice the cooled pork against the grain as thinly as possible. Season the slices lightly with salt. Place the rolls, cut sides up, on a work surface, and spread the cut sides with the mayonnaise and then the mustard. Divide the pork slices evenly among the rolls, placing them on the bottom half. Top with 2 ham slices and 2 cheese slices, then divide the dill pickle and pickled chile slices evenly among the sandwiches. Close the sandwiches with the roll tops.

Smear the top and bottom of each sandwich with the butter. Heat a large frying pan over medium heat. Add as many sandwiches as will fit comfortably and heat for 3 to 4 minutes, or until browned on the first side. Carefully flip the sandwiches over and place a sandwich press (or a brick covered with aluminum foil) on top of the sandwiches. Cook for 1 minute, then transfer to a sheet pan.

When all of the sandwiches have been browned, put the sheet pan in the oven for about 6 minutes, or until the sandwiches are hot throughout. Serve at once.

Luis's
ITALIAN SAUSAGE
SANDWICH WITH
PEPPADEW PEPPERS

Here is a proper sausage recipe from our butcher, Luis. I know that with the grinding, the casing, and the poaching it all sounds a bit daunting, but if you follow the instructions faithfully and see the process through to the end, you'll be rewarded. Combining freshly made sausages with sweet and spicy Peppadew peppers and simply dressed arugula makes this sandwich something truly special. If you're pressed for time, you can form the mixture into patties (see note). The flavor will still be great, though you will lose a little something in texture because you'll lose some of the fat. You can't get around it: fat is an important element in sausage making. Pork is a wonderful provider. After serving a platter of your own homemade sausage sandwiches, you'll be one, too.

MAKES 6 SANDWICHES

ITALIAN SAUSAGES

2½ pounds boneless pork butt, cut into chunks

1 tablespoon toasted fennel

1 tablespoon kosher salt

1¼ teaspoon freshly ground pepper

1 teaspoon dried chile flakes

½ cup Chicken Stock (page 250) or water, chilled

7 to 8 feet natural hog or sheep casings, well rinsed

2 cups arugula

Extra-virgin olive oil

Sea salt

Torpedo rolls, split horizontally and cut sides toasted

Mayonnaise (page 251)

12 to 14 pickled Peppadew peppers, seeded and chopped

To make the sausages, place the meat in a bowl and put the bowl in the freezer, along with the food grinder attachment of your stand mixer and the medium disk, for 15 minutes.

Meanwhile, in a small, dry frying pan, toast the fennel seeds over medium-high heat, shaking the pan often to avoid scorching, for about a minute or two, or until they just turn golden brown and are fragrant. Pour onto a cutting board and chop coarsely.

Fit the grinder attachment to the stand mixer and pass the pork through the grinder into the mixer bowl. Add the fennel, kosher salt, pepper, chile flakes, and stock to the ground pork. Fit the mixer with the paddle attachment and mix on low speed for 1 minute. Increase the speed one setting and mix for 1 minute longer, or until well combined.

Now fit the mixer with the sausage stuffer attachment. Transfer the sausage mixture to the stuffer, slip a casing onto the stuffer tube, and fill the casing. Repeat until you have used up all of the sausage mixture, then twist the stuffed casings into sausages 5 to 7 inches long. You should have 6 sausages.

Fill a large pot with water, place over low to medium-low heat, and heat until the water registers 160°F on an instant-read thermometer. Add the sausages to the water and poach, stirring occasionally, for about 15 minutes, or until the internal temperature of a sausage registers 140°F on the thermometer. Remove the sausages from the water.

You can now grill the sausages on a stove-top ridged grill pan over medium heat or over a medium-hot fire in a charcoal or gas grill until browned and warmed through, or you can panfry them over, you guessed it, medium heat until browned and warmed through.

TO ASSEMBLE THE SANDWICHES, in a bowl, toss the arugula with a little olive oil and sea salt. Spread the cut sides of the rolls with the mayonnaise, then place a hot sausage on each roll. Add some peppers and arugula to each sandwich, then close the sandwiches and serve immediately.

NOTE: If you don't have equipment to grind the meat at home, ask your butcher to grind it for you. If you don't have a sausage stuffer, shape the sausage mixture into patties to fit the rolls and about $1/4$ inch thick, then fry in a frying pan in a little olive oil until nicely browned and cooked through.

Smoked Andouille
sausage

199

CHAPTER FIVE *Smoke* AND FIRE

My brother, STEVEN, AND I have traveled all across the country sampling regional barbecue. We've tasted meats that have been rubbed, brined, and marinated, grilled or smoked or both. Our first barbecue trip was to the Texas Hill Country outside Austin. My friend Brett Anderson, food writer for the *Times-Picayune* in New Orleans, gave us a list of "must-try" barbecue joints. We ate at nine barbecue places in two and a half days. The one I remember most is Luling City Market in Luling, Texas. Brett said that they had the juiciest smoked sausage he had ever eaten—and he was right.

SINCE THAT FIRST TRIP, Steven and I have been to Memphis, Kansas City, and many other barbecue hot spots. I have taken all of this research back into the kitchen and created my own versions of our favorite dishes. In this chapter, both traditional and nontraditional barbecue methods are highlighted. The St. Louis ribs with a spicy bourbon sauce (page 138) and the pecan-smoked pulled pork (page 137) represent the low-and-slow approach, in which you smoke the meats for a longer period and over lower heat than is typical for most barbecue recipes. But this chapter also shows that there is so much more to barbecuing than ribs and pulled pork. The recipes for the paprika-rubbed skirt steak (page 146) and the grilled salmon with teriyaki sauce (page 133) introduce quick ways to get great barbecue flavor. This chapter also offers recipes for an array of side dishes that pair perfectly with anything cooked on a grill or in a smoker.

Tips on cooking with smoke and fire

SOUS VIDE, which calls for cooking food in a vacuum-sealed bag placed in a low-temperature water bath for a long period, is all the rage of late. While we occasionally employ this technique in the restaurants, I more often opt for the original low-and-slow approach: smoking. At Town Hall, we have two commercial electric smokers that can handle 140 pounds of meat at a time. In the summer, when we're running our outdoor barbecue, those smokers are pushed to the limit.

YOU CAN SMOKE MEATS using a variety of tools. I recently acquired a shiny new gas grill (primarily because it allows me to do up a burger quickly to please the strange and fickle palate of my son, Eli). Although it can be set up for use as a smoker (if you have one, check the instructions for your make and model), I decided to use a barrel-type charcoal grill with an offset smoke box for testing the recipes in this book. They come in many styles and sizes and vary in price from one hundred dollars to many thousands. I picked one up on the low-end of that scale and it performed beautifully. When I would get the fire going around 8:00 a.m. for a long day of smoking, and the scent of hickory would start to waft around our block, the neighbors would start meandering over from their gardens and driveways. They knew they would soon be the beneficiaries of the testing process: "Sure Mitch, I'll come back at lunch for some pulled pork," or "Hmmm, prime rib, well I guess so. . . ." A few folks were so impressed by the simplicity of that smoker that they went out and bought their own. I can't recommend the offset barrel smoker enough, and as an added attraction, it also functions as a standard charcoal grill—smoke *and* fire. But remember, the offset smoker isn't a necessity. If you have a charcoal grill with a lid, you need only make a few tweaks and you'll have the most popular house on the block.

Smoking technique

IF YOU DO HAVE AN OFFSET SMOKER, first place whatever variety of woodchips you'll be using in water (you want them to soak for at least half an hour), then light the coals in the smoke box. When you reach the desired temperature, add a handful of the soaked chips and place your meat on the grate. Remember to watch your temperature and add charcoal and woodchips as necessary, usually about every hour.

IF YOU ARE GOING TO SMOKE IN A KETTLE GRILL, you need to set it up for indirect heat. Some grills, such as the Weber, have wire inserts for this purpose, a kind of basket to keep the coals to one side of the bottom grate. But they are not absolutely necessary. So, if you don't have the inserts what you want to do is light your coals and bank them against one side of the bottom grate. Then, place a foil pan of hot water next to the coals to add moisture. When the coals are ready, add your soaked woodchips and then place your meat on the grill, opposite side with the coals. Cover with the lid, and open the top vent about half way. Be sure to watch your temperature and regulate it using both the top and bottom vents. And, of course, add coal and woodchips as necessary.

How hot is your grill?

I'M GUESSING MOST FOLKS KNOW how to get a fire going in their outdoor grill. You might use briquettes and lighter fluid, or maybe lump charcoal and starter sticks. I find that what's known as a "chimney starter," and some crumpled newspapers, do the trick and splendidly. The best way to start a fire in your grill is to start it the way that makes you the most comfortable. I'm guessing, too, that you know what to do once those coals are lit. To wit: Let them ash over and distribute them evenly across your cooking area. While we mostly call for a hot grill, you might find yourself needing to cook over a variety of temperatures. Here's a "handy," literally, tip to get a pretty good approximation of the heat of your grill: use your hand. Place your palm about 4 inches above the coals. If you can stand it for just 2 or 3 seconds before it's necessary to pull your hand away, you've got yourself a hot grill. If it's 4 or 5 seconds before the heat gets to you, you're in the medium-high range. If you're able to count "six-one-thousand, seven-one-thousand," that's about medium heat, and 8 or 9 seconds, that's medium-low. Now, if you have a gas grill, for a hot fire, turn the knob to "high," for medium...you get the picture.

Creamy Smoked
TOMATO BISQUE

When we started our outdoor lunch at Town Hall, we wanted to see how a soup infused with the flavors associated with barbecue would go over with the lunchtime crowd. This is what we came up with, and it went over big. What makes this soup special—and also makes it a bisque—is the addition of cream, which softens the smoky edges of the tomatoes. Don't just take my word for it: taste the soup before you add the cream and then taste it again after. Finally, you should use plum tomatoes, which are meatier and less watery than many other varieties and therefore hold up better during the two to three hours they need to take on the smoke flavor.

❦ SERVES 6 TO 3 ❦

2 pounds plum tomatoes

2 to 3 large handfuls of hickory chips, soaked

1 tablespoon olive oil

1 tablespoon unsalted butter

1 large yellow onion, diced

Salt and freshly ground pepper

1 clove garlic, minced

1 teaspoon chopped fresh thyme leaves

2 cups Chicken Stock (page 250) or water

$^{1}/_{2}$ cup heavy cream

PREPARE A BARREL SMOKER with an offset firebox according to the directions on page 126 (or adapt you charcoal or gas grill). You want the temperature to be between 225° and 250°F.

Cut 1 pound of the tomatoes in half lengthwise and place them in the smoker on a grill screen. Add half of the soaked hickory chips and smoke for $2^{1}/_{2}$ hours, taking care to add more charcoal after about 1 hour to keep the temperature at around 225°F. Add the remaining hickory chips halfway through the cooking time.

When the tomatoes are ready, transfer them to a cutting board, let cool, then peel and dice.

Dice the remaining 1 pound tomatoes. In a heavy-bottomed pot, heat the oil and butter over low heat. Add the onion and a few pinches of salt, cover, and sweat for about 15 minutes, or until soft. Add the garlic and cook uncovered, stirring occasionally, for a few minutes, or until fragrant. Add the fresh and smoked tomatoes, the thyme, and 1 teaspoon salt, stir well, raise the heat to medium, and cook for 5 to 10 minutes, or until the tomatoes break down. Add the stock, bring to a simmer, and simmer for 10 minutes to blend the flavors.

Remove from the heat and let cool slightly. Working in batches, add the mixture to a blender and process until smooth. For a silkier texture, pass the puree through a fine-mesh strainer.

Return the puree to the pot over medium heat. Add the cream, stir well to incorporate, and heat until piping hot. Ladle into individual bowls and serve right away.

Herb Fired
RAINBOW TROUT
with **APPLE** and **HORSERADISH**
SALSA VERDE

Rainbow trout is one of the good fish. By that I mean rainbow trout are farmed in an environmentally friendly manner. They are labeled a "Best Choice" by the Monterey Bay Aquarium's Seafood Watch program, which helps consumers make sound selections based on what is fished or farmed sustainably.

I learned this Italian quick-smoking technique during my time at New York's Coco Pazzo, where it was used to prepare squab. Here, I apply it to make a good American fish even better. The play of sweet and savory—maple syrup and herbs—in the cooking of the trout is also present in the *salsa verde*, with the pairing of apples and horseradish.

The trout is cooked whole, with the skin on. The fat in the skin helps keep the fish moist. Also, make sure you soak the herbs well (as you would wood chips) so that they smolder. This will protect the skin from charring, which can sometimes impart a bitter flavor. And go ahead and try different variations and ratios of the herbs.

❧ SERVES 6 ❧

2 bunches thyme

2 bunches oregano

2 bunches sage

2 bunches rosemary

1/2 cup maple syrup

2 tablespoons cider vinegar

1/2 teaspoon salt

6 whole rainbow trout, head and tail on, cleaned

SALSA VERDE

1/2 cup chopped fresh flat-leaf parsley

1 heaping tablespoon chopped fresh tarragon leaves

1 tablespoon chopped fresh chives

1/4 cup walnuts, toasted and chopped

1 Fuji or other sweet, crisp apple, peeled, halved, cored, and finely diced

2 tablespoons grated fresh horseradish

1 cup extra-virgin olive oil

1 tablespoon walnut oil

1 large shallot, finely diced

1 teaspoon salt

Grated zest and juice of 1 lemon

Lemon wedges for garnish

LOOSEN THE THYME, oregano, sage, and rosemary bunches, place the sprigs in a large bowl, and mix well. Add water to cover and let soak for about 45 minutes.

Meanwhile, make the salsa. In a bowl, combine all of the ingredients and mix well. Set aside at room temperature.

Prepare a hot fire for direct-heat grilling in a charcoal or gas grill.

While the grill is heating, in a bowl, whisk together the maple syrup, vinegar, and salt. Working with 1 trout at a time, open up the cut along the belly to expose the interior flesh, and season the flesh with salt and pepper. Then, using a basting brush, generously coat the interior of the fish with the maple syrup mixture.

When the fire is ready, shake the excess water off of the herbs and divide into 4 equal piles. Spread 2 of the piles evenly on the grill rack directly over the fire to make beds for the trout, making sure each bed is wide enough to accommodate 3 trout. Lay 3 trout down on each of the herb beds, and cover each trio with 1 of the remaining herb piles. Place a large pot lid over each set of trout and cook for 4 minutes. Then, using a spatula, turn each of the trout, along with the herbs covering it (the herbs you had placed on top of the fish should now be in contact with the grill rack). Re-cover

continued

the trout with the lids and cook for an additional 4 minutes, or until the flesh is opaque when tested near the backbone with the tip of a knife and the skin is crispy.

To serve, discard the herbs and place the trout on individual plates. Drizzle with the salsa, garnish with a wedge of lemon, and serve, passing the remaining salsa at the table.

GRILLED SALMON
with *Tokyo Teriyaki*
BARBECUE GLAZE

I once took a trip to Japan with Seis Kamimura, who I had the pleasure of cooking with for many years at Postrio. One night when I was staying with his family, his grandmother came out of the kitchen carrying a salmon dish that including a rich, amazing sauce, much like you might find served with unagi (that's eel). At the table, I asked Seis what his grandmother called the sauce. "Tokyo barbecue sauce," he replied. The dish stayed with me, and because I didn't see her prepare it, I asked Seis to make it for me. When he did, I noticed that he brought his formidable classical technique to bear on this Japanese sauce. In fact, it was as if he was making a bordelaise. He caramelized the beef chuck, but replaced the Bordeaux with sake and rice vinegar. So, I'm not sure if he was being totally honest.

SERVES 6

GLAZE

1 tablespoon canola oil

1/2 pound boneless beef chuck, cubed

3-inch piece fresh ginger, peeled and sliced

3 cloves garlic, sliced

1 small jalapeño chile, seeded and sliced

1 bunch green onions, white parts sliced and tender green parts reserved whole

1/2 cup firmly packed dark brown sugar

3 tablespoons rice vinegar

1 cup sake

1 cup mirin

1 cup soy sauce

6 skinless center-cut salmon fillets, preferably wild, about 6 to 8 ounces each

To MAKE THE GLAZE, in a large, heavy-bottomed frying pan, heat the canola oil over high heat. Add the beef and brown, turning as needed, until well caramelized on all sides. Lower the heat to medium and add the ginger, garlic, chile, and the white parts of the green onions and cook, stirring occasionally, for 3 to 4 minutes, or until the aromatics are soft. Add the brown sugar and stir until fully dissolved and integrated into the mixture. Add the vinegar, raise the heat to high, cook, stirring to scrape up any browned bits on the pan bottom, for 30 to 45 seconds. Add the sake, mirin, and soy sauce and then lower to a simmer. Cook, stirring occasionally, for about 8 minutes, or until the liquid reduces slightly and lightly coats the back of a spoon.

Strain the glaze through a fine-mesh strainer into a baking dish just large enough to accommodate the salmon in a single layer and let cool. Remove 1/4 cup of the glaze from the dish and reserve for serving with the salmon. Add the salmon to the dish, turn to coat with the glaze, cover, and refrigerate for 30 minutes, turning after 15 minutes to ensure the fish marinates evenly.

Meanwhile, prepare a hot fire for direct-heat grilling in a charcoal or gas grill. Slice the green parts of the green onions as thinly as possible and set aside.

Remove the salmon from the marinade, allowing the excess to drip off, and discard the marinade. Place the salmon on the grill rack. Grill, turning once, for 2 to 2 1/2 minutes on each side, or until just cooked through. (The timing will vary depending on the thickness of the salmon.)

Transfer the salmon to individual plates, top with a splash of the reserved marinade and a sprinkling of green onion tops, and serve.

Tea-Smoked DUCK with

NECTARINE, AVOCADO, and WILD ARUGULA SALAD

Here's an unconventional way to put smoke on meat and to do it quickly—so quickly, in fact, that you don't even have to fire up the grill. You do this smoking in your kitchen. The duck is smoked on your stove top over an aromatic combination of rice, sugar, and tea. This recipe may be the most interesting way you'll ever use that collapsible metal steamer basket that's been knocking around your bottom cupboard for years. While nectarines are featured in the salad, you can try other seasonal fruits.

❀❧ SERVES 4 ❀❧

1 cup basmati rice

¼ cup sugar

½ cup loose green tea

2 duck breasts, skin on (about 1½ pounds)

SALAD

1 tablespoon champagne vinegar

1 tablespoon freshly squeezed lemon juice

Salt and freshly ground pepper

2 tablespoons extra-virgin olive oil

1 tablespoon canola oil

1 green zucchini

1 yellow zucchini

3 nectarines, halved, pitted, and thinly sliced

½ pound romano or other green beans, trimmed, halved on the diagonal, and blanched for about 3 minutes

¼ pound wild arugula

½ cup chiffonade-cut fresh basil (long, narrow strips)

¼ cup salted pistachios

1 avocado, halved, pitted, peeled, and thinly sliced

Line a large heavy-bottomed pot with a double layer of aluminum foil to protect the surface. Add the rice, sugar, and green tea to the pot and stir to mix well. Place a collapsible metal steamer basket on top of the dry ingredients and place the pot over high heat. When the mixture starts to smoke, place the duck breasts, flesh side down, in the steamer basket. Cover the pot, lower the heat to medium (and turn on the fan), and let smoke for 12 to 15 minutes for medium-rare to medium. When done, remove the duck from the steamer and let cool completely on a rack. Discard the contents of the pot.

TO MAKE THE VINAIGRETTE, in a small bowl, whisk together the vinegar, lemon, and a few pinches of salt. Whisk in both oils and season with pepper and with more salt, if needed. Set aside.

TO MAKE THE SALAD, trim the zucchini, then slice crosswise as thinly as possible, preferably on a mandoline. Place the zucchini in a large bowl, add the nectarines, beans, and arugula, and season lightly with a pinch of salt. Drizzle with the vinaigrette, toss lightly, and divide among individual plates. Garnish with the pistachios and avocado.

Thinly slice the smoked duck, place on top of the salads, dividing it evenly, and serve immediately.

Pecan-Smoked
PULLED PORK,
CAROLINA STYLE

Barbecue is perhaps the American staple with the strongest regional identification. Kansas City is known for its long smokes and sauces. In Memphis, get the pork ribs. And in Texas, order the brisket. In the Carolinas, the specialty is pulled pork slathered in a vinegary sauce. That Carolina style serves as the inspiration here.

Don't be shy when you apply the rub. It will form a thick crust in the smoker that, when chopped up and mixed back in with the pulled meat, provides wonderful texture and flavor. Remember, you are cooking to temperature, not time, and I can't stress enough the importance of finishing the pork by wrapping it in plastic wrap. The meat steams in the wrapping, a simple technique that results in the moistest barbecued pork you will ever eat.

SERVES 6 TO 8

6 pounds boneless pork butt, in one piece

¹/₂ cup firmly packed golden brown sugar

¹/₄ cup Town Hall Spice Mixture (page 253)

About 6 large handfuls pecan wood chips, soaked

Plenty of time (not the herb)

VINEGAR BARBECUE SAUCE

1 cup Spicy Bourbon Barbecue Sauce (page 253)

³/₄ cup distilled white vinegar

³/₄ cup water

1 teaspoon dried chile flakes

6 to 8 brioche buns or hamburger buns, split horizontally

Unsalted butter, at room temperature

GET UP EARLY and prepare a barrel smoker with an offset firebox according to the directions on page 126 (or adapt you charcoal or gas grill). You want the temperature to be between 225° and 250°F. Take the meat out of the refrigerator and allow it to sit at room temperature for about 30 minutes while you get the fire ready.

In a small bowl, mix together the brown sugar and spice mixture. Coat the meat liberally with the sugar mixture.

Place the pork in the smoker and add a handful of the soaked pecan chips. Cook the pork until an instant-read thermometer inserted into the center registers 185°F. This will take 10 to 12 hours. Be sure to add charcoal every hour or so to maintain the temperature inside the smoker at about 225°F. When you add the charcoal, give the meat a quarter turn. Add more soaked wood chips about every 2 hours to keep the smoke flowing. After 6 hours, cover the meat with aluminum foil.

When the meat reaches 185°F, discard the foil and remove the meat from the smoker. Wrap the pork as tightly as possible in plastic wrap and let it sit for 45 minutes.

The slow smoking gives you plenty of time to make the sauce. In a saucepan, combine the barbecue sauce, vinegar, water, and chile flakes over medium heat, stir well, and heat for about 2 minutes, or until warm. Set aside.

After the pork has rested for 45 minutes, reheat the sauce over very, very low heat in a pan large enough to accommodate the sauce and the meat. Preheat the oven to 350°F.

Unwrap the pork and, using either two forks or gloved hands, pull the meat apart, taking care to remove as much fat and gristle as possible. I like the larger, chunkier style of pulled meat, but you can chop the meat with a large kitchen knife, if you prefer. Transfer the pulled meat to the sauce, stir well to coat, and immediately take the pan off the heat. Cover and let stand for 4 to 5 minutes.

Butter the cut sides of the buns and arrange them, cut sides up, on a sheet pan. Toast in the oven for about 5 minutes, or until golden brown.

To serve, pile the pulled pork high on the toasted buns.

NOTE: If you don't have time to make the ketchup barbecue sauce, go ahead and vinegar-up a cup of store-bought sauce.

Apple-Glazed
ST. LOUIS RIBS
WITH SPICY BOURBON
Barbecue Sauce

While doing "field research" on barbecue a few years back, Steven and I somehow ended up in Hillsdale, Kansas, a tiny town in the middle of nowhere. There we discovered The Bank, a place that serves beautifully smoked meats and perhaps the greatest barbecue sauce I've ever tasted. A conversation with the pit boss revealed that his 'cue method was to forgo the dry rub and use hickory at a very low temperature, giving the meat more time in the smoker. Everything about those ribs told us that these were good ideas, and as soon as we got back in our rental car, we called Town Hall and told the staff to change our preparation immediately.

After you make these ribs the first time, you'll realize that the hardest thing about preparing a batch is the cooking time. By that I mean when the air starts smelling of smoke and the ribs begin taking on a gorgeous deep color, well, you're going to want them right away. But, as I said, these ribs are of the low-and-slow variety and patience is necessary. I often cook these ribs for parties, and guests inevitably ask me for the recipe. "No need to write it down," I'll say. "It takes 4 to 4$\frac{1}{2}$ hours. Just some salt and pepper, and after a half hour, baste them with some apple juice, and then again after 2$\frac{1}{2}$ hours. That's how you get that paper-thin, candylike glaze." For your convenience, I've written the instructions below.

At the restaurant and in this recipe, we use St. Louis–style ribs, which are the spareribs trimmed of the tips. But you can use regular spareribs or even baby back ribs. Make sure to ask your butcher to remove the membrane from the rib racks, to let more of the hickory-smoke flavor in.

❧ SERVES 6 ❧

3 racks St. Louis ribs, about 10 pounds total

Salt and freshly ground pepper

3 to 4 handfuls hickory chips, soaked

1 cup apple juice

PREPARE a barrel smoker with an offset firebox according to the directions on page 126 (or adapt you charcoal or gas grill). You want the temperature to be between 225° and 250°F. Take the rib racks out of the refrigerator and allow them to sit at room temperature for about 30 minutes while you get the fire ready.

Season the ribs liberally with salt and pepper. Place the racks, bone side down, in the smoker, and add a handful of the soaked hickory chips. Smoke the ribs for 30 minutes, then baste them well with half of the apple juice. Smoke for 2$\frac{1}{2}$ hours longer, then baste again with the remaining apple juice. Rotate the ribs every hour, moving the racks closest to the heat source to the farthest point. Be sure to add charcoal every hour or so to maintain the temperature inside the smoker at about 225°F. Add more soaked wood chips about every 2 hours to keep the smoke flowing. The ribs will be ready in 4 to 4$\frac{1}{2}$ hours. They will be tender and pull easily from the bone.

Remove the racks from the smoker, cut the ribs apart, and serve with Spicy Bourbon Barbeque Sauce (page 253).

Blackened

BURGER *with*

BLUE CHEESE AND

RUSSIAN DRESSING

Blackening is a kind of accelerated form of smoking. Although it might seem like an old-fashioned technique practiced for generations in the bayous of Louisiana, it was actually invented by Paul Prudhomme. When I was at K-Paul's, the kitchen had three cast-iron frying pans dedicated to blackening. They were over the flame from the beginning of service to the end.

Blackening can be a challenge for the home cook. It is affected by a few variables, such as the quality and fat content of the meat and, most important, the consistency of the heat source. It might take you a few tries to perfect your own technique, but when you do, it's going to be perfect and you'll know it.

❧ SERVES 6 ❧

2 pounds boneless beef chuck, cut into 1-inch cubes, or ground beef chuck (15 percent fat)

2 tablespoons salt

RUSSIAN DRESSING

¼ cup well-drained jarred pimiento

1 cup Mayonnaise (page 251)

¼ cup chili sauce

¼ cup sweet pickle relish

1 tablespoon chopped green onion

2 tablespoons capers, rinsed and coarsely chopped

1 tablespoon chopped fresh flat-leaf parsley

¼ teaspoon sweet smoked paprika

1 tablespoon freshly squeezed lemon juice

Salt and freshly ground pepper

4 tablespoons clarified butter (see page 254), melted

2 tablespoons Town Hall Spice Mixture (page 253)

1½ cups crumbled blue cheese (optional)

6 hamburger buns, split horizontally and toasted

Lettuce leaves, tomato slices, red onion slices, or other condiments

IF GRINDING your own meat, place a meat grinder or the food grinder attachment of a stand mixer and the medium disk in the freezer for 30 minutes. Spread the cubed chuck on a sheet pan, sprinkle with the salt, and refrigerate for 30 minutes.

When ready to grind, fit the grinder with the disk and pass the well-chilled meat through the grinder twice. The ground meat should have a firm texture. If after the first pass through the grinder the meat feels soft and "mushy," you might want to refrigerate it for a bit longer, along with the grinder attachment.

Divide the meat you have ground (or two pounds of ground chuck you have purchased) into 6 equal portions, and shape each portion into a patty about ½ inch thick. (If you like rare burgers, make the patties thicker.) Set aside.

TO PREPARE THE DRESSING, in a mini processor or a blender, combine the pimiento and 1 tablespoon of the mayonnaise and process until smooth. Transfer to a bowl and add the remaining mayonnaise, chili sauce, pickle relish, green onion, capers, parsley, paprika, and lemon juice and stir to mix well. Season with salt and pepper, then cover and refrigerate until serving. (The dressing will keep for up to 4 days.)

TO COOK THE BURGERS, place a dry cast-iron frying pan over high heat. You want it very, very hot. Meanwhile, baste both sides of each patty with clarified butter, and then dust each side with a liberal amount of the spice mixture.

When the pan is superhot, place 2 patties in it. They will give off a lot of smoke, so make sure you have the fan on

continued

high. Cook for 2¹/₂ to 3 minutes. Flip the burgers, lower the heat to medium, top each burger with ¹/₄ cup of the cheese, and cook for 2¹/₂ to 3 minutes longer for medium.

Spread the cut sides of the buns with the dressing, and top the bottom halves with the burgers. Serve with the condiments for diners to add as desired.

Slow-Smoked
BARBECUED
MEAT LOAF

Inspiration can hit at the oddest times. One morning, I was looking through the refrigerator for something for my kids' breakfast. As I reached for the eggs, I noticed a package of ground beef and suddenly thought, "What if I smoked a meat loaf?"

The ingredients here are basic. They include the same trio of meats—veal, pork, and beef—used in the Town Hall meatballs. But the low-and-long smoking gives the dish a surprising complexity. Oddly enough, it makes it almost delicate, a word not often associated with meat loaf. You can either hand-shape it on a sheet pan, or pack the meat loaf into a tureen. We tried it both ways. The former will give you more intensity of smoke while the latter has a lighter smoke flavor, and also offers a nice French presentation, again something not normally associated with meat loaf.

SERVES 6

1 pound ground beef

1/2 pound ground pork

1/2 pound ground veal

1 tablespoon olive oil

1 cup yellow onion, finely chopped

1 1/2 cups white bread, torn into small pieces (3 or 4 slices, depending on the thickness)

1/2 cup whole milk

2 large eggs

1/2 cup grated Parmesan cheese

1/3 cup Spicy Bourbon Barbecue Sauce (page 253), or barbecue sauce of your choice

1 tablespoon Worcestershire sauce

1 tablespoon Dijon mustard

2 tablespoons Town Hall Spice Mixture (page 253)

1 tablespoon salt

2 or 3 handfuls hickory chips, soaked

PREPARE a barrel smoker with an offset firebox according to the directions on page 126 (or adapt you charcoal or gas grill). You want the temperature to be between 225° and 250°F. Take the meats out of the refrigerator and allow them to sit at room temperature for about 30 minutes while you get the fire ready.

In a frying pan, heat the oil over medium heat. Add the onion and cook, stirring occasionally, for 8 to 10 minutes, or until soft and slightly caramelized. Remove from the heat and let cool. While the onion is cooling, combine the bread and milk in a bowl and let stand for about 2 minutes, or until the milk is completely absorbed.

In a stand mixer fitted with the paddle attachment, (or in a large bowl using a wooden spoon) combine the soaked bread, cooled onion, eggs, Parmesan, barbecue sauce, Worcestershire sauce, mustard, spice mixture, and salt. Beat on low speed just until combined. Shape the mixture into loaf on a sheet pan, or pack into a standard loaf pan.

Place the meat loaf in the smoker and add a handful of the soaked hickory chips. Smoke the meat loaf for 3 to 3 1/2 hours, or until an instant-read thermometer inserted into the center of the loaf registers 165°F. Be sure to add charcoal every hour or so to maintain the temperature inside the smoker at about 225°F. Add more soaked wood chips as necessary to keep the smoke flowing.

Remove the meat loaf from the smoker and let rest for 15 to 20 minutes before serving. Any leftovers will make a great sandwich.

Smoked Paprika-Rubbed SKIRT STEAK with Fried YUKON GOLD POTATOES

with SWEET PEPPERS and Sage

A couple of things about the preparation of this dish: One, if you have time, marinate the steak overnight. But if the idea of a delicious skirt steak catches your fancy in the afternoon, you can marinate it for as little as an hour and still get great flavor. That's because of the second thing, which is that you're kind of cheating here. See, the paprika gives you a wonderful smoky flavor without hours of actual smoking. That's cheating we can all abide, however.

Now, two other things: First, you want to cook this steak as rare as you can eat it. And second, I can't stress enough the importance of slicing it *against the grain*. If you don't, the steak will be too chewy. Also, never slice this steak near a crowd. This dish lends itself to picking, and by the time the platter gets to the table, it will be shy a few pieces.

You can use this marinade on a rib-eye, a flank steak, or a tri-tip, but I especially like it on skirt steak.

❧ SERVES 6 ❧

MARINADE

3 large cloves garlic, thinly sliced

$\frac{1}{2}$ teaspoon salt

1 cup loosely packed fresh flat-leaf parsley sprigs coarsely chopped

3 sprigs rosemary

$\frac{1}{4}$ cup olive oil

$1\frac{1}{2}$ teaspoons hot smoked paprika

$\frac{1}{8}$ teaspoon dried chile flakes

2 pounds skirt steak, trimmed of excess fat and silvery membrane

Salt and freshly ground pepper

POTATOES

2 pounds medium-size Yukon gold potatoes

Canola oil for frying

2 tablespoons olive oil

4 cloves of garlic, sliced

2 bell peppers (green, red or yellow, or a mix thereof), seeded and diced

2 tablespoons chopped sage

TO MAKE THE MARINADE, put the garlic and salt in a mortar and pound with a pestle until a paste forms. Add the parsley and work together with the garlic to a paste. Add the rosemary, oil, paprika, and chile flakes and stir to combine.

Place the skirt steak in a shallow dish. Season with salt and pepper and rub with the marinade, making sure to cover the meat completely. Marinate at room temperature for at least 1 to 2 hours, or preferably overnight in the refrigerator.

TO MAKE THE POTATOES, place them in a large pot, cover with cold water by about 2 inches and add 2 tablespoons salt. Bring to a boil over high heat. When it reaches the boiling point, reduce the heat slightly and continue boiling for 15 minutes. They should still be firm in the center when tested with a fork. Strain gently, and then set aside to cool.

continued

When cool, peel the potatoes and cut into 1-inch chunks. Heat a deep fryer or a large cast iron pot with oil at a depth of about 3 inches to 375 degrees. Fry the potatoes (in 2 batches) until golden brown, about 4 to 6 minutes per batch. Drain on paper towels.

In a large sauté pan, heat the olive oil over medium, add the garlic slices and cook, stirring, for about 15 seconds, then add the green and red peppers and cook, stirring, for 2 to 3 minutes until they begin to become tender. Add the fried potatoes and sage and cook for about 2 minutes more. Keep warm.

When ready to cook the steak, prepare a hot fire for direct-heat grilling in a charcoal or gas grill.

Place the steak on the grill rack directly over the fire and grill, turning once, for $2^1/_2$ minutes on each side for medium-rare. Transfer to a platter and let rest for 5 minutes.

Thinly slice the steak against the grain and serve at once with a side of the potatoes.

MUSTARD SEED–
Marinated Pulled
CHICKEN THIGHS

The hallmark of Carolina 'cue is the vinegary sauce—the more vinegary, the better. But this recipe is given an extra vinegary kick in the marinade, which uses ground mustard seeds infused with the stuff. Be sure to let the chicken cool before you take off the skin and pull the meat. If you don't, the meat will dry out. Take my advice, hurry up and wait. The spicy slaw that goes into our fried chicken sandwiches is good with this smoky chicken.

SERVES 6

2 tablespoons mustard seeds

3 tablespoons water

3 tablespoons cider vinegar

3 tablespoons distilled white vinegar

1 teaspoon salt

2 cloves garlic, sliced

2 tablespoons Town Hall Spice Mixture (page 253)

2 tablespoons firmly packed golden brown sugar

1/2 cup olive oil

2 tablespoons Tabasco sauce

12 bone-in, skin-on chicken thighs

2 to 3 handfuls hickory chips, soaked

VINEGAR BARBECUE SAUCE

1/2 cup Spicy Bourbon Barbecue Sauce (page 253)

6 tablespoons distilled white vinegar

6 tablespoons water

1/2 teaspoon dried chile flakes

6 brioche buns or hamburger buns, split horizontally
Buttermilk-Jicama Slaw (page 116) or your favorite slaw.

In a small saucepan, combine the mustard seeds, water, and both vinegars over medium heat. Bring to a boil and boil until all of the liquid has evaporated, about 5 minutes. Remove from the heat and let the mustard seeds cool.

Transfer the cooled mustard seeds to a mortar, add the salt, and mash for a minute or two, until a paste just begins to form. Add the garlic, spice mixture, and brown sugar and work together all of the ingredients for 4 to 5 minutes, or until a paste forms. Add the oil and work it into the mixture for a minute or so, or until it just starts to emulsify. Finally, mix in the Tabasco sauce.

Place the chicken thighs in a large bowl, pour the mustard seed mixture over the top, and toss to coat the thighs evenly. Cover and refrigerate for 1 hour.

Prepare a barrel smoker with an offset firebox according to the directions on page 126 (or adapt you charcoal or gas grill). You want the temperature to be 250°F.

Place the chicken thighs, skin side down, on the grill rack in the smoker and add the soaked wood chips. Smoke for 45 minutes. Turn the thighs over and rotate the thighs closest to the heat source to the farthest point. Smoke for an additional 45 minutes, or until meat is firm and cooked through.

Transfer the chicken thighs to a pan and let cool (remember picking it hot will dry it out). While the chicken is cooling, make the sauce. In a saucepan large enough to accommodate the sauce and the pulled chicken, combine the barbecue sauce, vinegar, water, and chile flakes over medium heat, stir well, and heat for about 2 minutes, or until warm. Set aside.

When the chicken is cool, remove and discard the skin, then pick off all of the meat from the bones, discarding any sinew or fat and the bones. Place the picked chicken meat in the sauce and warm over very low heat.

To serve, divide the pulled chicken evenly among the buns and top with the slaw.

Black Pepper
and CORIANDER CRUSTED
PASTRAMI

In my earliest days at Jack's Celebrity Deli, I was always fascinated by the pastrami man. He knew exactly how to keep the meat at a perfect temperature, a kind of artist at the steam table. This recipe reminds me of Jack's—specifically Jack's famous No. 4, an extremely popular sandwich featuring a combination of pastrami, corned beef, slaw, and Russian dressing.

Here's a recipe for the lamb pastrami we serve at Irving Street Kitchen. But if you're a traditionalist, you can use the same process to make a pastrami from a beef brisket. Whatever you chose, I can't stress enough the importance of cleanliness during the brining. You *need* to sterilize everything, you *need* to wear gloves and use tongs . . . the whole nine yards. In fact, you had better make it ten.

I'm from Jersey. I'm used to hot pastrami. But at Irving Street Kitchen, up in Portland, chef Sarah Schafer sometimes serves it cold as part of a charcuterie plate. It was unusual for me to have it served that way. Beautiful thin slices of pastrami laying on a wooden board seemed out of place. But they were delicious, incredibly delicious. I couldn't stop eating them. You might want to give cold pastrami a try.

SERVES 6 TO 3

1 gallon cold water

1¹/₃ cup salt

1¹/₃ cup sugar

1 head of garlic, cloves separated, peeled, and crushed

1 small leg of lamb, split in two, butterflied and sinews removed

CRUST

1 cup black peppercorns, toasted

¹/₂ cup coriander seeds, toasted

2 large handfuls hickory chips, soaked

BEFORE YOU BRINE THE LAMB, sterilize a large pot, or covered container large enough to hold the lamb, that will fit in your refrigerator, as well as any utensils you will be using (you can do this in your dishwasher). When ready, mix together the water, salt, and sugar in a large pot and stir to dissolve. Next, wearing sterile gloves, place the crushed garlic in cheese cloth, dip into the water and squeeze as hard as you can, extracting as much of the juice as possible. Repeat this process twice.

Place lamb in the large covered container. Pour the brine over the lamb and position the lamb so that it is completely submerged. Cover and place in refrigerator. Let sit for 7 days, rotating the lamb daily with gloved hands or sterile tongs.

TO PREPARE THE CRUST, first toast the peppercorns and coriander by placing them in a dry pan over medium-high heat. Cook, shaking the pan often for a minute or two, or until fragrant and the coriander begins to color. Remove from heat, and let cool.

Set up an offset smoker (see page 126) and bring the temperature to about 250°F.

Remove the lamb from the brine and rinse lightly in cold water. Next, place the toasted black peppercorns and coriander in spice grinder and pulse until coarse. Encrust lamb completely with pepper/coriander mix, pressing it in firmly.

Place the lamb in the smoker, adding a handful of hickory chips to the firebox. Add more hickory chips after about two hours. The cooking time will be somewhere between 4 and 5 hours. The pastrami is ready when the internal temperature has reached 155°F on a meat thermometer.

Serve with mustard on sliced rye.

Garlic-Studded Hickory-Smoked PRIME RIB

The recipe here, an elemental combination of salt, pepper, meat, and heat (okay, and a little olive oil), comes from a mistake—a failure, really. Steven and I were trying to approximate a slow-smoked prime rib that we had at a Kansas City barbecue joint. But no matter how we tried, we couldn't get it right. In that process, however, I found this method, and the failure is better than the original. Plus, it's ready in just three hours or so.

You can use a boneless cut, but a bone-in prime rib will retain more moisture. Either way, ask your butcher to keep some of the so-called fat cap on the meat because, in this instance, fat is good. As the smoke and heat circulate around the prime rib, the fat melts, dripping and flowing and keeping everything beautifully tender and so moist that if you don't want to make the sauce, the prime rib is still great without it.

The idea of studding the rib with garlic comes from Paul Prudhomme. At K-Paul's, he would stud a prime rib before roasting it extremely rare, then he would chill the prime rib, cut it into thick steaks, and blacken the steaks in a cast-iron pan. (Consider this a lagniappe recipe.)

❦ SERVES 6 TO 3 ❦

Three-bone prime rib, about 8 pounds

4 cloves garlic, halved

1/4 cup olive oil

Salt and freshly ground pepper

2 large handfuls hickory chips, soaked

HORSERADISH SAUCE

1/2 cup sour cream

1/2 cup crème fraîche

1/4 cup grated fresh horseradish

1 tablespoon Dijon mustard

2 tablespoons freshly squeezed lemon juice

1 tablespoon juices from prime rib

PREPARE A BARREL SMOKER with an offset firebox according to the directions on page 126 (or adapt you charcoal or gas grill). You want the temperature to be between 275° and 300°F. Place a tray underneath the area where you will be placing the meat to collect juices for the horseradish sauce. Take the prime rib out of the refrigerator and allow it to sit at room temperature for about 30 minutes while you get the fire ready.

With a sharp paring knife, cut 8 slits each 1 inch deep in the top part of the meat, and stuff each slit with a halved garlic clove. Rub the oil over the entire prime rib, and finally, season with salt and pepper.

Place the prime rib in the smoker and add one-third of the soaked hickory chips. Smoke the prime rib until an instant-read thermometer inserted into the center of the meat away from bone registers 135°F. This will take somewhere in the neighborhood of 2 1/2 to 3 hours. Start checking the temperature at the 2-hour mark. While the prime rib is smoking, give it a quarter turn every 30 minutes. Be mindful of the temperature inside the smoker, adding charcoal as needed to keep it between 275° and 300°F. Also, add more soaked hickory chips twice to keep the smoke flowing.

TO MAKE THE SAUCE, in a bowl, stir together the sour cream, crème fraîche, horseradish, mustard, and lemon juice, mixing well. Cover and refrigerate.

When the prime rib is ready, remove it from the smoker and let rest for at least 20 to 25 minutes before serving to allow the internal juices to redistribute evenly.

Meanwhile, add the 1 tablespoon juices from the smoker to the sauce and mix well.

To serve, carve the prime rib into thick slices. Serve the sauce alongside.

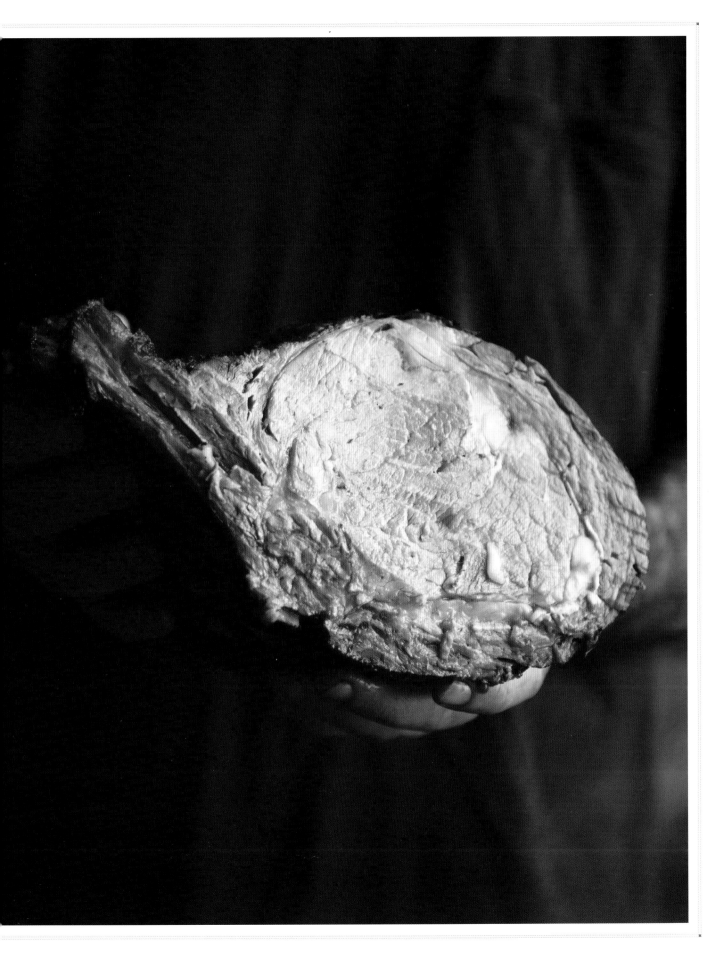

SIDE DISHES

With a couple of exceptions here, cooking with "smoke and fire" means cooking outdoors. It follows that most of the recipes above are perfect to cook up at a cookout. Whether in the kitchen or the courtyard, it's always a good idea to have plenty of sides to offer with the main event. Here are half-a-dozen that pair up well with most everything that will come out of your smoker or off of your grill. And if you're having a get-together, it might be a good idea to have some of these sides prepared before things get rolling, just in case your guests have to wait for the meats to be ready. That's because with the smell of smoke and fire thick in the air, trust me, you'll want to have a little something to placate the folk while you finish cooking those ribs.

Collard Greens

Some southern collard recipes dispense with exacting measurements and merely call for a "mess o' greens." I suggest that 4 bunches can rightly be considered a "mess." The liquid that remains after the greens have cooked down is known as "Pot Likker," and is delicious sopped up with corn bread. One southern tradition has it that if you eat collards on New Year's Day, along with some black-eyed peas, you'll have good luck. And if it doesn't pan out, well, at least you had a pretty delicious meal on the first of the year.

SERVES 6

2 tablespoons canola oil

2 medium onions, diced

1 ham hock

³/₄ cup unsalted butter

3 quarts Chicken Stock (page 250)

1³/₄ cups red wine vinegar

²/₃ cup hot sauce, such as Crystal

²/₃ cup firmly packed golden brown sugar

4 bunches collard greens, tough stems removed

IN A LARGE POT, heat the oil over medium heat. Add the onions and ham hock and cook, stirring occasionally, for about 10 minutes, or until the onions have caramelized. Add the butter, and once it melts, add the stock, vinegar, and hot sauce, followed by the brown sugar. Bring the mixture to a boil, stirring to dissolve the sugar, and add the greens. Lower the heat to low, cover, and simmer for about 2¹/₂ hours, or until the greens are tender.

Remove the ham hock and let cool until it can be handled. Then pick the meat, discarding any fat and gristle, and return it to the pot. Stir well, then heat over medium-low heat until heated through and serve.

Corn MAQUE CHOUX

What a great name for a dish, Corn *Maque Choux*. Say it again, Corn *Maque Choux*. It's a kind of Cajun creamed corn and is yet another, and very fine, play on the sweet/spicy theme. If your corn is super sweet, leave the sugar out. At the restaurants, we've served this with everything from grilled rib-eye to blackened salmon.

SERVES 6

10 ears corn, silk and husks removed

4 cups heavy cream

1 cup whole milk

3 tablespoons unsalted butter

1 tablespoon canola oil

1 small white onion, diced

1 pasilla chile, diced

3 tablespoons sugar

2 tablespoons Town Hall Spice Mixture (page 253)

1 tablespoon salt

USING A SHARP KNIFE, cut the kernels from the ears of corn. Set the kernels aside.

Snap the corncobs in half and place them in a wide pot. Add the cream and milk, place over medium heat, bring to a simmer, and simmer for about 30 minutes, or until the liquid is reduced to 2 cups. Remove and discard the cobs, strain the liquid through a fine-mesh strainer, and set aside.

In a large pot, combine 2 tablespoons of the butter with the oil over medium heat. When the butter starts to melt, add the onion and chile and cook, stirring occasionally, for 10 minutes, or until softened. Add the remaining 1 tablespoon butter, the corn kernels, the sugar, the spice mixture, and the salt and stir well to combine. Cook for 10 minutes, stirring often with a wooden spoon and making sure you scrape the bottom of the pan to prevent the mixture from caramelizing.

Turn the heat to low, add the strained corn cream, and cook, stirring occasionally, for 8 to 10 minutes, or until the mixture starts to thicken. Serve immediately.

Dirty Rice

This rice isn't just dirty, it's also screaming hot. You can cut the spice mixture down by half and the dish will still have plenty of heat. But don't you occasionally find something terribly exciting about something with a high-level of spicy heat? You know what I mean, that kind of heat where it's almost painful, but you can't wait to get to the next bite? When we tested this, I had that feeling and was reminded of a rice dish I had for breakfast in Thailand. I couldn't believe how hot it was, but I couldn't stop eating

it. By the time I was done I had blisters on my lips, but I was more than satisfied. Don't worry, this dirty rice isn't that hot.

SERVES 6

2 tablespoons unsalted butter

1 tablespoon canola oil

1/2 pound ground pork

1/4 cup ground chicken gizzards (optional)

1/2 cup diced yellow onion

1/2 cup diced celery

1/2 cup diced mixed red and green bell peppers

1 tablespoon minced garlic

2 tablespoons Town Hall Spice Mixture (page 253)

2 bay leaves

2 cups Chicken Stock (page 250)

1 rosemary sprig

1 teaspoon salt

1/4 pound ground chicken livers

1 cup long-grain white rice

IN A HEAVY-BOTTOMED POT, melt the butter with the oil over high heat until almost smoking. Add the pork and gizzards and cook, breaking up the pork with a wooden spoon and stirring occasionally, for about 5 minutes, or until browned. Add the onion, celery, peppers, and garlic and cook, stirring occasionally and allowing the vegetables to sweat slightly, for 5 minutes more. Add the spice mixture and bay leaves and continue to cook, stirring occasionally, for 5 minutes more. Pour in the stock, add the rosemary sprig and salt, and bring to a boil. Add the chicken livers, stir well, and cook for 2 minutes.

Add the rice, return the mixture to a boil, cover, and turn the heat down to low. Cook for 20 minutes, or until the rice is tender and the liquid is absorbed.

Remove and discard the bay leaves and the rosemary sprig. Serve immediately.

Spicy
RED POTATO
SALAD

Like the song says, this is a "Solid Potato Salad" (look it up, it's by the Ross Sisters . . . you'll be amazed). Our version of the cookout staple uses red potatoes and benefits from the kick provided by the combination of horseradish mustard, Tabasco, and our spice mix. That kick has made it a favorite at Town Hall's BBQ.

❧ SERVES 6 TO 8 ❧

2 pounds small red potatoes

6 large eggs

1 cup Mayonnaise (page 251)

1/3 cup finely diced celery

1/3 cup finely diced red onion

1 bunch green onions (including tender green parts), thinly sliced

1 1/2 tablespoons horseradish mustard

1 tablespoon Worcestershire sauce

1 tablespoon Town Hall Spice Mixture (page 253)

1 tablespoon Tabasco sauce

1 tablespoons distilled white vinegar

Salt and freshly ground pepper

IN A SAUCEPAN, combine the potatoes with salted water to cover by 2 inches, bring to a boil over high heat, then lower the heat to medium, and cook for about 20 minutes, or until fork-tender. Remove from the heat, drain, and spread out in a single layer on a sheet pan to cool and dry.

While the potatoes are cooking, you can hard-boil the eggs any way you'd like. I bring a saucepan filled with water to a boil, carefully add the eggs, and cook for 8 minutes. Then I remove the pan from the heat and transfer the eggs to a large bowl of cold water. However you boil your eggs, when they are cool, peel them, separate the whites and yolks, and chop them separately.

In a bowl, combine the mayonnaise, celery, red onion, green onions, mustard, Worcestershire sauce, spice mixture, Tabasco sauce, and vinegar and mix well. Fold in the egg whites and yolks and season with salt and pepper.

When the potatoes are cool, quarter them lengthwise and place in a large bowl. Add the mayonnaise mixture and stir to coat the potatoes evenly. Taste and adjust the seasoning, then serve.

Jalapeño
CORN BREAD
with HONEY BUTTER

Sweet and spicy again. Corn, too. This is not only a great side dish, it's a great side dish to many of the side dishes. At the restaurant, we cook and serve up this corn bread in little cast-iron pans shaped like ears of corn. If you can find them, well, I'm just saying it makes a nice presentation.

❧ MAKES 12 MUFFINS ❧

1 1/2 cups all-purpose flour

2/3 cup sugar

1/2 cup cornmeal

1 tablespoon baking powder

1 teaspoon salt

1 1/4 cups whole milk

2 large eggs

1/3 cup canola oil

4 tablespoons unsalted butter, melted

3 jalapeño chiles, seeded and finely diced

5 tablespoons unsalted butter, melted, mixed with 2 tablespoons honey

PREHEAT the oven to 350°F. Grease 12 standard muffin-tin cups with butter or line the cups with paper liners. (If you've got little cast-iron pans shaped like ears of corn, use them.)

In a large bowl, stir together the flour, sugar, cornmeal, baking powder, and salt. In a medium bowl, stir together the milk, eggs, oil, and butter until well blended. Add the wet ingredients to the dry ingredients and mix well to combine. Finally, add the chiles and, you guessed it, mix again until well combined.

Distribute the batter evenly among the 12 prepared muffin cups. Bake for about 20 minutes, or until light golden brown and a toothpick inserted into the center of a corn bread comes out dry. When done, immediately brush the tops of the hot breads with the butter-honey mixture and then let rest in the pan on a wire rack for a few minutes. Serve hot.

BAKED BEANS

Music is a big part of the atmosphere at Town Hall, an engaging mix of Delta and Chicago blues, roots music, and jazz, both hot and cool. Every once in a while you might hear Louis Armstrong sing, "People say, in Boston even beans do it, ummph," while riffing on the Cole Porter classic, "Let's Fall in Love." If you're interested in doing Boston Beans, look no further than this rich and hearty version. These baked beans have ummph.

SERVES 6

2 cups dried navy beans, picked over

¼ pound thick-cut sliced bacon, diced

1 small yellow onion, finely diced

½ cup ketchup

¼ cup dark molasses

¼ cup firmly packed dark brown sugar

2 tablespoons Dijon mustard

1 tablespoon Worcestershire sauce

1 tablespoon salt

1 teaspoon freshly ground pepper

1 teaspoon dry mustard

1 small ham hock

PLACE THE BEANS in a saucepan, add water to cover by 2 inches, and let soak overnight. The next day, drain, cover with fresh water, and place the pan on the stove top over medium heat, bring to a simmer, and cook for about 1 hour, or until they start to become tender. Drain the beans and reserve the beans and liquid separately.

Preheat the oven to 325°F. Put the beans in a 2-quart bean pot or deep baking dish. Add the bacon and onion and toss to combine. In a saucepan, combine the ketchup, molasses, brown sugar, Dijon mustard, Worcestershire sauce, salt, pepper, and dry mustard and stir well. Bring the mixture to a boil over medium-high heat, stirring to dissolve the sugar, and then pour it over the beans. Add the ham hock and pour in just enough of the reserved bean cooking liquid to cover the beans. Cover the bean pot with its lid (or the baking dish with aluminum foil).

Bake for 3 to 4 hours, or until the beans are tender. Remove the lid about halfway through cooking and add more liquid if necessary to prevent the beans from getting too dry. You shouldn't need to add any more salt, but taste and adjust if necessary.

Slowed
COOKING

The dishes IN THIS CHAPTER reflect the communal spirit of our restaurants and can set the tone for both small, casual gatherings and large, boisterous blowouts. Unlike a "composed" dish, where the star attraction is enhanced in flavor and texture by a sometimes disparate supporting cast, here the emphasis is on the ensemble, each ingredient playing an important role in the quality of the finished product. I love this kind of cooking: it is a form of alchemy in which simple, humble ingredients are transformed into culinary gold. I'll never forget watching Paul Prudhomme walking among the pots, tasting the gumbo or the jambalaya, making sure that the transformations were taking place.

ONE OF THE MOST IMPORTANT INGREDIENTS in all of these recipes is time. The jambalaya (page 175), the lamb shank (page 184)—these are just some of the dishes that are cooked slowly to develop deep, burnished flavors. You will also find that if you let, say, the jambalaya sit for a few hours, or even overnight, the flavors will mature even further, sometimes dramatically. That complexity of flavor does not necessarily mean that these dishes are difficult to prepare, however. Some of the techniques might initially intimidate. For example, braising or making a roux might not yet be in your cooking repertoire. But you will master them with some practice, and will soon view them as just another step in the dish you are building—part of the architecture at work.

THE DISHES HERE also demand your attention. When tending any pot, you must observe the subtle changes in color and taste as the flavors meld and develop. Be mindful of the importance of each step, because everything matters. How you caramelize the lamb shank at the beginning of a recipe will affect not only how the lamb looks, but also the complexity of the finished sauce.

FOR ME, cooking on the line at a restaurant is a form of meditation. The pace is lightning quick, the quarters are close, and a great swirl of activity is all around you. You have to be completely focused; you have to be in a zone. The home kitchen naturally lacks that intensity. Yet I find a meditative quality in cooking the dishes here. I find myself getting into that zone, focusing on that one thing, that single pan or pot.

COOKING YOUR WAY through this chapter, layering elements, finding the right balance of flavor and texture, and doing it all in one pot, will sharpen your senses and sensitivities in the kitchen. Perhaps you'll find a zone of your own.

Semolina
GNOCCHI *with*
WILD MUSHROOM
❧ *Ragout* ❧

I'll be honest: most of my childhood memories about food are unpleasant—nightmares, really. A particularly vivid one is of eating gummy, tough potato gnocchi at the cheap Italian joints my parents would take the family. I liked gnocchi, so this nightmare recurred frequently. Thankfully, I discovered a way to make gnocchi that has finally put those nightmares to rest: using semolina flour has occasioned sweeter dreams.

What's interesting about this gnocchi recipe is that it's more akin to making polenta. The semolina flour is added to milk, thickened, and spread out to cool. I learned this method at Coco Pazzo, where we browned the crescent-shaped gnocchi, layered them in a crock, and poured a ladleful of wild mushroom sauce on top. Here, I show you how to do the same, thus guaranteeing you a good night's sleep.

❧ SERVES 6 ❧

GNOCCHI

4 cups whole milk

1¹⁄₂ cups semolina flour

1¹⁄₂ cups grated Parmesan cheese

2 large egg yolks

4 tablespoons unsalted butter

1 teaspoon salt

Freshly ground pepper

MUSHROOM RAGOUT

¹⁄₂ cup unsalted butter

¹⁄₂ yellow onion, finely diced

1 carrot, peeled and finely diced

1 celery stalk, finely diced

1 tablespoon chopped fresh thyme leaves

1 tablespoon chopped fresh oregano leaves

1 cup peeled, seeded, and chopped tomatoes (see How to Peel and Seed Tomatoes, page 254)

1¹⁄₂ pounds wild mushrooms or crimini mushrooms, sliced

1 cup Chicken Stock (page 250)

¹⁄₂ cup heavy cream

¹⁄₃ cup chopped fresh flat-leaf parsley

Salt and freshly ground pepper

1 cup grated Parmesan cheese

2 to 3 tablespoons unsalted butter, cut into small pieces for finishing

To make the gnocchi, in a heavy-bottomed pot, bring the milk to a boil over medium-high heat. Lower the heat so the milk simmers, then slowly whisk in the semolina flour. Then, switching to a wooden spoon, continue to stir for 8 to 10 minutes. The mixture will get pretty thick. If it gets too thick, and starts sticking to the spoon, add a little more milk. Stir in the Parmesan, egg yolks, and butter, mixing well, and season with the salt and a few grinds of pepper. Remove from the heat.

Dampen a sheet pan with water and shake off any excess. Pour the gnocchi mixture onto the pan and, using the spoon, spread it out evenly about ¹⁄₂ inch thick. Let cool completely for 15 to 20 minutes, or until firm. (At this point, you can cover and refrigerate the gnocchi mixture for up to 2 days before continuing.)

To make the ragout, in a saucepan with a lid, melt 4 tablespoons of the butter over low heat. Add the onion, carrot, and celery, stir well, cover, and cook for about 10 minutes, or until the vegetables are soft. Uncover, add the chopped herbs and tomatoes, and cook, stirring occasionally, for 5 minutes. Raise the heat to medium, add the remaining 4 tablespoons butter and the mushrooms and continue to cook, stirring occasionally, for 8 to 10 minutes, or until the mushrooms release their liquid and begin to take on some color. Add the stock and cream, stir well, and bring to a simmer. Continue to cook for 10 to 15 minutes, or until the mixture has reduced to the consistency of a cream sauce. Stir in the parsley and season with salt and pepper. Remove from the heat and cover to keep warm.

Preheat the oven to 400°F. Butter a 9-by-13-inch baking dish or 6 individual gratin dishes.

Using a 2-inch round cookie cutter, cut out the gnocchi. (I like to cut them into three-quarter moons because it creates less waste, so if you can find a cutter in that shape, use it.) Place the gnocchi in a single layer in the prepared dish (or dishes), slightly overlapping each row. Sprinkle the Parmesan evenly over the top, reserving a few spoonfuls for garnish, and dot with the butter.

Bake the gnocchi for 15 to 20 minutes, or until lightly browned and bubbly. Reheat the ragout gently just before the gnocchi are ready.

To serve, divide the gnocchi among individual plates if baked in a large dish. Spoon the ragout over the top and sprinkle with the reserved Parmesan. Serve immediately.

SEAFOOD RISOTTO
with Lemongrass

Here's an example of how recipes get passed along. When I was running the kitchen at Postrio, my sous chef Gerard Darian taught me this recipe. He had learned it from François Kwaku-Dongo, the chef at Spago. They are both elegant cooks, as evidenced by this risotto, which is all about finesse. It takes a delicate hand to blend the Asian flavors with Italian rice and truffle oil without having one element overwhelm the others. When that balance is achieved, the aromatic ginger and lemongrass marry beautifully with the earthy truffle oil.

SERVES 6

BROTH

6 cups Shrimp Stock (page 250)

2 lemongrass stalks

3-inch piece fresh ginger, sliced

$1/2$ leek (white and tender green parts), sliced

1 jalapeño chile, seeded and sliced

2 tablespoons unsalted butter

1 tablespoon olive oil

1 small yellow onion, finely diced

$1^1/2$ cups Arborio rice

1 cup dry white wine

Salt

$1/2$ pound sea scallops

$3/4$ pound shrimp, peeled and deveined

1 cup peeled, seeded, and chopped tomatoes
(see How to Peel and Seed Tomatoes, page 254)

$1/2$ pound freshly cooked lump crabmeat,
picked over for shell and cartilage bits

2 teaspoons chopped fresh flat-leaf parsley

2 teaspoons chopped fresh tarragon

2 tablespoons grated Parmesan cheese

2 teaspoons grated lemon zest

$1/2$ teaspoon white truffle oil

Freshly ground pepper

To make the broth, trim the leafy tops and root end from the lemongrass stalks, pound the bulblike base with the back of a knife, then cut crosswise into $3/4$-inch-thick slices. Add the shrimp stock to a large pot and bring to a boil, turn the heat down to low so the stock maintains a simmer. Add the lemongrass, ginger, leek, and chile to the pot along with the onion and other vegetables. Simmer for 20 minutes, then strain through a fine-mesh strainer and measure out 5 cups into a clean saucepan. Bring to a bare simmer and keep hot.

In a heavy-bottomed pot, melt 1 tablespoon of the butter with the oil over medium heat. Add the onion and cook, stirring occasionally, for about 5 minutes, or until soft. Do not allow the onion to color. Add the rice and stir for minute or so to coat well. Pour in the wine and simmer for 2 to 3 minutes.

Add about $1/2$ cup of the hot stock and let simmer, stirring occasionally, for 2 or 3 minutes, or until the most of the liquid is absorbed. Add a pinch or two of salt, then continue to add the stock, about $1/2$ cup at a time, simmering and stirring occasionally for 2 to 3 minutes after each addition, or until most of the liquid is absorbed. After about 15 minutes, add the scallops, shrimp, tomatoes, and another $1/2$ cup of the stock. Turn up the heat a bit to help cook the seafood. This should take just a few minutes. At this point, your rice should be creamy and cooked but still have a bit of a bite to it. If it is too hard, add additional stock or hot water and cook for a few minutes longer to soften a bit more.

Add the crabmeat, the remaining 1 tablespoon butter, the parsley, the tarragon, the Parmesan, the lemon zest, the truffle oil, 1 tablespoon salt, and several grinds of pepper. Mix gently to distribute all of the ingredients evenly. Taste and adjust the seasoning, then serve.

CACCIUCCO

With three restaurants in San Francisco, you would think we would serve cioppino, the famous seafood stew invented by Italian fishermen on the city's waterfront in the nineteenth century. But we don't. One reason is that cioppino, like, say, gumbo in New Orleans, is one of those big "personality" dishes that defines a city's cuisine and therefore stirs up all sorts of opinions about how it should be made. I hate conflict, so to steer clear of it we serve a different fish stew, cacciucco, which originated in the Tuscan port city of Livorno. It has a cleaner, fresher flavor than cioppino because of how the shellfish is added. Now, if you happen to be from Livorno, please excuse my addition of white beans. Although not an element of the traditional preparation, I think the beans bring extra body and richness, resulting in a dish that is "personality-plus."

The explosion that occurs when you add the shellfish and sauce to the hot olive oil is integral to the dish and provides a moment of excitement for culinary thrill seekers. It allows the shellfish to release their juices, and immediately incorporates the olive oil into the broth. Make sure you pull the pan from stove top when you do it. Then cover the pan and get it back on the flame quickly.

SERVES 4 AS A MAIN COURSE OR 6 AS A FIRST COURSE

5 tablespoons tomato paste

2 cups dry white wine

1 pound mussels, well scrubbed and any beards removed

1 pound clams, well scrubbed

1 cup tomato sauce or tomato puree

1½ teaspoons dried chile flakes

¼ cup extra-virgin olive oil

6 cloves garlic, sliced

2 cups Shrimp Stock (page 250) or, in a pinch,
Chicken Stock (page 250)

1 pound shrimp in the shell

2 cups cooked white beans

1 teaspoon chopped fresh oregano

Salt and freshly ground pepper

Grilled coarse country bread rubbed with garlic for serving

In a large bowl, combine the tomato paste and wine and stir well to combine. Add the mussels, clams, tomato sauce, and chile flakes, stir, coating the shellfish with the tomato and wine mixture, and set aside.

In a large pot, heat the oil over medium heat. Add the garlic and cook for about 30 seconds, or until fragrant, being careful not to let it color. Remove the pot from the heat, quickly add the mussel and clam mixture, and cover at once with a tight-fitting lid. Return the pot promptly to high heat and cook for about 8 minutes, or until the mussels and clams open.

With a slotted spoon, remove the clams and mussels to a bowl, discarding any that failed to open, and set aside. Add the stock to the pot and let simmer over medium heat for about 5 minutes. Add the shrimp, beans, and oregano and continue to simmer, stirring occasionally, for about 2 minutes, or until the shrimp are cooked through and the beans are hot. Return the mussels and clams to the pot and stir. Season with salt and pepper.

To serve, divide the mussels, clams, shrimp, and beans evenly among individual bowls and top each bowl with a nice helping of the sauce. Accompany with the grilled bread.

Butter-Baked
SEAFOOD-Stuffed
MAINE LOBSTER

This is an elegant way to serve lobster, and especially nice for those who balk at wearing a bib. When you mix the stuffing, make sure all of the ingredients are at the same temperature so you get the correct consistency. Also, when you remove the lobster from the refrigerator, put it into the pan right away so the butter stuffing doesn't start to melt before it goes into the oven. And once the lobster is in the pan, leave it alone. That way you'll get the proper caramelization. Serve the lobster with a salad of mixed greens—that's all you'll need.

❧ SERVES 6 ❧

3 lobsters, each 1½ pounds, cooked (see How to Cook and Clean a Lobster, page 255)

STUFFING

1 cup chopped shrimp

1 large egg

1 teaspoon Wondra or other instant flour or cake flour

1 cup (½ pound) unsalted butter, at room temperature, cut into pieces

1 teaspoon chopped fresh chervil

1 teaspoon chopped fresh tarragon

1 teaspoon chopped fresh flat-leaf parsley

Salt and freshly ground pepper

Wondra or other instant flour or cake flour, for dusting

1 tablespoon extra-virgin olive oil

2 tablespoons unsalted butter, melted

6 thyme sprigs

3 lemons, halved

ONE AT A TIME, hold each lobster, back side up, on a cutting board and cut in half lengthwise: Insert the tip of a large knife where the body and head meet and cut the head in half lengthwise. Then rotate the knife 180 degrees and cut the body and tail in half lengthwise. Remove the claws and legs from each half. Remove the head meat from the lobster halves and set it aside to use in the stuffing. Discard the tomalley and roe. Remove the meat from the claws and from any large legs and set aside with the head meat. Clean well the head portion of each lobster half, as it will hold the stuffing. Place the halved lobsters in the refrigerator.

TO MAKE THE STUFFING, bring all of the ingredients to room temperature. Place the shrimp and lobster in a food processor and pulse until the mixture is finely chopped. Add the egg and pulse a few more times. Add the flour and pulse a few times to blend and bind. Add the butter a few pieces at a time to the seafood mixture and pulse until incorporated. Then add the herbs, a couple of pinches of salt, and a few grinds of pepper and pulse just to combine. Cover and refrigerate for a minimum of 30 to 45 minutes.

After the stuffing is properly chilled, preheat the oven to 350°F. Fill the top portion of each lobster half with the stuffing. Dust each lobster half on both sides with the flour.

In a large ovenproof sauté pan, heat the oil over medium-high heat. (If all of the lobster halves will not fit comfortably in a single pan, use 2 pans.) Place the lobster halves, stuffing side down, in the pan and sear until golden brown, about 5 minutes. Then, flip the lobster halves over onto the shell side and place in the oven for 15 to 20 minutes, or until the stuffing is golden brown and the lobster is cooked through. Remove from the oven and drain off any excess liquid.

To serve, place a lobster half on each plate, and baste each half with 1 teaspoon of the butter. Garnish each serving with a thyme sprig and a lemon half.

Shrimp
ÉTOUFFÉE

Picking crawfish is an art, and among the many masterpieces you can create with their succulent meat is crawfish étouffée, one of my favorite New Orleans classics. To make a great crawfish étouffée, you need to start with a sack of live crawfish. We get them shipped in from Sal's Riverside Seafood outside New Orleans. But since fresh crawfish are not only hard to pick, but also hard to come by, we often use shrimp, and this shrimp étouffée is one of the most requested dishes at Town Hall. Along with gumbo and jambalaya, étouffée can be considered part of a Holy Trinity of Louisiana cooking. And they all use that other Holy Trinity, which is how Louisiana cooks refer to onions, peppers, and celery. Indeed, this trinity is so important that you can buy it buy pre-diced and packaged in New Orleans grocery stores. Here, the trio is sliced rather than diced, and not as deeply caramelized as it is in other dishes. That's because it is used, along with shrimp shells, to make the stock. That stock serves as the basis for the marriage of the roux and shrimp, the real stars of this particular show.

❧ SERVES 6 ❧

1½ pounds extra-large shrimp (about 36 shrimp), preferably with heads intact

Shrimp Stock (page 250)

1 cup Roux (page 48)

Salt and freshly ground pepper

3 tablespoons unsalted butter

1 tablespoon canola oil

Steamed white rice, for serving

Thinly sliced green onions, for garnish

PEEL THE SHRIMP, reserving the shells and heads. Devein the shrimp and refrigerate until needed. Using the shells and heads, make the stock as directed on page 250. When the stock is ready, strain through a fine-mesh strainer, measure out 4 cups, and set aside in a saucepan. Reserve the remaining stock for another use.

TO MAKE THE ÉTOUFFÉE, prepare the roux as directed on page 48. Bring the stock to a boil and stir in the roux and 1 teaspoon salt. Return the mixture to a simmer and cook, stirring occasionally for about 15 minutes, or until slightly thickened to a nice sauce consistency.

In a frying pan, melt 1 tablespoon of the butter with the oil over medium-high heat. Add the shrimp and sauté for 2 minutes. Pour in the sauce, add the remaining 2 tablespoons butter, and cook for 1 minute more, or until the shrimp are cooked through. Season with salt and pepper.

To serve, put a spoonful of hot rice on each plate, and spoon the shrimp and sauce over the top. Garnish with the green onions.

Chicken

and SMOKED ANDOUILLE

JAMBALAYA

When we make jambalaya at Town Hall, we make it in very large portions. In other words, we start the pot with a twenty-five-pound sack of onions. Just to caramelize those onions takes the better part of an hour, and by the time we have finished adding the other base ingredients, the cook charged with minding the pot has been stirring and scraping for more than an hour. Restaurants necessarily work in these outsized portions, but the process, though not the size, is the same at home. So here is another instance in which you have a long-term relationship with your dish. Although you're starting with just a couple of large onions and not a sack, the scraping and stirring step, as well as every other step, is just as important, because following those steps is the only way to get the flavor you want.

SERVES 6 AS A MAIN COURSE OR 12 AS A SIDE DISH

1/3 cup canola oil

1 whole chicken, 3 1/2 to 4 pounds, boned and cut into 3-inch pieces, or about 2 1/2 pounds boneless, skinless chicken (thighs and breasts)

1 tablespoon butter

2 large yellow onions, diced

2 cups (about 3/4 of a pound) andouille sausage cut into 1/2-inch pieces

1 cup (about 1/4 pound) tasso, cut into 1/2-inch pieces

2 tablespoons Town Hall Spice Mixture (page 253)

2 large green bell peppers, seeded and diced

3 celery stalks, diced

1 jalapeño chile, seeded and finely diced

1 tablespoon minced garlic

Salt and freshly ground pepper

One 15-ounce can tomato sauce or crushed tomatoes

1 tablespoon tomato paste

2 cups long-grain white rice

3 cups Chicken Stock (page 250)

2 bay leaves

Thinly sliced green onions, for garnish

PREHEAT the oven to 375°F.

In a heavy-bottomed ovenproof pot, heat the oil over high heat. Working in batches, add the chicken pieces, skin side down, and cook for 2 minutes, or until browned. Transfer to a plate and set aside. When all of the chicken has been browned, drain the oil from the pot into a measuring cup and return 1/4 cup of the oil to the pot (discard the remainder). Add the butter and heat over high heat until the butter melts. Add the onions and stir vigorously with a wooden spoon, scraping the bottom of the pot to loosen up any little browned bits that might be sticking. Cook, stirring occasionally, for about 5 minutes, or until the onions just begin to brown. Add the andouille, tasso, and 1 tablespoon of the spice mixture and cook, continually scraping the bottom of the pot, for about 10 minutes, or until the meat and onions are caramelized. Add the green peppers, celery, chile, garlic, the remaining 1 tablespoon seasoning mixture, and 1 teaspoon salt and cook for 10 more minutes, scraping the pot bottom every so often to loosen any browned bits that might be sticking.

Stir in the tomato sauce and the tomato paste and return the chicken to the pot. Let cook for a few minutes over medium heat. Add the rice, stock, and bay leaves and bring to a boil. Cover, transfer to the oven, and cook for 30 minutes, or until the rice is tender and the liquid has been absorbed.

Remove from the oven and let rest for 5 minutes before serving. Remove and discard the bay leaves. Spoon onto individual plates or shallow bowls, garnish with the green onions, and serve.

LEMON CHICKEN

with OLIVES AND FETA

I learned this dish from Tom Plaganis, the towering Greek chef at the Celebrity Deli. Tom used skinless chicken strips, and served the whole thing on a bed of noodles. I'm following his lead on the skinless strips of chicken, but if you're feeling adventurous you can butcher a bird, keep the skin on and prepare it the same way, just make sure you cook it through. The key to this recipe is the balance of sugar to lemon, a play on sweet and sour. You'll note that I call for dried oregano. While I usually prefer fresh herbs, here I use the dried because that's how Plaganis did it. Dried herbs need to be cooked longer, so they are added at the beginning of the cooking, which also incorporates their flavor more deeply. When my family comes to visit me from Jersey, they always request the lemon chicken. And I'm always happy to oblige.

SERVES 6

6 boneless, skinless chicken breasts, each cut on the diagonal into 3 pieces

Salt and freshly ground pepper

$1/3$ cup all-purpose flour

$1/4$ cup canola oil

4 tablespoons unsalted butter

8 cloves garlic, finely chopped

1 tablespoon dried oregano

1 tablespoon sugar

$1/2$ cup dry white wine

$1/4$ cup freshly squeezed lemon juice

$1^{1}/2$ cups Chicken Stock (page 250)

1 tablespoon fresh flat-leaf parsley

GARNISH

1 cup niçoise olives, pitted and quartered

$1/2$ cup crumbled feta cheese

2 tablespoons chopped fresh flat-leaf parsley leaves

SEASON THE CHICKEN PIECES with salt and pepper. Put the flour in a shallow dish and dredge each piece of chicken in the flour, lightly shaking off the excess. In a heavy-bottomed frying pan, heat the oil over medium heat. Working in batches to avoid crowding, add the chicken pieces and cook, turning once, for $2^{1}/2$ to 3 minutes on each side, or until they just start to become golden. Transfer to a plate and set aside.

Turn down the heat to low and add 2 tablespoons of the butter to the pan. When the butter has melted, scrape up any browned bits stuck to the pan bottom. Add the garlic and cook, stirring, for about 30 seconds. Add the oregano and sugar and cook, stirring, for about 30 seconds more. Then add the wine and lemon juice, raise the heat to high, and simmer for about 2 minutes. Pour in the stock and cook, stirring occasionally, for 4 minutes more. Turn down the heat to medium-low, return the chicken to the pan, and add the remaining 2 tablespoons butter. Stir well to coat each chicken piece with the sauce and simmer for 2 minutes, or until the chicken is cooked through. Add the parsley and stir well again. Season with salt and pepper.

To serve, place 3 pieces of chicken on each plate and top with several tablespoons of the pan sauce. Garnish with the olives and feta and a scattering of parsley.

Slow-Braised
PORK POZOLE

Growing up in New Jersey, my early knowledge of Mexican cooking didn't go much past Taco Bell's Enchirito. That all changed when I got to San Francisco. Oddly enough, my first encounter with authentic Mexican cooking wasn't a taco or a burrito but a goat stew called "birria," and frankly, I'm not sure I liked it. I was unaccustomed to the flavors. Now, though, I appreciate the fresh, earthy tastes of Mexican cuisine. Pozole is a hominy stew laced with meat and vegetables. In this recipe, the broth is reduced a little more than usual to give the dish extra body.

SERVES 6

Canola oil, for sautéing

3 pounds boneless pork shoulder, cut into 1-inch pieces

2 large yellow onions, diced

4 cloves garlic, finely chopped

1 teaspoon ground cumin

1 teaspoon dried Mexican oregano

1 bay leaf

1 cinnamon stick

2 tablespoons chopped fresh cilantro

1 slice bacon

8 cups Chicken Stock (page 250)

4 dried guajillo chiles, seeded and stemmed

2 ancho chiles, seeded and stemmed

2 dried chipotle chiles, seeded and stemmed

Two 28-ounce cans hominy, drained

GARNISHES

Lime wedges

Thinly sliced radishes

Cilantro sprigs

Diced avocado

Finely shredded napa cabbage

Fried tortilla strips

POUR THE OIL to a depth of 1/8 inch into a sauté pan and heat over medium-high heat. Working in batches to avoid crowding, add the pork and sauté, turning as needed, until browned on all sides. Transfer to a plate.

When all of the meat has been browned, in a large pot, add 2 tablespoons oil and heat over medium heat. Add the onions, garlic, cumin, oregano, bay leaf, cinnamon stick, chopped cilantro, and bacon and cook, stirring occasionally, for 5 to 8 minutes, or until the onions are soft. Add the browned pork and the stock and bring to a vigorous simmer. Turn down the heat to low, cover, and cook for 1 hour.

Meanwhile, seed and stem the guajillo, ancho, and chipotle chiles. In a dry sauté pan, toast the chiles over medium heat for a few minutes, or until fragrant. Transfer to a heatproof bowl, add boiling water to cover, and set aside for 30 minutes. Remove the chiles from the water and place in a blender. Add 1/4 cup of the soaking water and process to a smooth puree.

When the pork has been cooking for 1 hour, uncover, add the chile puree and hominy, stir well, and simmer uncovered, skimming any fat and scum that rise to the surface, for about 50 minutes, or until slightly thickened.

Remove and discard the bacon, bay leaf, and cinnamon stick and season with salt and pepper. At this point, the pozole should be slightly thickened. If it has become too thick, add a little water or stock.

To serve, spoon the pozole into shallow individual bowls. Garnish with the lime wedges, radish slices, cilantro sprigs, avocado, cabbage, and tortilla strips.

Guajillo Chile
and PORK STEW

You might be asking, "What's a guajillo chile?" Don't worry. When Bob Leva put this stew on the menu at Salt House, I asked the same question. Like me, you'll like the answer. I was amazed and pleasantly surprised at the depth of flavor that both the guajillo and the ancho chile added to this dish. Guajillo has a spicy, bright flavor, and the ancho is deep and earthy. I also like the way the stew is thickened by pureeing the peppers, a neat technique. Pork shoulder or "butt" is sold under a variety of names (pork butt, Boston butt, shoulder roast and country roast among many), whatever your butcher calls it, just make sure you don't overcook it and dry it out.

SERVES 6

4 pounds boneless pork shoulder, cut into 2-inch cubes

Salt and freshly ground pepper

Canola oil, for sautéing

4 cups Chicken Stock (page 250)

1 cup dry white wine

2 cups peeled and diced carrots

2 cups diced yellow onion

³/₄ cup diced celery

3 cloves garlic, minced

6 dried guajillo chiles, stemmed and seeded

3 ancho chiles, stemmed and seeded

2 cinnamon sticks

1 tablespoon cumin seeds

POLENTA

5 cups water

1 cup polenta

4 tablespoons unsalted butter

2 teaspoons salt

Freshly ground pepper

BRAISED PEARL ONIONS

1 pound pearl onions

1 tablespoon olive oil

Salt and freshly ground pepper

1 tablespoon unsalted butter

¹/₂ cup Chicken Stock (page 250)

Cilantro sprigs and thinly sliced radishes, for garnish

SEASON THE PORK with salt and pepper. In a sauté pan, pour the oil to a depth of ¹/₄ inch and heat over medium-high heat. Working in batches to avoid crowding, add the pork and sauté, turning as needed, until well browned. Using a slotted spoon, transfer the pork to a roasting pan.

When all of the pork has been browned, pour the fat out of the pan and return the pan to medium-high heat. Add the stock and wine, bring to a simmer, and deglaze the pan, stirring to scrape up any browned bits from the pan bottom. Stir well and pour the mixture over the pork in the roasting pan.

Preheat the oven to 350°F. Return the sauté pan to medium heat and add 2 tablespoons of oil. Add the carrots, onions, and celery and sauté until they just begin to soften. Add the garlic and stir for a few minutes until the garlic is fragrant.

Add the contents of the sauté pan to the roasting pan along with the guajillo and ancho chiles. Wrap the cinnamon sticks and cumin seeds in a piece of cheesecloth, tie securely with kitchen string, and place in the roasting pan. Cover the pan with aluminum foil, place in the oven, and bake for 2 hours, or until the meat is tender.

TO MAKE THE POLENTA, bring the water to a boil in a heavy-bottomed saucepan. Add the polenta in slow, steady stream while whisking constantly, then continue to whisk just until polenta begins to thicken. Turn down the heat to low and cook, stirring occasionally, for about 1 hour, or until it begins to pull away from the sides of the pan. If it begins to get too thick before it is cooked, just add some water. Add the butter, salt, and a few grinds of pepper, stir well, and keep warm until serving.

TO PREPARE THE PEARL ONIONS, bring a saucepan filled with water to a boil. Meanwhile, cut a thin slice off the stem end of each pearl onion. Add the onions to the boiling water, blanch for about 2 minutes, and drain. When cool enough to handle, squeeze each onion to free it from its skin, then trim the root end. In an ovenproof sauté pan, heat the oil over medium-high heat. Add the onions, season with salt and pepper, and cook, stirring occasionally, for about 3 minutes, or until they start to caramelize. Add the butter and stock and cook, stirring occasionally, for 2 minutes more,

then remove the pan from the heat and cover the onions with a round of parchment paper that fits just inside the pan rim.

When the pork is ready and remove the pan from the oven. Raise the oven temperature to 375°F, slip the pan holding the onions into the oven, and cook for about 20 minutes, or until the onions are tender.

Meanwhile, using a slotted spoon, remove the pork and chiles to separate bowls and set aside. Strain the liquid in the roasting pan through a fine-mesh strainer into a measuring cup. In a blender, combine the chiles and $1/2$ cup of the strained liquid and process to a smooth puree. Pour the puree into the roasting pan and add the remaining strained liquid along with the braised onions. Return the pork to the pan and stir to mix. Place the pan on the stove top over medium heat, bring to a simmer, and simmer, stirring, until nicely blended and the sauce coats the meat.

To serve, spoon the polenta onto individual plates and ladle the stew over the top. Garnish with the cilantro sprigs and radish slices.

Parmesan-Crusted
LAMB SHANK
with GARLIC
Mashed Potatoes

When I think lamb, I think spring. But here I am using lamb shank, so let me rephrase: When I think lamb shank, I think winter. Braised for hours and served with garlic mashed potatoes, it makes a perfect partner to a chilly evening. A joint cut, the shank is more economical than, say, a prime chop, and while tough by nature, it is made tender by the long braise. Don't rush the browning of the meat. You want to let it burnish deeply to build up the flavor. It will be time well spent. You can even braise the shanks a day before and, like a stew, the flavors will mature overnight. The Parmesan crust adds both taste and texture. *Cavolo nero*—also known as Tuscan kale, black cabbage, and even dinosaur kale—is a beautiful leafy vegetable with heavily veined, crinkly leaves and a deep purplish-green color that darkens to near black as it cooks.

— ❄ SERVES 6 ❄ —

6 lamb shanks

Salt and freshly ground pepper

1/4 cup canola oil

1 small yellow onion, diced

1 celery stalk, diced (about 1 cup)

2 carrots, peeled and diced (about 1 cup)

1/2 leek (white and tender green parts), sliced (about 1/2 cup)

2 tablespoons tomato paste

1 cup dry white wine

1 rosemary sprig

2 bay leaves

1/2 head garlic, cloves separated and peeled

6 cups Chicken Stock (page 250) or lamb stock

6 tablespoons Dijon mustard

PARMESAN CRUST

4 cups torn day-old coarse country bread such as pain levain (1 1/2- to 2-inch pieces)

Equal parts olive oil and canola oil, for frying the bread

3 tablespoons chopped fresh flat-leaf parsley

2 tablespoons chopped fresh oregano

3/4 cup grated Parmesan cheese

GARLIC MASHED POTATOES

3 pounds Yukon gold potatoes, peeled and cut into 2-inch pieces

1 cup heavy cream

2 cloves garlic, smashed

1/2 cup unsalted butter, at room temperature, cut into 4 or 5 pieces

Salt and freshly ground pepper

CAVOLO NERO

1 pound cavalo nero, tough stems removed

1/2 cup extra-virgin olive oil

1 yellow onion, diced

Salt and freshly ground pepper

1/4 teaspoon dried chile flakes

PREHEAT the oven to 375°F.

Season the lamb shanks well with salt and pepper. In a large, wide, shallow, heavy-bottomed ovenproof pot, heat the oil over high heat. Add the shanks and cook, turning as needed, until browned on all sides. Remove the lamb shanks to a plate and set aside.

Pour out all but 1 tablespoon of the oil and return the pot to medium heat. Add the onion, celery, carrots, and leek and sweat, stirring occasionally, for about 5 minutes, or until the vegetables begin to soften. Add the tomato paste, mix well, and add the wine. Bring to a boil and return the browned lamb shanks to the pot, along with the rosemary sprig, bay leaves, garlic, and stock. Stir and bring to a boil.

Cover the pot, transfer to the oven, and braise for $1^1/_2$ to 2 hours, or until the meat is tender.

When the shanks are ready, remove them from the pot and set aside. Pour the contents of the pot through a fine-mesh strainer placed over a small saucepan and discard the contents of the strainer. Place the saucepan over high heat, bring to a boil, and boil until reduced by half, constantly skimming off any fat that rises to the surface. This should take about 30 minutes. Set the reduced liquid aside.

TO PREPARE THE PARMESAN CRUST, in a large sauté pan, pour equal parts canola and olive oil to a depth of $^1/_4$ inch and heat over medium-high heat. Add the bread pieces and fry, tossing gently with tongs, for about 3 to 5 minutes, or until nice and brown on all sides. Transfer to paper towels to drain. When cool enough to handle, chop the bread pieces with a knife or pulse in a food processor. You should have $^3/_4$ cup coarse crumbs. In a bowl, stir together the crumbs, parsley, oregano, and Parmesan and set aside.

TO PREPARE THE MASHED POTATOES, in a large pot, combine the potatoes with salted water to cover, place over medium-high heat, and bring to a boil. Lower the heat to a simmer and cook for about for about 20 minutes, or until the potatoes are fork-tender. Just before the potatoes are ready, in a small saucepan, combine the cream and garlic, bring to a boil over medium-high heat, lower the heat to a simmer, and simmer for a few minutes. Remove from the heat, strain through a fine-mesh strainer, and keep warm.

Drain the potatoes, then pass them through a ricer or food mill back into the pot, or return them to the pot and mash with a potato masher. Add the warm cream and the butter and whisk or stir until well blended. Season with salt and pepper and keep warm.

TO PREPARE THE CAVOLO NERO, bring a large pot filled with salted water to a boil, add the greens, and blanch for 2 minutes. Drain well, and when cool enough to handle, squeeze out any excess water. In a large pot, heat the oil over medium heat. Add the onion, season with salt and pepper, and cook, stirring occasionally, for 5 minutes. Add the chile flakes and the blanched greens and continue to cook over medium heat, stirring occasionally, for 30 minutes, or until the greens are tender and turn a very dark purple. Taste and adjust the seasoning, then keep warm.

Now it is time to put everything together. Preheat the oven to 350°F. Place the shanks in a roasting pan just large enough to accommodate them, pour the reduced braising liquid over the top, and turn the shanks as needed to coat evenly. Spread 1 tablespoon of the mustard on one side of each shank. Cover the mustard with the Parmesan crust, dividing it evenly. Bake for 10 to 15 minutes, or until the shanks are hot and the crust is golden brown.

To serve, place a goodly amount of mashed potatoes on each plate. Top with the *cavolo nero*, then with a shank, and finally with the pan sauce.

ROASTED

Cooking IS A SERIES OF CHOICES. Each dish brings with it a set of possibilities in terms of preparation. So instead of titling this chapter Entrées or Main Courses, I've titled it Grilled, Roasted, and Fried, to show how choices are made, choices that reflect the characteristics of the ingredients at hand. How you cook something should be determined by what it is you're trying to cook.

FOR EXAMPLE, the slow-roasted duck preparation solves the problem of roasting a duck whole, which often results in a dry, unevenly cooked bird. By stuffing the duck with a mixture of onions, peppers, and duck fat and roasting it for several hours at a very low temperature, you are essentially confiting the duck from the inside out, thereby ensuring even cooking.

WITH STEAK, the nature of the cut will affect how it is prepared. The fatty rib-eye lends itself to a hot grill (which also imparts a smoky flavor, thus enhancing the effect of the brown butter–garlic sauce). The leaner filet mignon develops a beautiful crust when pan roasted. That's not to say you can't grill a filet or pan roast a rib-eye, but these are the choices I've made, and I think they are the right ones. Chefs are know-it-alls, trust me.

MEAT is more forgiving than fish. Halibut has very little natural fat content, and as a result has a tendency to dry out. That's why I've chosen to coat the fillets with olive oil and cook them in the oven, a technique that keeps everything moist and lets the delicate flavor of the fish shine through. And a lesser fish than tuna would have trouble holding its own paired with Italian sausage. Yes, these are all choices. When frying chicken or fish, we play with the type and temperature of the oil, and consider the type and quality of batter, seemingly small distinctions that can change the character of a dish.

SEARED TUNA

with GIGANTE BEANS,
CHARD, and
Italian Sausage

Because of its texture and its ability to stand up to bold flavors (as well as to the introduction of fat), tuna cooks more like meat than fish. Put another way, tuna is a man's fish. Here, to prove its mettle, we put the tuna to the test by rubbing it with a mixture peppercorns, cumin, coriander, and fennel, and pair it with Italian sausage, chard, and Gigante beans. As their name implies, Gigante beans are gigantic. Don't let their size fool you, however. They are incredibly creamy and have great mouthfeel. If you must, you can substitute smaller white beans, but for this dish, don't skimp on the tuna. Try to find sushi-grade yellowfin (ahi) or bigeye. That's what we use in the restaurants, and they are worth their lofty price tag.

Like a nice cut of beef, tuna should be served rare to medium-rare, with the center slightly warm. Make sure you cook all sides evenly, and never over too high a flame. If you cook it in a pan that is too hot, the center will be cold and the fish will be hard to slice.

❧ SERVES 6 ❧

GIGANTE BEANS

1 rounded cup (1/2 pound) dried Gigante beans, picked over

2 cups Chicken Stock (page 250)

2 cups water

2 oregano sprigs

1 clove garlic, smashed

1 teaspoon salt

1 tablespoon extra-virgin olive oil

PEPPERCORN SPICE RUB

1 teaspoon peppercorns

1 tablespoon coriander seeds

1 tablespoon cumin seeds

1 tablespoon fennel seeds

OREGANO VINAIGRETTE

1 tablespoon red wine vinegar

1 teaspoon minced fresh oregano or a few pinches dried

Salt and freshly ground pepper

1/4 cup extra-virgin olive oil

2 tablespoons canola oil, or as needed

1/2 pound hot Italian sausages

1 bunch Swiss chard, stems removed and leaves cut crosswise into 1/2-inch-wide strips (about 3 cups)

4 tablespoons unsalted butter

2 tablespoons chopped fresh flat-leaf parsley

3 tablespoons freshly squeezed lemon juice

Salt and freshly ground pepper

2 pounds sushi-grade tuna fillet, cut into 6 equal pieces

To PREPARE THE BEANS, in a pot, combine the beans, stock, water, oregano sprigs, and garlic, bring to a simmer over medium heat, and simmer for 45 to 60 minutes, or until tender. Add the salt and oil, stir well, and set aside.

TO PREPARE THE SPICE RUB, in a small, dry frying pan, toast the peppercorns, coriander, cumin, and fennel seeds over medium heat, shaking the pan often to avoid scorching, for about a minute or two, or until fragrant and just turning color. Let cool completely, then finely grind in a spice grinder or in a mortar with a pestle.

TO PREPARE THE VINAIGRETTE, in a small bowl, stir together the vinegar, oregano, and a pinch or two of salt. Slowly whisk in the oil, then season with a few grinds of pepper and with more salt, if necessary. Set aside.

continued

TO FINISH THE DISH, in a large sauté pan, heat 1 tablespoon of the oil over high heat. Pinch off (or cut) 1-inch pieces of the sausages, add to the pan, and brown well on all sides. Add the cooked beans with their liquid and cook over high heat for about 2 minutes, or until the liquid reduces a bit (you should have at least ¼ cup liquid remaining in the pan). Add the chard and cook, stirring once or twice, for about 1 minute, or until it wilts. Add the butter, parsley, and lemon juice and stir well until the butter melts. Season with salt and pepper and set aside. If the bean mixture gets a little dry, you can add a little water to bring back the creaminess.

Season the tuna pieces with salt, then cover with spice rub. In a sauté pan, heat the remaining 1 tablespoon oil over medium-high heat until it shimmers. Working in batches (and adding more oil if needed), cook the tuna pieces, turning once, for about 1 minute on each side, or until nicely seared on the outside and rare to medium-rare at the center.

To serve, divide the bean mixture evenly among individual plates. Slice each piece of tuna against the grain into 3 or 4 pieces each about ½ inch thick. Arrange the tuna slices on top of the bean mixture , and spoon a few teaspoons of the vinaigrette over the tuna.

PETRALE SOLE

with *Wild Mushrooms,*

CHARD, AND TRUFFLE
LEEK CREAM

This dish has sole . . . petrale sole, that is (which is actually a flounder). A seasonal Pacific flatfish, and San Francisco favorite, Petrale is highly sought after for its mild and tender flesh. Here we have a preparation brought to Salt House by chef Bob Leva, served atop a rich and creamy combination of sautéed leeks, chard, and wild mushrooms, finished with delicately pungent black truffle oil, all together giving a flatfish some real dimension.

❦ SERVES 6 ❦

6 (6-ounce) sole fillets

2 leeks, white and tender green parts, split lengthwise and cut in thirds

3 bunches chard, destemmed

1/2 pound crimini, morels, or black trumpet mushrooms, cleaned

3 tablespoons unsalted butter

4 1/2 tablespoons extra-virgin olive oil

2 teaspoons black truffle oil

1 1/2 cups heavy cream

3/4 cup Chicken Stock (page 250)

Salt and freshly ground pepper

First, bring a large pot of salted water to a boil. In a large bowl prepare an ice bath. Blanch the chard for 2 to 3 minutes in the boiling water, until tender. Drain, and transfer to ice bath to stop the cooking, about two minutes. Drain again and then squeeze out as much liquid from the chard as possible. Set aside on paper towels.

Next, in a medium saucepan over medium heat add the butter and leeks and stir regularly with a wooden spoon for 5 minutes. You don't want any color on the leeks so adjust heat as necessary. After 5 minutes turn heat to medium-low and cover. Cook for an additional 10 minutes, stirring occasionally. Add the cream and stock and cook, stirring occasionally for 3 or 4 minutes. Set aside.

Next, in a large sauté pan heat 3 tablespoons of the olive oil over high heat. When the oil is shimmering add the mushrooms and cook, shaking the pan occasionally, until they begin to release their liquid and become tender, about 2 to 4 minutes. Reduce the heat to medium and add the blanched chard and leek and cream mixture. Cook over medium heat for 3 to 4 minutes until the chard is warmed through and the sauce begins to thicken. Take off the heat and add the truffle oil and stir to incorporate. Set aside and keep warm. If the sauce becomes too thick, stir in a few tablespoons of water to thin it out.

Season the sole fillets with salt and pepper. Working in batches (or in two pans), heat 1 1/2 tablespoons of oil over medium high heat in a large sauté pan until shimmering. Place 3 filets, (flesh side down) in the pan and cook for 3 to 4 minutes. When golden brown, flip the fish and cook for another minute or two.

While the fish is cooking, distribute the leek and chard mixture evenly among six serving bowls. When the fish is done, place a fillet on top and serve immediately.

Pan-Roasted HALIBUT with TOMATO Soffritto, CRANBERRY BEANS, and Zucchini

At Salt House, we pan roast Alaskan halibut, which, due to colder waters, are fattier than our local variety. But halibut, if not cooked perfectly, has a tendency to become dry. To avoid that possibility, this recipe calls for a slow bake covered in olive oil, a gentle approach that ensures a beautifully moist piece of fish. Why fresh cranberry beans? Well, they are in season in the summertime, same as halibut, so it's a natural pairing. Tomatoes, garlic, and peppers complete the plate.

SERVES 6

SPICE MIXTURE

1½ teaspoons coriander seeds

1½ teaspoons cumin seeds

1½ teaspoons fennel seeds

SOFFRITTO

¼ cup extra-virgin olive oil

2 cups diced yellow onion

Salt

3 cloves garlic, finely diced

1½ tablespoons spice mixture (above)

3 pounds tomatoes, preferably heirlooms, diced

Freshly ground pepper

CRANBERRY BEANS

2½ cups shelled fresh cranberry beans

1 teaspoon salt

1 tablespoon extra-virgin olive oil

6 halibut fillets, each 5 ounces and about 1 inch thick

About ⅔ cup extra-virgin olive oil

Sea salt and freshly ground pepper

3 zucchini, trimmed, quartered lengthwise, and sliced crosswise

½ teaspoon dried chile flakes

½ cup fresh basil leaves, cut in chiffonade (long, narrow strips), plus more for garnish

TO MAKE THE SPICE MIXTURE, in a small, dry frying pan, toast the coriander, cumin, and fennel seeds over medium heat, shaking the pan often to avoid scorching, for about a minute or two, or until fragrant and just turning color. Let cool completely, then grind in a spice grinder or in a mortar with a pestle to a medium-fine grind.

TO MAKE THE SOFFRITTO, in a pot, heat the oil over low heat. Add the onion, season with a few pinches of salt, and cook, stirring occasionally, for 5 minutes, or until transparent. Add the garlic and spice mixture and cook for 3 minutes more. Add the tomatoes, a few more pinches of salt, and simmer over low heat for 45 minutes to 1 hour, or until the tomatoes break down, the mixture thickens and the flavors are well blended. Remove from the heat, pass through a food mill into a bowl, season with salt and pepper, and set aside.

TO PREPARE THE CRANBERRY BEANS, in a saucepan, combine the beans with water to cover by 2 inches. Bring to a boil over high heat then lower to a simmer, and cook for 30 to 45 minutes, or until tender. Remove from the heat, season with the salt and oil, and drain, reserving the beans and liquid separately.

TO COOK THE FISH, preheat the oven to 375°F. Cut 12 pieces of parchment paper several inches bigger than each piece of fish. Place 6 of the parchment pieces on a sheet pan, and spread 1 teaspoon oil on each piece. Season the fish

continued

pieces with salt and pepper, and place a piece of fish on top of each piece of oiled parchment. Spread 1 teaspoon oil on top of each piece of fish, and cover the fish pieces with the remaining parchment pieces. Bake in the oven for 8 minutes.

Meanwhile, heat 2 tablespoons oil in a sauté pan over medium heat. Add the zucchini slices and sauté for about 2 minutes, or until beginning to soften and trying not to put any color on them. Add the chile flakes, the cranberry beans and ¼ cup of their cooking liquid, and the soffritto

and simmer for a few minutes. Just before serving, add 2 tablespoons oil and the basil. Season with salt and pepper and stir well.

To serve, divide the cranberry bean–zucchini mixture among shallow individual bowls. Remove the parchment from the fillets, and place one on each serving, then garnish with a drizzle of olive oil, a sprinkle of sea salt, and scattering of basil.

Pan-Roasted
MUSSELS *with*
OLD BAY Broth

Moules frites—"mussels and fries"—is a simple classic. In Belgium and France, entire restaurants are dedicated to mussels and fries paired with different sauces: tarragon and shallots, white wine, even beer. Mussels can make their home in just about any kind of water—salt, fresh, or brackish—and they are also at home in all types of cuisines.

Since we swing southern at Town Hall, we use Old Bay Seasoning when preparing mussels. Old Bay, in its familiar yellow, blue, and red package, hails from Chesapeake Bay in Maryland. It is generally used to season crabs and shrimp, but it's a great addition to all sorts of seafood. It's also terrific on potato chips. Here, we serve the mussels with toasted bread, but they are also delicious with shoestring potatoes.

Here are four tips for dealing with mussels: (1) rinse them well in cold water to remove any sand; (2) throw out any with cracked or broken shells; (3) tap an open mussel, and if it does not clam up (to mix our bivalve metaphors), throw it out; and (4) if a clutch of thready fibers (a beard) is poking out where the shells meet, pull it taut and cut it off with a paring knife.

❧ SERVES 6 ❧

1 tablespoon extra-virgin olive oil

6 cloves garlic, thinly sliced

2 shallots, thinly sliced

2 tablespoons Old Bay Seasoning

¼ teaspoon Town Hall Spice Mixture (page 253)

2 cups peeled, seeded, and diced tomatoes (see How to Peel and Seed Tomatoes, page 254)

3 pounds mussels, well scrubbed and any beards removed

½ cup dry white wine

½ cup Chicken Stock (page 250), warmed

2 tablespoons unsalted butter

2 tablespoons chopped fresh flat-leaf parsley

1 tablespoon chopped fresh tarragon

Toasted coarse country bread rubbed with garlic, for serving

IN A LARGE POT with a tight-fitting lid, heat the oil over medium heat. Add the garlic and shallots and cook for a few minutes, or until softened. Add the Old Bay, the spice mixture, and the tomatoes, stir well, and add the mussels. Pour in the wine and stock, raise the heat to high, cover, and cook until the mussels open. This usually takes about 5 minutes.

Using a slotted spoon, transfer the mussels to individual serving bowls, discarding any that failed to open. Simmer the cooking liquid over medium heat for about 2 minutes to reduce slightly, then add the butter, parsley, and tarragon. Ladle the cooking liquid over the mussels, dividing it evenly. Serve at once with the toasted bread.

SAUTÉED SCALLOPS
with *Spiced Couscous*
and PRESERVED
LEMON–CURRY SAUCE

Nine times out of ten, when I'm out to eat and scallops are on the menu, I order them. That's because I'm crazy about scallops. If you are too, you would be crazy not to request the dry-packed variety. It's imperative if you like your scallops medium-rare and beautifully caramelized. The alternative is wet-packed scallops, which are full of additives and have usually been frozen. When they hit the pan, water comes oozing out. You don't want any part of that. Here, the scallops are served with Israeli couscous, which is larger than the standard issue and stands up better to the curry sauce. Like most fish dishes, scallops benefit from a heavy shot of lemon. We use both fresh lemon juice and preserved lemon to brighten the whole affair. Although you can purchase preserved lemons in specialty-food stores, I have included a recipe for them in the Basics chapter (page 246), in case you want to make your own.

SERVES 6

CURRY SAUCE

2 tablespoons curry powder

1 tablespoon canola oil

1/2 carrot, halved lengthwise and sliced crosswise

1/2 celery stalk, sliced

1/2 leek, white and tender green parts, halved lengthwise and sliced crosswise

3-inch piece fresh ginger, peeled and thinly sliced

1 green onion, white and tender green parts, sliced

2 teaspoons rice vinegar

1/3 cup mirin

1/2 cup dry vermouth

2 cups Shrimp Stock (page 250)

1/4 cup heavy cream

Salt and freshly ground pepper

3 tablespoons unsalted butter, cut into tablespoons

SPICED COUSCOUS

1 3/4 cups (1/2 pound) Israeli couscous

1 teaspoon olive oil

1 teaspoon canola oil

1/3 cup fennel, finely diced

1/4 cup finely diced preserved lemon (page 254)

2 teaspoons chopped fresh dill

1/8 teaspoon cayenne pepper

Salt and freshly ground pepper

5 ounces mustard greens, trimmed, parboiled for 3 to 5 minutes, drained, squeezed dry, and coarsely chopped

2 tablespoons unsalted butter

FENNEL SALAD

1/2 fennel bulb, thinly sliced

1 tablespoon olive oil

Juice of 1/2 lemon

Salt and freshly ground pepper

2 pounds dry-packed scallops

Canola oil, for sautéing

To MAKE THE SAUCE, in a small, dry frying pan, toast the curry powder over medium heat, stirring often, for about 1 minute, or until fragrant. Set aside. In a saucepan, heat the oil over medium heat. Add the carrot, celery, leek, ginger, and green onion and cook for about 5 minutes, or until the vegetables start to soften. Stir in the curry powder, turn down the heat to low, add the vinegar, and deglaze the pan, stirring to scrape up any browned bits from the pan bottom. Cook until the vinegar evaporates, then add the mirin and simmer for 2 minutes. Add the vermouth and simmer for

continued

2 minutes, then add the stock and simmer for 10 minutes, or until then mixture reduces slightly and the flavors are well blended. Add the cream, season with salt and pepper, and then cook for a few more minutes.

Remove the sauce from the heat, strain through a fine-mesh strainer, and then return to the saucepan. Bring to a simmer over medium heat, and whisk in the butter, 1 tablespoon at a time, whisking after each addition until fully incorporated. When done, remove from the heat and keep warm.

TO PREPARE THE COUSCOUS, cook the couscous according to the package directions, then toss with the olive oil and set aside. In a large sauté pan, heat the canola oil over low heat. Add the fennel and preserved lemon and cook, stirring, until the fennel is soft. Add the dill and cayenne pepper and stir well. Add the fennel mixture to the couscous along with 1 teaspoon salt and the mustard greens. Mix well and season with salt and pepper. Set the sauté pan aside to use for finishing the couscous.

TO PREPARE THE SALAD, in a bowl, combine the fennel, oil, and lemon juice and toss to coat the fennel evenly. Season with salt and pepper and set aside.

TO COOK THE SCALLOPS, heat a large sauté pan over high heat. When the pan is hot, add a thin layer of oil and heat until it shimmers. Add the scallops and cook, turning once, for 3 to 4 minutes on each side, or until nicely caramelized on the exterior and medium-rare at the center.

TO FINISH THE COUSCOUS, return the sauté pan to medium heat and add the butter. When the butter melts, add the couscous and cook, stirring gently, until heated through.

To serve, divide the couscous among individual plates. Arrange some of the fennel salad and 3 scallops on top of each serving. Pour some sauce around the edge of the couscous on each plate, then drizzle some on top of each scallop.

Paulie's ALE-BATTERED FISH and CHIPS

One of the benefits of working in restaurants is "research and development." I've mentioned the barbecue road trips I have taken with Steven. Another time, we had to go to London. Work, work, work. This particular trip was focused on some important R & D into the world of gastropubs. Part of the journey was devoted to the quest for the finest fish and chips in London. A friend directed us to the Golden Hind on Marylebone Lane, where you had your choice of fish (cod, haddock, or pollock) served as a whole fillet rather than in large chunks. Our opening chef at Town Hall, Paul O'Brien, developed the batter for our fish and chips. At the restaurants, we use local halibut or cod, depending on what's swimming. You should use the freshest eco-friendly fish possible.

For this recipe, peanut oil works best, and when you're frying, try not to pick up the basket of fish too often to check if the fish is done. Taking the basket out of the oil and then dropping it back in tends to make the fish taste a little greasy.

❊ SERVES 6 ❊

Pictured on pages 202–203.

BATTER
1 cup all-purpose flour

¹/₂ cup cornstarch

¹/₂ teaspoon salt

¹/₈ teaspoon baking soda

1¹/₂ cups Smithwick's Irish ale or other red ale

Peanut oil, for deep-frying

2 pounds Kennebec or Russet potatoes

2¹/₂ pounds cod, haddock, or pollock fillet, cut into 12 equal pieces

Malt vinegar and tartar sauce, for serving

TARTAR SAUCE
1 cup Mayonnaise (page 251) or store-bought

¹/₄ cup dill pickles finely diced

1 tablespoon rinsed and chopped capers

2 teaspoons chopped tarragon

1 teaspoon Dijon mustard

1 tablespoon lemon juice

¹/₂ shallot finely diced (about 2 teaspoons)

1 tablespoon finely diced cornichons

¹/₄ teaspoon Tabasco or other hot sauce

A few grinds of black pepper

To make the batter, in a large bowl, whisk together the flour, cornstarch, salt, and baking soda. Add the ale and mix well. Cover and refrigerate.

To fry the "chips," pour the oil to a depth of 3 to 3¹/₂ inches into a deep fryer or deep, heavy-bottomed pot and heat to 300°F. Have ready a large bowl of cold water. Cut the unpeeled potatoes lengthwise into large, flat, thick or wedge-shaped fries (like steak fries). As the pieces are cut, add them to the water.

When all of the potatoes are cut, drain them well and pat dry. Working in batches to avoid crowding, add the potatoes to the hot oil and blanch for 8 to 10 minutes, or until the potatoes begin to soften and just start to turn color. Using a wire skimmer, transfer to paper towels to drain.

Raise the heat to bring the oil to 375°F. Fry the potatoes a second time for 8 to 10 minutes, or until golden brown. Using the wire skimmer, transfer to paper towels to drain. Keep warm.

To fry the fish, heat the oil you used for frying the potatoes to 365°F. Working in batches to avoid crowding, dip the fish pieces into the batter, allowing the excess to drip off, and then carefully slip them into the hot oil. Fry for 4 to 6 minutes, or until golden brown and just cooked through. Using the wire skimmer, transfer to paper towels to drain briefly.

To serve, place 2 pieces of fish and a handful of chips on each plate. Pass the vinegar and tartar sauce at the table.

NOIRE DE BRUXELLES

HTACHI...
Osrai-ka...

SCHONRAMER...
schon...

...ng that are...

...EAD 'FESTINA PE...
...ware

BLONDE...

Light bodied ales with...

...ROUWERIJ DE DOCHTER VAN DE...
...aarle-hertog, belgium

SCHONRAMER GOLD 16.9OZ
schonram, germany

CASTELAIN BLONDE 'BIERE DE GARDE' 11.2...
benifontaine, france

AFFLIGEM BLONDE 330ML
opwijk, belgium

DUVEL GOLDEN ALE, 11.2OZ
brendonk-puurs, belgium

UNIBROUE 'DON DE DIEU' 750ML
chambly, quebec

LA BRASSERIE DES ORVAL 11.2OZ
villers-devant-orval, belgium 6.9% ABV

HITACHINO NEST 'RED RICE' 330ML
kananaski naka-gun, japan 7% ABV

BROUWERIJ HET ANKER 'LUCIFER' 11.2OZ
mechelen, belgium

BRASSERIE HUYGHE 'DELIRIUM TREMENS' 11
belgium

INFERNO 750ML

11% A

NG DARK ALE
flavors.

10% ABV

BELGIAN DUBBEL
marked X's on beer   rength of the
or Dubbel xxx for Tripel in ascend   bels have
with dark fruit flavors that finish dry   n strong with
ht orange hue loaded with fruit, hops and spice.

PIST DUBBEL 11.2OZ
7% ABV

DUBBEL 11.2OZ
9% ABV

MONDE' TRIPEL 11.2OZ
9% ABV

ROTHER DAVID'S' DOUBLE 22OZ
10% ABV

UADRUPEL 11.2OZ
ands 10% ABV

'KASTEEL' TRIPLE 330ML
um 11% ABV

EL ALES

SAMUEL
balanc

OMMEGANG 7%
cooperstown, ny

GREEN FLASH 'L'
san diego, californ

UNCOMMON BREWI
santa cruz, california (d.

BREWDOG 'DOGMA'
fraserburgh, scotland (

38
13
14
13
12

50

16.
12.
12.
9.
12.
12.

20.
15.

Tabasco-Spiked

SLOW-COOKED

FRIED CHICKEN

It took two giants in the food world to teach me how to make the perfect fried chicken. Mike Boylan, a good friend of mine, invited me to his house for a demonstration on deep-frying turkey presented by the McIlhenny family (the makers of Tabasco sauce). About ten of us were huddled around a huge vat of oil on Boylan's backyard deck in Marin County, just north of San Francisco. What was especially interesting to me, even more than the deep-frying, was the mixture of garlic juice, onion juice, clarified butter, and Tabasco that was injected into different parts of the bird. The next step was to rub the bird with flour, and then lower it *very slowly* into a pot of oil—slowly because if you dropped it in quickly, we were told, the moisture in the bird would cause it to shoot out of the pot like a cannonball. This sense of danger only added to the experience. It took all of thirty minutes to cook a sixteen-pound turkey. The first bite was incredible: crispy, garlicky, and moist.

The second thing that influenced me was a discussion with Wolfgang Puck about how his mother used to cook fried chicken. Her secret was frying the chicken at 300°F, a much lower temperature than normal. With a lower temperature, the chicken is able to cook evenly and the skin becomes crispy without burning. At Town Hall, we soak the chicken pieces in buttermilk, inject the Tabasco mixture, and then dredge the pieces in a seasoned flour mixture. A flour mixture (versus a wet batter) allows you to taste the flavors of the chicken and still gives you a crispy skin.

⋙ SERVES 6 ⋘

TABASCO JUICE

1 1/2 cups (3/4 pound) unsalted butter

4 cloves garlic, coarsely chopped

1/2 yellow onion, coarsely chopped

1/4 cup Tabasco sauce

Salt and freshly ground pepper

2 whole chickens, 3 to 3 1/2 pounds, each cut into 8 pieces (2 breasts, 2 thighs, 2 legs and 2 wings), or 6 or 7 pounds mixed chicken pieces

4 cups buttermilk

Canola oil, for deep-frying

2 cups all-purpose flour

1/2 cup cornstarch

1 1/2 tablespoons Old Bay Seasoning

1 tablespoon Town Hall Spice Mixture (page 253)

To PREPARE THE TABASCO JUICE, clarify the butter as directed on page 254, then let cool. You should have 1 cup. In a food processor, combine the garlic, onion, and Tabasco sauce and process until smooth. Pass the puree through a fine-mesh strainer into a measuring cup. You should have 1/2 cup. Mix together the clarified butter and the strained mixture and set aside.

TO PREPARE THE CHICKEN, salt and pepper the pieces. Using a meat injector, inject each piece of chicken with 2 shots of juice, using about 1 1/2 teaspoons for each shot. Place the chicken pieces in a single layer in a large baking dish (or 2 dishes), and pour the buttermilk over the top. Cover and refrigerate for at least 3 hours or up to overnight.

TO FRY THE CHICKEN, pour the oil to a depth of 3 to 3 1/2 inches into a deep fryer or deep, heavy-bottomed pot and heat to 325°F. While the oil is heating, in a shallow bowl, stir together the flour, cornstarch, Old Bay, spice mixture, and 1 teaspoon salt. Coat the chicken pieces with the seasoned flour, lightly shaking off the excess.

Working in batches to avoid crowding, add the chicken pieces to the hot oil and fry for 8 to 10 minutes, or until golden brown and cooked through. Drain on paper towels and serve hot.

Bacon-Wrapped
QUAIL with CLAMS
and CRISPY POTATOES

My introduction to this dish, which has its roots in Portugal, was at a big food event in New York City, where chef Jasper White used pork as the centerpiece. When I became the chef at Postrio, we were getting quail from Brent Wolfe, who raises quail on his ranch near Dixon, California. And because I love pairing game with seafood, I thought of those Wolfe Ranch quail (which are larger than the typical farmed quail and have an incredibly clean flavor). The instinct was right.

Because of its size, quail is more apt to dry out than, say, chicken. Wrapping the bird in bacon keeps the meat nice and moist. Keep in mind, too, that quail, unlike chicken, can be served a little on the pink side.

SERVES 6

POTATOES

1½ pounds Yukon gold potatoes

3 sprigs thyme

3 cloves garlic

2 tablespoons extra-virgin olive oil

Salt and freshly ground pepper

6 cups spinach, stemmed and chopped

QUAIL

6 quail

Salt and freshly ground pepper

¾ cup Dijon mustard

12 thin slices bacon

2 tablespoons extra-virgin olive oil

SAUCE

2 tablespoons extra-virgin olive oil

12 cloves garlic, slivered

2 pounds Manila clams, well scrubbed

1 cup dry white wine

1 cup Chicken Stock (page 250)

6 tablespoons unsalted butter, chilled and cut into tablespoons

2 tablespoons chopped fresh flat-leaf parsley

1 tablespoon freshly squeezed lemon juice

1 teaspoon dried chile flakes

TO PREPARE THE POTATOES, in a large saucepan, combine the potatoes, thyme, garlic, and 1½ teaspoons salt with water to cover by 1 inch. Place over medium-high heat and bring to a boil. Lower the heat to a simmer and cook for about 30 minutes, or until the potatoes are fork-tender. Remove from the heat and drain. While the potatoes are still warm, peel them and cut them in half and then cut each half into thirds.

In a large sauté pan, heat the oil over medium-high heat. Add the potatoes and cook, turning as needed, until crispy on all sides. Season with salt and pepper. Add the chopped spinach and mix with the potatoes until just wilted. Keep warm.

TO PREPARE THE QUAIL, preheat the oven to 375°F. Season the quail inside and out with salt and pepper, then stuff 2 tablespoons of the mustard inside the cavity of each bird. Make a little slit in the bottom of the skin of 1 leg on each quail, and pull the other leg through it so the legs are crisscrossed. Or, tie the legs together with kitchen string. Wrap 2 slices of bacon around each quail, overlapping them slightly.

Place 2 large sauté pans over medium-high heat, and pour 1 tablespoon of the oil into each pan. When the oil is hot, divide the quail between the pans and cook for about 4 minutes, or until the bacon is crispy and nicely browned on the first side. Turn the quail over and cook for about 4 minutes, or until the bacon is crispy and nicely browned on the second side.

Remove from the heat and pour any fat in the sauté pans into a sheet pan, coating the bottom, then transfer the quail to the sheet pan. Place the quail in the oven and roast for 15 minutes, or until meat is slightly pink.

TO MAKE THE SAUCE, in a heavy-bottomed pot with a tight-fitting lid, heat the oil over medium heat. Add the garlic and sauté for 1 minute, or until fragrant. Toss in the clams, pour in the wine, stir, and cover the pot. The clams should open in 3 to 5 minutes. When they do, using a slotted spoon, remove them to a bowl, discarding any that failed to open, and set aside.

Add the stock to the liquid remaining in the pan bring to a simmer until reduced by half. Turn down the heat to low and add the butter, 1 tablespoon at a time, whisking after each addition until fully incorporated. Finally, stir in the parsley, lemon juice, and chile flakes. Toss the clams back into the sauce and stir to warm through.

TO SERVE, place a quail in the middle of each plate and surround with the potato and spinach mixture. Scatter the clams evenly among the plates, and top the quail off with the sauce .

Slow-Roasted DUCK with Spicy FIG JUS

Who would have thought to confit a duck from the inside out? I must give credit where credit is due. Paul Prudhomme, that's who. Wow. Just wow. The hardest part of this recipe is deboning the duck and removing the skin. It works easiest if the duck is at the right temperature. You want it to cool down so you can handle it, but you want it warm enough so it sort of falls off the bone. If you will be reheating the duck to serve it, be sure to put it into the oven preheated to the same temperature at which you cooked it to ensure it won't dry out.

The sauce for this dish is usually made by making a sugar syrup, adding fruit to it, and cooking it for quite a long time. My friend Janet Rikala, a pastry chef, suggested this method, which cuts the sugar out and the cooking time down and results in a fresher fruit flavor.

SERVES 6

3 ducks, 4 to 4½ pounds each

3 yellow onions, diced

2 green bell peppers, seeded and diced

Leaves from 2 rosemary sprigs

1½ cups rendered duck fat, congealed

1¼ cups Town Hall Spice Mixture (page 253)

SPICY FIG JUS

¼ pound dates, pitted

½ pound fresh figs

Grated zest and juice of 1 orange

2 tablespoons canola oil

Reserved wings, necks, and gizzards, excluding the hearts

½ yellow onion, diced

1 celery stalk, diced

1 green bell pepper, diced

1 dried chipotle chile stemmed, seeded, and coarsely chopped

2 tablespoons Town Hall Spice Mixture (page 253)

½ cinnamon stick

3 cups Chicken Stock (page 250)

Dirty Rice (page 157), for serving

PREHEAT THE OVEN to 275°F. Remove the neck and giblets from the duck cavities, then cut the wings off each duck, and set the necks, giblets, and wings aside.

In a bowl, combine the onions, bell peppers, rosemary, duck fat, and ¼ cup of the spice mixture. Season the outside of the ducks, with the remaining 1 cup spice mixture, using about ⅓ cup for each bird. Fill each duck cavity with one-third of the vegetable mixture. Then, push 2 long wooden skewers through the legs of each duck to close the cavity.

Place the ducks on a rack on a large sheet pan and roast for 4 to 4½ hours. Halfway through the cooking, rotate the pan, back to front. After 3½ hours, pull the pan out of the oven and drain off the fat, then return to the oven. The ducks are done if when you twist a leg bone, it pulls right out. Let the ducks rest for at least 45 minutes before you begin portioning them.

While the ducks are resting, make the fig jus. In a food processor, combine the dates, figs, and orange zest and juice and process until smooth. Set aside.

In a large sauce pan, heat the oil over medium-high heat. Add the necks, wings, and gizzards and cook, turning as needed, until browned. This should take about 10 minutes. Add the onion, celery, and bell pepper and continue cooking, scraping the bottom of the pan, for about 5 minutes more, or until the vegetables begin to caramelize. Add the chipotle chile, spice mixture, and cinnamon stick and continue cooking, scraping the pan, for a few minutes more. Pour in the stock and bring to a boil. Turn down the heat to a simmer and cook for about 10 minutes, or until reduced by half. Stir in the date–fig mixture and simmer for a few minutes more to blend the flavors. Remove from the heat, strain through a fine-mesh strainer, and season with salt and pepper. Reheat gently just before serving.

To portion the ducks, make a slice down the center, along the breastbone and remove the skin from each breast in one piece (you should have two pieces for each duck). Now, pull the meat from each breast off in one piece and place each piece on a plate. Next, pull off the meat from each leg, and lay it next to each of the pieces of the breast meat on each plate. Lay a piece of duck skin on top of the pile of meat on each plate. Portion the remaining 2 ducks the same way. You will have 6 plated portions. See photos page 210–211.

To serve, pour about ¼ cup fig jus over each duck portion. Accompany with the rice.

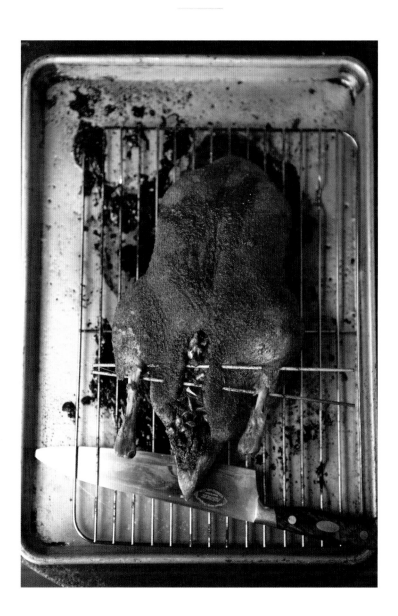

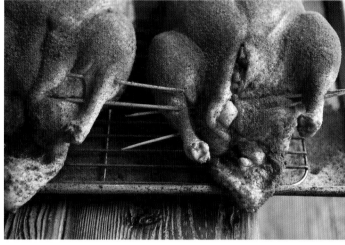

Peanut and TASSO Crusted

PORK CHOP

with HOT MUSTARD

4 pork chops

2 tablespoons unsalted butter

2 ounces tasso or ham, finely diced (about ¹/₂ cup), mixed with
1¹/₂ teaspoons Town Hall Spice Mixture (page 253)

1 cup roasted peanuts, coarsely chopped

2 teaspoons Worcestershire sauce

1 teaspoon maple syrup

4 tablespoons whole grain mustard

This pork chop was on Town Hall's opening menu, and it has become one of our signature dishes, but due to seasonal changes, every once in a while it comes off the list. When it returns, it does so triumphantly, creating excitement among the regulars in need of a fix. This is another dish where spicy and sweet intermingle. There's hot mustard, which not only adds flavor, but also acts as glue for the crust. The maple syrup also pulls double duty, imparting sweetness and acting as a binder for the peanut and tasso mixture. And as I've said before, seek out that spicy Cajun tasso. But if you can't get your hands on it, substitute regular ham sautéed in our spice mixture.

The process of brining intensifies the flavor of the meat and keeps it moist during the cooking process. You can play with different ingredients in the brine, but the salt content needs to be strong to penetrate to the center of the meat.

To make the brine, in a container, mix together all of the ingredients and stir to dissolve the salt and sugar. Add the pork chops to the brine, cover, and refrigerate for at least 24 hours or up to 3 days.

When you are ready to cook the pork chops, prepare a hot fire for direct-heat grilling in a charcoal or gas grill.

In a heavy-bottomed frying pan, melt 1 tablespoon of the butter over medium-high heat. Add the tasso and sauté until crispy. Remove from the heat and let cool.

In a food processor, combine the cooled tasso, peanuts, Worcestershire sauce, maple syrup, and the remaining 1 tablespoon butter. Pulse a few times to blend. Set aside.

Take the pork chops out of the brine and rinse them off under cold running water. Pat dry with a kitchen towel. Place the chops on the grill rack directly over the fire and grill, turning once, for 5 to 6 minutes on each side, or until pale pink at the center when tested with a knife. The timing will depend on the thickness. Two minutes before the chops are ready to come off the fire, smear 1 tablespoon of the mustard on top of each chop, then cover each chop with one-fourth of the tasso mixture and continue to grill just until the tasso topping is warm. Serve at once.

SERVES 4

BRINE

²/₃ cup kosher salt

³/₄ cup sugar

2 cloves garlic, smashed

¹/₄ cup peppercorns

¹/₂ bunch thyme

4 quarts water

FILET MIGNON
with Corn Mulch
and PORCINI BUTTER

What I call "corn mulch," some people call "corn pudding." Whatever you call it, the sweetness of the corn paired with the deep, earthy flavor of the mushrooms (accentuated by the bitter touch of coffee) makes for an amazing combination. You can substitute most wild mushrooms for the chanterelles in the ragout, and if you can't find porcini powder, you can grind dried porcini mushrooms in a spice grinder.

New Jersey is known for a few great food items and corn is one of them. I still associate corn with summer, when the roadside stands would start selling it.

❧ SERVES 6 ❧

PORCINI BUTTER
¼ cup porcini powder

1 stick unsalted butter at room temperature

1 shallot coarsely chopped

1 teaspoon whole grain mustard

1 tablespoon roasted garlic (see page 81)

1 teaspoon brewed espresso or double-strength coffee

Salt and freshly ground pepper

CORN MULCH
8 ears corn, silk and husks removed

Salt and freshly ground pepper

1 tablespoon unsalted butter

MUSHROOM RAGOUT
2 tablespoons extra-virgin olive oil

¼ pound chanterelle mushrooms, trimmed

Kernels from 4 ears corn (about 3 cups)

1 tablespoon unsalted butter

Salt and freshly ground pepper

½ cup cherry tomatoes, halved

¼ pound sugar snap peas, blanched for 2 minutes, drained, and thinly sliced on the diagonal

1 tablespoon chopped fresh flat-leaf parsley

1 tablespoon olive oil

6 filets mignons, 6 ounces each and about 2 inches thick

PREHEAT the oven to 375°F.

TO MAKE THE PORCINI BUTTER, place all of the ingredients in a food processor and pulse until combined. Season with salt and pepper and set aside.

TO MAKE THE CORN MULCH, grate the corn on the large holes of a hand grater placed over a saucepan. Place the pan over medium heat and cook the corn, stirring with a wooden spoon, for about 10 minutes, or until soft and just turning golden. Season with salt and pepper and stir in the butter. Keep warm.

TO MAKE THE RAGOUT, in a sauté pan, heat the oil over high heat. Add the mushrooms and sauté for 2 minutes. Add the corn and sauté for a few minutes more, or until the mushrooms begin releasing their liquid and the corn softens. Add the butter, a few pinches of salt, and a few grinds of pepper and stir to mix. Add the tomatoes and sugar snap peas and cook, stirring, for 1 minute, or until they become tender. Stir in the parsley and keep warm.

TO COOK THE STEAKS, in a large cast-iron frying pan, heat the olive oil over medium-heat. When the oil shimmers, add the steaks and cook, turning once, for about 4 minutes on each side, or until nicely seared. Transfer the pan to the oven and cook for 5 minutes more for medium-rare or until done to your liking. Pull the pan out of oven, transfer the steaks to a platter, and let rest for 4 to 5 minutes.

To serve, divide the corn mulch evenly among individual plates. Top each serving with some of the mushroom ragout and then with a steak. Place a heaping tablespoon of the porcini butter on top of each steak and serve right away.

Grilled
RIB-EYE STEAK
with BROWN BUTTER–GARLIC SAUCE
and *Hash Browns*

The rib-eye is my favorite steak. It's tender and well marbled, which means it's fatty. At the restaurant, our servers always let the guest who orders the rib-eye know to expect some fat. But this is a case in which fat is good because fat means flavor. It is also what makes this cut a great candidate for a hot grill. When you're grilling, vote rib-eye.

When making the sauce, it is important to let the butter brown before you add the garlic. If you add it too early, the garlic will burn before it's time to add the stock. Although we use a veal demi-glace at the restaurant, I prefer chicken stock, which brightens the other flavors.

SERVES 4

HASH BROWNS

2 pounds small Yukon gold potatoes, peeled and cut into slices about 1 inch in diameter and 1/4 inch thick

Salt and freshly ground pepper

1 tablespoon plus 1/3 cup olive oil

1 yellow onion, sliced

2 teaspoons Town Hall Spice Mixture (page 253)

1 tablespoon freshly squeezed lemon juice

4 rib-eye steaks, about 11 to 12 ounces each and 1 to 1 1/2 inches thick

Salt and freshly ground pepper

BROWN BUTTER–GARLIC SAUCE

6 tablespoons unsalted butter

8 large cloves garlic, sliced

2 teaspoons Town Hall Spice Mixture (page 253)

1 cup Chicken Stock (page 250)

2 tablespoons Worcestershire sauce

1 teaspoon freshly squeezed lemon juice

Salt and freshly ground pepper

Prepare a hot fire for direct-heat grilling in a charcoal or gas grill.

To prepare the hash browns, in a large pot, combine the potatoes and 1 teaspoon salt with water to cover. Bring to a boil over high heat and parboil for about 10 minutes, or until half cooked. Drain well and spread the slices on a sheet pan to cool.

In a sauté pan, heat the 1 tablespoon oil over medium-high heat. Add the onion and sauté for 10 minutes, or until soft and turning golden. Add the spice mixture and 1 teaspoon salt and cook for 5 minutes more. Remove from the heat.

In large sauté pan, heat the remaining 1/3 cup oil over high heat. Add the potatoes and sauté for 8 to 10 minutes, or until crispy and brown. Add the sautéed onion and the lemon juice, stir well, and season with salt and pepper. Keep warm.

Season the steaks with salt and pepper. Place on the grill rack directly over the fire and grill, turning once, for 4 minutes on each side for medium-rare, or until done to your liking. Transfer to a platter and let rest for 4 to 5 minutes.

While the steaks are resting, make the sauce. In a sauté pan, melt 2 tablespoons of the butter over medium heat, then continue to heat the butter until it turns a nutty brown. Add the garlic and when it starts to brown, add the spice mixture, the stock, and the Worcestershire sauce. Stir well, then reduce for 1 minute. Add the remaining 4 tablespoons butter in pieces, the parsley, and the lemon juice and stir until the butter melts. Season with salt and pepper.

To serve, place the steaks on individual plates, top each steak with a big spoonful of the sauce, and place a generous portion of the hash browns alongside.

Desserts

chapter DESSERTS eight

Dessert—IT'S A KIND OF TEMPTRESS, ISN'T IT? You know what I mean. Even the way the waitstaff handles the menu, offering it to you but still holding it just out of reach, while asking, "Will you be having dessert?" The question comes off as a challenge, almost a taunt. Should you or shouldn't you?

YOU SHOULD. I don't remember who it was, but one of the chefs I worked for argued that dessert was actually the most important part of a meal, the final course and thus the last impression a guest has of a restaurant. Not surprisingly, I'd like to think otherwise. But that's because I'm not a pastry guy. As I've already mentioned, before I began working on this book, I didn't go in much for precision when it came to measurements. But my approach, cooking by feel, doesn't cut it in the pastry kitchen where exacting measurements are the backbone of the art. My only experience anywhere near the pastry area consists of a stint working garde-manger at Le Cirque in Manhattan, a position responsible for preparing the restaurant's legendary crème brûlée (that's a recipe I wish I would have written down). Couple my inexperience with pastry with the fact that I rarely eat sugar, and you'll understand why when it comes to sweets, I gladly hand over the reins at our restaurants and for this chapter.

LUCKILY FOR ME, and for you, those reins have been picked up by two of the best pastry chefs I've ever known, Janet Rikala and Christine Law. I first worked with both of them when I was at Postrio. When we opened Town Hall, Janet guided our dessert menu and is responsible for the most popular item on that list, the Butterscotch-Chocolate Pot de Crème (page 223). She got the sweet things going at Salt House, as well. As for Christine, she now oversees the pastry departments at all of our restaurants. And because of both Janet and Christine, people leave happy.

Butterscotch-
CHOCOLATE
POT DE CRÈME

This dessert—rich bittersweet chocolate pudding layered with silken butterscotch pudding and topped with chocolate-dipped buttercrunch candy—has been on the menu at Town Hall since the doors opened in 2003. It definitely makes a lasting impression on diners, many of whom come back to the restaurant again and again just for this dessert.

At the restaurant, we ladle warm chocolate pudding into oversized soup bowls, some sixty orders at a time. By the time we have ladled the last bowl of pudding, the first ones have set up enough that we can add the butterscotch layer without it sinking into the chocolate. For small home batches, you can refrigerate ramekins of chocolate pudding to firm the layer while you prepare the butterscotch pudding.

SERVES 6

CHOCOLATE PUDDING

2 tablespoons high-quality Dutch-process cocoa powder

2 tablespoons cornstarch

$^2/_3$ cup sugar

$^1/_8$ teaspoon kosher salt

1 vanilla bean

1 cup heavy cream

2 large egg yolks

2 cups whole milk

6 ounces bittersweet chocolate (62 % percent cacao), chopped

1 tablespoon unsalted butter

BUTTERSCOTCH PUDDING

$1^1/_2$ cups heavy cream

A pinch of kosher salt

$^1/_2$ vanilla bean, split lengthwise and seeded

$^1/_4$ cup sugar

4 ounces Guittard butterscotch chips

6 large egg yolks

BUTTERCRUNCH CANDY (OPTIONAL)

1 cup ($^1/_2$ pound) unsalted butter, plus more for pan

$1^1/_4$ cups sugar

$^1/_3$ cup light corn syrup

$^1/_3$ cup water

1 teaspoon kosher salt

$^1/_2$ teaspoon baking soda

8 ounces bittersweet chocolate (62% percent cacao), chopped

TO MAKE THE CHOCOLATE PUDDING, in a 4-quart heavy-bottomed pot, whisk together the cocoa powder, cornstarch, sugar, and salt. Using the tip of a sharp knife, scrape the seeds from the vanilla bean halves into the pot, then add the pods. Pour in the cream in a steady stream while whisking constantly to make a smooth paste. Whisk in the egg yolks, followed by the milk.

Place the pot over medium heat and heat, whisking frequently, until the mixture registers 140°F on an instant-read thermometer. Add the chopped chocolate and whisk until smooth. Continue cooking, whisking constantly and making sure to scrape the bottom of the pot to keep any chocolate particles from sticking and scorching, until the mixture reaches 185°F. At this point, the pudding should appear slightly thickened. Whisk in the butter and then strain the pudding through a fine-mesh strainer into a container.

Ladle $^2/_3$ cup of the pudding into each of 6 bowls. Refrigerate the bowls to allow the pudding to set for at least 2 to 3 hours before you add the butterscotch layer.

TO MAKE THE BUTTERSCOTCH PUDDING, first place a strainer and a bowl together in an ice bath. Next, in a

continued

medium-sized pan, combine the cream, salt, and vanilla bean and gently bring to a boil. Add the sugar and butterscotch chips, stirring constantly until the butterscotch has melted and the mixture is smooth. In a separate bowl, lightly whisk the egg yolks and then, whisking constantly, very slowly pour the butterscotch into the bowl. Once incorporated, return the mixture to the pot and bring to boil over medium heat, stirring constantly. Once it reaches a boil, remove from the heat and strain into the bowl placed in the ice bath. Set aside, and whisk occasionally while it cools.

When cool (about 15 to 20 minutes), ladle about $1/3$ cup of the butterscotch over the chilled chocolate pudding in each bowl. Cover and refrigerate until firm, at least 8 hours or up to overnight.

TO MAKE THE BUTTERCRUNCH CANDY, butter a 10 by 13-inch sheet pan, or line the pan with a silicone baking mat. Have ready a large offset spatula. In a 4-quart heavy-bottomed pot, combine the sugar, corn syrup, water, and butter over medium heat until the sugar dissolves (use a clean wet pastry brush to wash down any sugar crystals that form on the sides of the pot). When the sugar has dissolved, continue to cook over high heat, stirring frequently, until the mixture is the color of peanut butter. This will take about 5 to 7 minutes. Remove from the heat and stir in the baking soda and salt.

Immediately pour the mixture out onto the prepared pan and quickly spread it into a thin, even layer with the offset spatula. Let cool to room temperature.

TO TEMPER THE CHOCOLATE, put the chocolate pieces in a heatproof bowl. Rest the bowl over (not touching) barely simmering water in a saucepan and heat, stirring occasionally, until the chocolate is completely melted and smooth. Remove the bowl from over the water and set it in a cool part of the kitchen for about 15 minutes. As the chocolate along the sides of the bowl begins to set, stir it back into the rest of the melted chocolate. Let the chocolate sit again, and again, as the chocolate begins to set, stir it back into the melted chocolate. Repeat this process until the chocolate feels cool on your lip. It will have a nice shine and register 88°F on the instant-read thermometer.

Using a clean, dry pastry brush, quickly and evenly spread the warm chocolate over the room-temperature buttercrunch candy. Let cool completely, then break into shards and store in an airtight container in the refrigerator until ready to use. (The buttercrunch can be made up to a week in advance.)

To serve, top each bowl of pudding with 3 shards of the buttercrunch.

Town Hall's
INFAMOUS
HOT CHOCOLATE

On a cold, foggy night by the bay, nothing satisfies like a cup of decadent, ultrarich hot chocolate. The partners at Town Hall all agreed: "Let's have the best cup of hot chocolate in San Francisco." After endless tries, we actually have come up with the best cup of hot chocolate in town.

Hot chocolate is only as good as the quality of the chocolate used. Fine chocolates are distinguished not only by the origin of the beans, but also by the total cacao content (or chocolate liquor, that is, what actually comes from the cacao bean) in the bar, with the balance made up of sugar, vanilla, and emulsifiers. Cacao percentages are printed on the labels of chocolate bars, though what they define differs from country to country and manufacturer to manufacturer. Here are the general guidelines we use: 38 to 41 percent cacao is milk chocolate, 55 to 59 percent cacao is semisweet chocolate, 60 to 66 percent cacao is bittersweet chocolate, 68 to 72 percent cacao is extra-bitter dark chocolate, and 100 percent cacao is unsweetened, or baking, chocolate. Different chocolate manufacturers have different flavor profiles within these ranges, so the best thing to do is to taste them all and see which one you prefer.

SERVES 6

½ cup whole milk

½ cup heavy cream

¼ cup brewed strong coffee

¼ cup sugar

1 tablespoon unsweetened cocoa powder, preferably Sharffen Berger or Valrhona

4 ounces milk chocolate (40 percent cacao), chopped

3 ounces extra-bitter dark chocolate (70 percent cacao), chopped

4 ounces bittersweet chocolate (62 percent cacao), chopped

IN A SAUCEPAN, combine the milk, cream, and coffee and heat gently over medium-low heat to a simmer, with bubbles forming around edges of the pan. Do not allow the mixture to boil.

Remove from the heat and whisk in the sugar, cocoa powder, and the chocolates until the sugar dissolves and the chocolates are melted. Pour through a fine-mesh strainer into individual cups, or a thermos to keep warm before serving.

Sticky
TOFFEE PUDDING

When Americans hear the name of this recipe, they usually picture something like Town Hall's famous Butterscotch-Chocolate Pot de Crème (page 223), which celebrates the stove-top custard-style puddings many of us grew up on. (Thanks, Jell-O.) In fact, this toffee pudding is an ultramoist date cake that originated in Britain, where soft, steamed cakelike desserts are called puddings. When the dates are pureed and added to the butter and sugar, they compose a flavor reminiscent of toffee candy, and contribute to the cake's delicate texture. We serve this dessert family style, in a pool of bourbon sauce with loads of fresh bananas that will make you wonder how on earth it didn't come from the South.

❖ SERVES 3 ❖

Unsalted butter, for pan

PUDDING BATTER
18 Medjool dates, pitted and chopped

1⅓ cups water

1 teaspoon baking soda

5 tablespoons unsalted butter

⅔ cup firmly packed golden brown sugar

2 large eggs

1 teaspoon vanilla extract

1 cup cake flour

1½ teaspoons baking powder

½ teaspoon salt

BOURBON TOFFEE SAUCE
½ cup buttermilk

1 cup granulated sugar

1 tablespoon light corn syrup

½ teaspoon baking soda

½ teaspoon vanilla extract

½ cup (¼ pound) unsalted butter, cut into ½-inch pieces

¼ cup bourbon

TO SERVE
1 banana, peeled and cut on the diagonal into 10 to 12 slices ¼-inch-thick

Chopped toasted walnuts

PREHEAT the oven to 350°F. Butter a 9-inch square cake pan, then line the bottom with parchment paper.

TO MAKE THE BATTER, put the dates in a heatproof bowl. In a small saucepan, combine the water and baking soda and bring to a boil. Remove from the heat, pour the boiling water over the dates, and let cool to room temperature.

When the dates are cool, transfer them and their soaking liquid to a food processor. Add the butter and brown sugar and process until mostly smooth with some flecks of date (do not whip!) Add the eggs and the vanilla, process briefly to mix, then scrape down the sides of the bowl with a rubber spatula.

In a bowl, sift together the flour, baking powder, and salt. With the processor running, stream in the flour and process just until combined. Pour the batter into the prepared pan.

Bake for 45 to 50 minutes, or until the top is golden and a toothpick inserted into the center comes out clean.

TO MAKE THE SAUCE, in a small, deep saucepan, combine the buttermilk, sugar, corn syrup, baking soda, and vanilla over medium heat. Once the mixture is hot, add the butter and cook over medium-high heat, whisking periodically to incorporate the butter as it melts (the sauce will foam up considerably, so be sure there is plenty of headroom in

continued

the pot). Once the mixture comes to a boil, reduce the heat to a low simmer and continue cooking until the sauce is the color of dark brown sugar. Remove from the heat, add the bourbon, and whisk to combine.

When the pudding is ready, remove from the oven and let cool on a wire rack for about 15 minutes. When ready, loosen the edges with a knife and unmold onto a serving plate.

Heat the toffee sauce in a sauté pan until bubbly. Add the banana slices and sauté until warm but not mushy, and then add a sprinkling of toasted walnuts. To serve, place a slice of cake on the plate and top with a few tablespoons of the hot sauce.

Maple
WHOOPIE PIES

There are many different stories behind the origin of whoopie pies, but my favorite is that the Amish used to bake their extra cake batter into cookie rounds and put them into their children's lunch boxes. On finding the cakey cookies at lunchtime, the children reportedly shouted "Whoopie!" Although it isn't the traditional filling, the maple marshmallow fluff used here pays extra homage to the undisputed New England roots of these cookies.

MAKES 12 WHOOPIE PIES

Pictured on page 230.

1 cup all-purpose flour

1/3 cup tablespoons unsweetened cocoa powder, preferably Valrhona

1/4 teaspoon baking powder

1/2 teaspoon baking soda

Scant 1/2 teaspoon kosher salt

1/2 cup whole milk

1 1/2 teaspoons freshly squeezed lemon juice

1 teaspoon vanilla extract

4 tablespoons unsalted butter, at room temperature

1/2 cup plus 2 tablespoons firmly packed dark brown sugar

2 egg yolks

MAPLE-MARSHMALLOW FLUFF FILLING

1/2 cup maple syrup

1/2 cup plus 1 teaspoon sugar

2 large egg whites

Pinch of kosher salt

Pinch of cream of tartar

1/4 teaspoon vanilla extract

Preheat the oven to 350°F. Line 2 large sheet pans with parchment paper.

In a bowl, sift together the flour, cocoa powder, baking powder, baking soda, and salt. Set aside. In a measuring cup, combine the milk, lemon juice, and vanilla and let stand for 5 minutes, or until the mixture thickens and curdles. Meanwhile, in a stand mixer fitted with the paddle attachment (or in a bowl with a handheld mixer), cream together the butter and brown sugar on medium speed until light and fluffy. Scrape down the sides of the bowl with a rubber spatula, add the egg yolks, and beat until incorporated. Reduce the speed to low and add the flour mixture in three additions and the milk mixture in two additions, beginning and ending with the flour mixture and mixing after each addition just until the batter is smooth.

Spoon the batter into a pastry bag fitted with a plain tip. Pipe mounds 2 inches in diameter onto the prepared sheet pans, spacing the mounds $1^1/2$ inches apart to make way for spreading. Dampen your fingertips with cold water and press down the point on each mound left by the pastry bag tip.

Bake for about 8 to 10 minutes, rotating the sheet pans back to front halfway through baking. The cakes are done when they are firm to the touch but not hard. Transfer to a wire rack and let cool completely before filling.

TO MAKE THE FILLING, in a small saucepan over low heat, combine the maple syrup and the $1/2$ cup sugar, stirring to dissolve the sugar. Use a clean, wet pastry brush to wash down any sugar crystals that form on the sides of the pan. Raise the heat to medium, and clip a candy thermometer onto the side of the pan and cook the syrup-sugar mixture, without stirring, for about 5 minutes, or until the thermometer registers 246°F, or the firm-ball stage. (This stage will yield a marshmallow filling that is soft and gooey, but won't ooze out when sandwiched between the cookies.)

While the syrup-sugar mixture is cooking, put the egg whites, salt, and cream of tartar in the clean, dry bowl of the stand mixer and fit the mixer with the whisk attachment. Beat on medium speed for about 2 minutes, or until creamy and foamy. With the mixer running on medium-high speed, sprinkle in the remaining 1 tablespoon sugar. Continue to beat on medium-high speed until the whites hold very soft peaks.

On low speed, carefully stream in the hot maple syrup, aiming it between the side of the bowl and the whisk to avoid spatters. Add vanilla and beat just until mixed.

Increase the speed to medium-high and beat for about 7 minutes, or until the mixture is thick, fluffy, and just warm. Turn the mixer to low speed and continue to beat for another minute or so, or until cooled to room temperature. The filling will be very thick and collect around the whisk.

Using a rubber spatula, transfer the filling to a clean pastry bag fitted with a plain tip $1/4$ inch in diameter. Turn half of the cooled cookies bottom side up, and pipe a generous mound of the filling onto each of them. Top with the remaining cookies, bottom side down, to make sandwiches. Serve immediately.

Coffee
MILK SHAKE

The idea of a recipe for a coffee milkshake may seem a little strange. However, in this instance you're not merely throwing some coffee ice cream and milk into a blender and calling it a day. No. While I'm pretty sure you'll agree that following this recipe will result in the best milkshake you've ever had, you're going to have to work for it. You'll make an extract of sorts and blend it with coffee liqueur. And be sure to use the best-quality vanilla ice cream you can find; it will make the shake that much better. At the restaurant, we serve this milkshake with the Maple Whoopie Pies (page 228).

MAKES 4 MILK SHAKES

COFFEE ESSENCE

3/4 cup ground espresso beans or other dark-roast coffee beans

1 1/3 cups plus 2 tablespoons water

2/3 cup sugar

Pinch of cream of tartar

6 tablespoons St. George Spirits Firelit coffee liqueur or other coffee liqueur

1/2 cup half-and-half

1 quart good-quality vanilla ice cream

Whipped cream and chocolate sprinkles, for garnish

TO MAKE THE COFFEE ESSENCE, in a 2-quart saucepan, combine the ground coffee and the 1 1/3 cups water and bring to a simmer over medium heat. Simmer gently for 4 to 5 minutes, stirring occasionally. Remove from the heat and strain through a fine-mesh strainer into a measuring cup, pressing on the grounds to extract as much liquid as possible. Check to see how much you have, then pour additional hot water over the grounds to measure 1 1/8 cups total. Set aside.

In a deep, 4-quart saucepan, combine the sugar, the remaining 2 tablespoons water, and the cream of tartar over medium heat, stirring to dissolve the sugar. Use a clean, wet pastry brush to wash down any sugar crystals that form on the sides of the pan. Cook the mixture over medium heat, without stirring, until it is deep amber and definitely starting to smoke.

Immediately remove from the heat and quickly and carefully stir in a little of the coffee liquid. The caramelized sugar will bubble up, so just keep adding the coffee liquid slowly until all of it has been added. Clip a candy thermometer onto the side of the pan, return the pan to medium heat, and simmer until the syrup registers 220°F on the thermometer. There should be large, foamy bubbles all over the surface of the syrup. Remove from the heat and let cool completely.

Add the liqueur to the cooled essence and whisk to combine. You should have about 1 cup, or enough for 4 milk shakes. Use immediately, or refrigerate in a plastic container with a tight-fitting lid for up to 1 month.

TO MAKE EACH MILK SHAKE, combine 1/4 cup of the coffee essence, 2 tablespoons of the half-and-half, and 4 scoops of the ice cream in a blender and process just until combined. Do not overblend or the ice cream will melt and the milk shake will be thin. Pour into a tall, chilled glass and garnish with whipped cream and chocolate sprinkles.

LEMON CHESS PIE

Here's another recipe where the origin of the name is murky. It is southern, so some have thought that it is a "chest" pie (to be kept in a pie chest) and was renamed because of a southerner's drawl. Another idea is that "chess" it's just a corruption of cheese, that is, the English tradition of a cheese-less cheesecake. In any event, the provenance of the name is less important than what you're going to take out of the oven—Christine Law's West Coast interpretation of a southern classic, made all the more appealing when you bake your own graham cracker for the crust.

❧ SERVES 8 ❧

GRAHAM CRACKER CRUST

1 cup (1/2 pound) unsalted butter, at room temperature, plus 3 tablespoons

6 tablespoons firmly packed golden brown sugar

5 tablespoons granulated sugar

1 tablespoon clover honey

1 1/2 teaspoons dark molasses

2 cups all-purpose flour

1/2 cup whole wheat flour

1 teaspoon ground cinnamon

1/2 teaspoon baking soda

1/8 teaspoon salt

Nonstick cooking spray

FILLING

1 1/2 cups granulated sugar

1 1/2 tablespoons stone-ground yellow cornmeal

1 1/2 tablespoons all-purpose flour

3/4 cup freshly squeezed Meyer lemon juice

1/4 cup freshly squeezed regular lemon juice

1 tablespoon grated lemon zest, preferably Meyer

3 large whole eggs

6 large egg yolks

5 tablespoons unsalted butter, melted

1/3 cup heavy cream

BLACKBERRY BASIL COMPOTE

2 1/2 cups fresh blackberries

1/2 cup granulated sugar

1 1/2 tablespoons water

1 1/2 tablespoons cornstarch

2 teaspoons basil chiffonade (cut into long, thin strips)

To MAKE THE CRUST, preheat the oven to 350°F. In a stand mixer fitted with the paddle attachment, combine the 1 cup room-temperature butter, the brown sugar, 2 tablespoons of the granulated sugar, the honey, and the molasses and beat on the lowest speed until smooth and shiny. Be careful not to incorporate too much air, and scrape down the sides of the bowl frequently with a rubber spatula.

In a bowl, sift together both flours, the cinnamon, the baking soda, and the salt. Add to the mixer all at once, turn on the mixer to the lowest speed, and mix just until the dough almost comes together (it will be pretty dry but not crumbly).

Remove the dough from the bowl, gather it into a ball, and place on a large sheet of parchment paper. Top with a second sheet of parchment, pat to flatten, then roll out 3/16 inch thick. Remove the top parchment sheet and slide the dough, still on the bottom parchment sheet, onto a sheet pan.

Bake for about 20 minutes, rotating the pan back to front halfway through baking. The crust is ready when it is a light golden brown and does not leave an indentation when gently pressed with a fingertip. Remove from the oven and let cool completely on the pan on a wire rack. When cool, break into big pieces, place in a food processor, and pulse to grind finely. You should have 1 3/4 cups crumbs.

TO FINISH THE CRUST, preheat the oven again to 350°F. Line the bottom of a 9 1/2-inch tart pan with a removable

continued

bottom with parchment paper, then spray the paper with nonstick cooking spray.

In a bowl, combine the crumbs and the remaining 3 tablespoons sugar and toss to mix with a fork. Melt the remaining 3 tablespoons butter, then slowly drizzle the melted butter into the crumbs while tossing with the fork, adding just enough butter for the crumbs to clump together when you squeeze them gently in your palm. Continue to toss with the fork until all of the crumbs are evenly moistened. Turn the crumb mixture into the prepared tart pan and press it evenly over the bottom and up the sides of the pan. Use a flat object, such as the bottom of a pot, to press the crust firmly into place.

Bake for 10 minutes, or until the crust smells toasted. Let cool completely on a wire rack before filling. Lower the oven temperature to 325°F.

TO MAKE THE FILLING, in a 2-quart saucepan, whisk together the sugar, cornmeal, and flour to remove any lumps. Pour in the lemon juices, add the lemon zest, and whisk to combine. Place over medium-high heat and bring to a boil while whisking gently. Remove from the heat.

In a bowl, lightly beat together the whole eggs and egg yolks just until blended, then add the melted butter and mix well. Pour in the hot lemon juice mixture while whisking constantly, then whisk until combined. Whisk in the cream until fully incorporated. Carefully pour the filling into the cooled crust.

Bake for 35 to 40 minutes, or until the filling is firmly set. It should jiggle like gelatin when the pan is shaken. Let cool completely in the pan on a wire rack, then remove the pan sides and slide the pie off the base onto a flat serving plate. Refrigerate until serving.

TO MAKE THE COMPOTE, in a 2-quart saucepan, combine 2^1/$_2$ cups of blackberries with the sugar over medium heat. Stir occasionally as the sugar melts and the berries release their juices. Meanwhile, in a small bowl, stir together the cornstarch and water to make a slurry. When the blackberry sugar mixture just starts to boil, whisk in the cornstarch slurry, then boil gently for a minute or two, or until slightly thickened. Whisk in the basil and remove from the heat. Let cool slightly, and fold in the reserved berries. Let cool completely and serve at room temperature. The compote can be covered and refrigerated for up to a week. Bring to room temperature before serving.

NOTE: This Lemon Chess Pie is also great with a brûlée crust. So, if you have a small kitchen torch, scatter 1 tablespoon of sugar evenly over the top of the pie and burn the sugar evenly keeping the torch an inch, to an inch of half away from the pie. Moving over the entire pie burning the sugar Repeat with the second tablespoon sugar

Chocolate Chunk
COOKIES

At the barbecue cart, we have parked behind Town Hall, people line up around the corner to pick up our signature ribs and these ultradecadent, oversized chocolate chip cookies for dessert. The Scharffen Berger chocolate sets these cookies apart from your mother's Toll House version, and a little bit of honey keeps them chewy and soft.

To make chewy, dense chocolate chip cookies, you must mix the ingredients on low speed at every stage. On higher speeds, too much air will be incorporated into the butter and eggs, causing the cookies to spread excessively and flatten. (They will still taste good, however.)

❧ MAKES ABOUT 24 COOKIES ❧

3¹/₂ cups all-purpose flour

¹/₃ cup whole wheat flour

1¹/₂ teaspoons baking soda

1 teaspoon salt

1 cup plus 4 tablespoons (10 ounces) unsalted butter, at room temperature

1¹/₄ cups granulated sugar

1¹/₂ cups firmly packed golden brown sugar

2 tablespoons honey

1 tablespoon vanilla extract

3 large eggs

1 pound bittersweet chocolate (62 percent cacao), chopped, or bittersweet chocolate chips, preferably Sharffen Berger

In a bowl, sift together both flours, the baking soda, and the salt. Set aside. In a stand mixer fitted with the paddle attachment, cream together the butter and both sugars on low speed until smooth, stopping to scrape down the sides and along the bottom of the bowl as needed. Add the honey and vanilla and mix until combined. Add the eggs, one at a time, mixing until fully incorporated and scraping down the sides of the bowl after each addition. Add the dry ingredients all at once and continue to mix on low speed until about three-fourths combined. Scrape down the sides of the bowl, add the chocolate, and continue to mix on low speed just until fully combined.

Slip the bowl into the refrigerator to chill the dough for about about an hour or until it is firm enough to shape into balls. Meanwhile, preheat the oven to 375°F. Line 2 sheet pans with parchment paper.

Shape the dough into 2-inch balls, rolling them between your palms, and place 2 inches apart on the prepared sheet pans.

Bake for 10 to 13 minutes, or until the edges are golden and the centers are still soft to the touch. Transfer the pan to a wire rack and let cool. Store in an airtight container at room temperature for up to 4 days.

WARM BEIGNETS
with *Powdered Sugar*

It's no surprise that the Town Hall menu, with its many nods south to New Orleans, includes that Café du Monde classic, beignets. Serve them with a strong cup of coffee and pretend you're on Decatur Street.

❧ MAKES 24 BEIGNETS; SERVES 6 ❧

½ cup plus 1 tablespoon warm water (110°F)

1 packet active dry yeast

⅓ cup sugar

2¾ cups all-purpose flour, plus more for dusting

2 large egg yolks

⅓ cup plus 1 tablespoon whole milk

1¾ teaspoons ground nutmeg

1¼ teaspoons salt

⅛ teaspoon baking powder

2 tablespoons unsalted butter, at room temperature, plus more for bowl

Canola oil, for deep-frying

Powdered sugar, for dusting

PLACE the warm water in the bowl of a stand mixer fitted with the dough hook attachment, sprinkle the yeast on top, and whisk to dissolve. Add a pinch of the granulated sugar and let stand for 5 minutes, or until foamy.

Add the flour, the remaining sugar, the egg yolks, milk, nutmeg, salt, and baking powder. Mix on low speed for about 30 seconds, or just until the dough comes together. Add the butter and mix on medium speed for 2 minutes, or until the butter is completely incorporated. Increase the speed to high and mix for about 2 minutes, or until the dough is smooth and shiny, stopping to scrape down the sides of the bowl as needed.

Butter a large bowl. Gather up the dough and form it into a loose ball (it will be sticky). Place it in the buttered bowl, cover the bowl tightly with plastic wrap, and place in a warm spot until the dough rises to 1½ times its original size, about 1½ hours.

Punch down the dough and turn it out onto a lightly floured work surface. Roll it out into a 8 by 2-inch rectangle about ¼ inch thick. Cut into twenty-four 2-inch squares and let rest for 10 minutes before frying.

Pour the oil to a depth of 3 to 3½ inches into a deep fryer or deep, heavy-bottomed pot, and heat to 370°F. Working in batches, add the dough squares and fry, turning once, for about a minute on each side, or until golden. Using a wire skimmer or slotted spoon, transfer the beignets to paper towels to drain briefly.

Dust the beignets generously with powdered sugar. Serve immediately.

Warm
APPLE-CHEDDAR
GALETTE

The Gravenstein is quite possibly the perfect baking apple, with a delicately balanced sweet-tart flavor. Lucky for us, Town Hall is just down the coast from Sonoma County, where Gravensteins thrive. Unfortunately, they have a short season, from late July to early September, and they are not good keepers. Once they are gone, pippins, Sierra Beauties, and Jonathans make fine substitutes in this galette, which is topped with an artisanal white Cheddar cheese, in an American tradition that few cooks still seem to practice. If you are among them, try this to see what you have been missing.

Frangipane, an incredibly versatile filling traditionally made from almond paste, eggs, sugar, butter, and flour, is used by French cooks in everything from petits fours to almond croissants. By substituting our homemade caramel applesauce for the almond paste in frangipane, we not only celebrate more apple flavor in the apple galette, but also provide a nut-free version of this classic preparation that is neutral enough to use in as many ways as the original.

The caramel applesauce has a wonderfully deep flavor. You can substitute store-bought applesauce, but it is mild and watery by comparison, so you'll need to cook it down to a dry paste in a frying pan and then measure out what you need. If you decide to make the caramel applesauce, you will have more than you need for this recipe. You can freeze the surplus and use it later in easy turnovers made with store-bought puff pastry, or you can serve it warm over vanilla ice cream with a splash of Calvados.

You need to freeze the assembled galette for at least 4 hours before baking, so you'll need to plan ahead.

Pictured on pages 238–239.

CHEDDAR DOUGH

1½ cups plus 2 tablespoons all-purpose flour, plus more for dusting

⅓ cup semolina flour

4 teaspoons sugar

1 teaspoon salt

2 ounces Vermont white Cheddar cheese, grated (about ½ cup)

½ cup (¼ pound) plus 3 tablespoons unsalted butter, chilled, cut into ½-inch pieces

½ cup ice-cold water

CARAMEL APPLESAUCE

⅔ cup sugar

1½ teaspoons freshly squeezed lemon juice

1 vanilla bean, split lengthwise

4 cups peeled and thinly sliced Gravenstein apples

Apple juice, if needed

FRANGIPANE FILLING

4 tablespoons unsalted butter at room temperature

⅓ cup sugar

¼ cup caramel applesauce (above)

1 large whole egg

1 large egg yolk

⅓ cup plus 1 tablespoon all-purpose flour, sifted

1 large egg lightly beaten with 1 tablespoon water and a pinch of salt, for wash

4 tablespoons granulated sugar mixed with ¼ teaspoon ground cinnamon

3 large Gravenstein apples, peeled, halved, cored, and sliced ⅛ inch thick

2 tablespoons unsalted butter, melted

1 tablespoon crystal sugar

¼ cup apricot jelly or jam

2 tablespoons water

¼ pound Vermont white Cheddar cheese, thinly sliced

To make the dough, in a stand mixer fitted with the paddle attachment, stir together the flour, semolina, sugar, and salt. Add the cheese and stir just to coat with the flour mixture. Scatter the butter over the flour mixture and mix on low speed until the largest chunks are about $1/4$ inch. Add the ice water and mix on low speed just until the dough comes together. Do not overmix. Gather the dough into a ball, wrap in plastic wrap, and refrigerate for at least 30 minutes or up to a day.

To make the caramel applesauce, in a small, deep saucepan, combine the sugar and lemon juice. Using the tip of a sharp knife, scrape the seeds from the vanilla bean halves into the pan. Place the pan over medium heat. As the sugar begins to melt, stir until all of the sugar has liquefied. Continue cooking over medium heat until the mixture is a medium amber. Add the apple slices and stir until they begin to release their juices. Turn down the heat to low and cook slowly until the liquid has evaporated and the apples have begun to break down. If the liquid evaporates before the apples have softened enough, add some apple juice, cover to steam the apples until they are soft, then uncover and cook off the excess liquid as before.

Remove from the heat and let cool slightly. Transfer to a blender or food processor and process until smooth. Let cool completely before using, then measure out $1/4$ cup to use for the frangipane. The applesauce can be made up to 1 week in advance and refrigerated. The leftover applesauce can be frozen for up to a month.

To make the frangipane, combine the butter and sugar in the stand mixer fitted with the paddle attachment and cream together on low speed until smooth. Add the applesauce and mix to combine. On low speed, add the whole egg and then the egg yolk, mixing until fully incorporated and scraping down the sides of the bowl after each addition. Add the flour all at once and mix on low speed just until incorporated. The frangipane can be made up to 4 hours in advance and refrigerated.

To assemble the galette, line a sheet pan with parchment paper. On a lightly floured work surface, roll out the dough into a round $1/8$ inch thick. Trim the edges

to form a 13-inch round. Carefully transfer the round to the prepared sheet pan. Brush a 1-inch border around the edge of the dough round with some of the egg wash. Spread the frangipane in the center of the round, stopping about 2 inches from the edge. Sprinkle 2 tablespoons of the cinnamon sugar over the frangipane. Arrange the apple slices on top of the frangipane in 3 concentric circles, overlapping them slightly. Brush the apples with the melted butter and sprinkle with the remaining 2 tablespoons cinnamon sugar. Fold up the uncovered edge of the dough around the apples, folding it onto itself to form uniformly spaced pleats every few inches around the perimeter and using the egg wash to seal each fold. Sprinkle the upturned edge with the crystal sugar. The finished galette should be about 11 inches in diameter.

Slip the assembled galette into the freezer for at least 4 hours or up to 1 week before baking. This will help it hold its shape in the oven.

To bake the galette, place a pizza stone on the lower rack of the oven and preheat to 425°F. When the oven is ready, remove the galette from the freezer and place it directly on the pizza stone. Bake for about 40 minutes, rotating the galette 180 degrees after 20 minutes. The top should be a dark golden brown. Slide a large, wide metal spatula under the galette to check the underside. It should be uniformly golden. Using the spatula, carefully transfer the galette to a wire rack. Let cool completely before glazing.

To make the glaze, in a small saucepan, combine the apricot jelly and water and bring to a boil over high heat while whisking constantly. As soon as the mixture boils, remove from the heat and immediately brush the glaze over the apples.

To serve, preheat the broiler. Slide the galette onto a sheet pan, and arrange the cheese slices around the outer edge of the crust Place under the broiler and broil just until the cheese melts. Watch closely, as this takes just a few minutes. Serve warm or at room temperature.

Mini Red Velvet
CUPCAKES *with*
CREAM CHEESE
Frosting

Town Hall has the perfect atmosphere for a celebration. When guests come in for an occasion, we inscribe plates with a chocolate message and deliver our take on the South's famed red velvet cake. The original version of this cake dates back to before cocoa powder was Dutch processed (which reduced the natural acids in the cocoa), so the acids in the buttermilk and vinegar reacted with the cocoa to give the cake a reddish hue. Over the years, red food coloring has become a standard ingredient to achieve the unique color and character.

MAKES 24 CUPCAKES

CUPCAKES

1¼ cups all-purpose flour

¾ cup sugar

½ teaspoon baking soda

½ teaspoon kosher salt

1 teaspoon unsweetened natural cocoa powder

¾ cup canola or safflower oil

½ cup buttermilk, room temperature

1 large egg, room temperature

1 tablespoon liquid red food coloring

½ teaspoon distilled white vinegar

¾ teaspoon vanilla extract

FROSTING

½ pound cream cheese, at room temperature

4 tablespoons unsalted butter, at room temperature

1⅓ cups powdered sugar

1 teaspoon vanilla extract

Toasted pecan pieces (optional)

Toasted shredded coconut (optional)

Preheat the oven to 350°F. Line 24 mini muffin-tin cups with paper liners.

To make the cupcakes, sift together the flour, sugar, baking soda, salt, and cocoa powder into the bowl of a stand mixer fitted with paddle attachment. In a separate bowl, whisk together the oil, buttermilk, egg, food coloring, vinegar, and vanilla. Add half of the wet ingredients to the dry ingredients and mix on low speed just until a paste forms, stopping to scrape down the sides and along the bottom of the bowl as needed with a rubber spatula. Add the remaining wet ingredients and mix until smooth. Do not overmix the batter or the cupcakes will be tough.

Fill the prepared muffin cups two-thirds full with the batter. Bake for 15 to 20 minutes, or until a toothpick inserted into the center of a cupcake comes out clean. Let cool completely in the pan on a wire rack, then remove from the pan.

To make the frosting, in the stand mixer fitted with the paddle attachment, beat the cream cheese on low speed until smooth. Do not whip! Add the butter and mix until incorporated. Use the rubber spatula to scrape down the sides and along the bottom of the bowl to check for lumps. Sift in the powdered sugar and mix on low speed until smooth. Add vanilla and mix until combined.

Spoon the frosting into a pastry bag fitted with a ¼-inch star tip and pipe a rosette onto the top of each cooled cupcake. Sprinkle with the pecans and coconut. Serve right away. They will keep for a day in an airtight container.

Chocolate
BLACKOUT CAKE

This cake, which Sarah Schafer offered up on the opening menu at Anchor and Hope, is a child's dream. Rich devil's food layered with chocolate pudding icing and topped with pistachio brittle for a sweet, salty crunch. What I mean to say is that this is a cake for children of all ages.

YIELD 16 SLICES

10 ounces (1¼ sticks) unsalted butter, plus more for pan

1⅔ cups all-purpose flour

2 tablespoons baking powder

½ teaspoon baking soda

½ teaspoon salt

1¾ cups unsweetened dark cocoa powder

1 cup brewed coffee

1 cup buttermilk

1 cup firmly packed golden brown sugar

1 cup granulated sugar

2 large eggs

1 teaspoon vanilla extract

CHOCOLATE ICING

8 ounces bittersweet chocolate (62 percent cacao), chopped

1¼ cups granulated sugar

3 tablspoon cornstarch

½ teaspoon salt

2 cups half-and-half

1 cup whole milk

½ teaspoon vanilla extract

PISTACHIO BRITTLE

¾ cup powdered sugar

½ cup (¼ pound) unsalted butter

2 tablespoons light corn syrup

1½ teaspoon powdered pectin

1 cup chopped pistachios

Sea salt

Preheat the oven to 350°F. Butter a 1-inch deep 13 by 18-inch sheet pan, then line with parchment paper.

TO MAKE THE CAKE, in a large bowl, sift together the flour, baking powder, baking soda, and salt until combined. In a saucepan, melt the butter over medium heat. Stir in the cocoa powder and cook stirring, for about 1 minute, or until fragrant. Transfer to a large bowl, add the coffee, buttermilk, and both sugars, and whisk until the sugars are dissolved. Whisk in the eggs and vanilla, and then slowly whisk in the flour mixture.

Pour the batter into the prepared pan. Bake for 20 to 25 minutes, or until a toothpick inserted into the center comes out clean. Let the cake cool completely in the pan on a wire rack.

TO MAKE THE ICING, place the chocolate in a large heatproof bowl. In a large saucepan, whisk together the granulated sugar, cornstarch, salt, half-and-half, and milk. Place over medium heat and heat, whisking constantly, until the mixture comes to a full boil. (It is important to continue to stir until the boil is reached or the cornstarch may burn. Remove from the heat, pour over the chocolate, and whisk constantly until the chocolate melts. Stir in the vanilla. Cover the bowl with plastic wrap, pressing it directly onto the surface of the frosting, and refrigerate for at least 4 hours, or until cold.

TO MAKE THE BRITTLE, preheat the oven to 350°F. Line a sheet pan with a silicone baking mat.

In a saucepan, combine the powdered sugar, butter, corn syrup, and pectin and bring to a full boil over medium heat, stirring occasionally as it comes to the full boil. Remove from the heat and immediately stir in the pistachios. Pour the mixture out onto the prepared sheet pan. Using a heat-resistant rubber spatula, spread into an even layer.

Bake for 5 to 7 minutes, or until golden brown. Remove from the oven and sprinkle immediately with a light dusting of sea salt. Let cool completely on a wire rack, then remove from the pan and, with a rolling pin, break up into small, rough chunks

TO ASSEMBLE THE CAKE, select a mold. We use a 4^1/$_2$ by 11-inch terrine, but you can also use a large loaf pan. Line the mold with plastic wrap, allowing it to overhang the edges by a few inches. Using a serrated knife, cut the cake into layers to fit your mold. You should be able to make 3 or 4 layers, depending on how high your cake is and the height of your mold. Place a cake layer in the bottom of the mold, and spread it with a thick layer of the icing. Repeat with another layer of the cake and spread it with icing until the mold is full, ending with a cake layer. Cover the top of the mold with the plastic-wrap overhang. Refrigerate for 3 to 4 hours.

TO UNMOLD THE CAKE, invert onto a serving platter, lift off the mold and peel away the wrap. Cover the top and sides with the remaining icing. Scatter the brittle evenly over the top. Slice and serve.

Peach-Blueberry— Brown Butter CRISP

The secret to creating the delicious brown butter for this peach-blueberry crisp is to brown it slowly so the milk solids toast to a lovely hazelnut brown. So be sure to keep a watchful eye as the butter can go from that nutty brown to black in a wink. And nobody wants a Black Butter Crisp.

SERVES 3 TO 10

6 to 8 peaches, halved, pitted, and sliced

1 pint blueberries

^{1}/$_4$ cup sugar

1 tablespoon tapioca flour

1^1/$_2$ tablespoons freshly squeezed lemon juice

TOPPING

1 cup (^{1}/$_2$ pound) unsalted butter

^{1}/$_4$ vanilla bean, split lengthwise

1^1/$_4$ cups all-purpose flour

1^1/$_4$ cups yellow cornmeal

^{3}/$_4$ cup coarsely ground toasted almonds

^{3}/$_4$ cup firmly packed dark brown sugar

^{1}/$_4$ cup granulated sugar

^{1}/$_2$ teaspoon ground cinnamon

^{1}/$_4$ teaspoon freshly grated nutmeg

Vanilla ice cream, for serving

PREHEAT the oven to 325°F. Have ready a 2-quart baking dish.

In a bowl, combine the peaches, blueberries, sugar, tapioca flour, and lemon juice and stir gently to combine thoroughly.

TO MAKE THE TOPPING, in a small saucepan, melt half of the butter with the vanilla bean over medium heat for 8 to 10 minutes, or until the butter is browned and has a nutty aroma. Remove and discard the vanilla bean and set the butter aside to cool.

In a second small saucepan, heat the remaining butter over low heat just until melted, then set aside to cool.

While the butters are cooling, in a bowl, stir together the flour, cornmeal, almonds, both sugars, cinnamon, and nutmeg.

When the butters have cooled, drizzle both of them over the flour mixture, then toss lightly with a wooden spoon, being careful not to overmix. You want to have small clumps.

Distribute the peach and blueberry mixture evenly on the bottom the baking dish. Spoon the topping evenly over the top. Bake for 35 to 45 minutes, or until the fruit is bubbling along the sides of the dish and topping is browned. Remove from the oven and let cool for about 10 minutes.

To serve, spoon the crisp onto individual plates and top with the ice cream.

chapter **BASICS** nine

A friend OF MINE OFTEN SAYS, "If you've got a good thing, stick with it." Below you'll find a few good things, recipes for ingredients and preparations that we used more than once while compiling this cookbook. Many of them are basics, stocks for example, or mayonnaise, while others, like the Harissa Vinaigrette or those buttermilk biscuits, are too good to use in just one dish. And it's good to know how to cook a lobster, don't you think?

IN A PROFESSIONAL KITCHEN, your basic ingredients are always at the ready—the *mise en place*, everything in its place. While I don't expect the home cook to have everything in place, it's nice if you can get *certains en place*, a term I just made up to mean "some in place." The stocks, the spice mix, the barbecue sauce, the clarified butter, these are things will keep for long periods and are great to prepare in advance so that they will be on hand when inspiration strikes. Get to work.

STOCKS

In the kitchen, good stock is one of the most important ingredients at your disposal. Although when a stock is called for in the pages of this, or any other, cookbook you can use one from the soup aisle at your grocery store, I don't recommend it. There are many reasons for this, but chief among them is salt. You'll note that in the three recipes below none is used. That way when you're making a dish that uses a stock you are in complete control of the seasoning. So be warned, if you have to use a commercial broth or stock, first make sure it's low sodium, and second be mindful of the amount of salt a recipe calls for directly and act accordingly, adjusting the amounts to compensate for the salt you're putting in with the store-bought stock (like I said, taste your food). The best way to avoid this possible pitfall is to make your own. Take a free day, buy a gang of vegetables and chicken bones, or shrimp, cook up some stock and tuck it away in your freezer. It will keep for months.

4 QUARTS

Chicken Stock

4½ pounds chicken bones (including wings and backs)

8 quarts water

1 leek, sliced

1 yellow onion, coarsely chopped

2 carrots, sliced

2 celery stalks, sliced

1 bay leaf

1 teaspoon black peppercorns

6 to 8 parsley stems

A few sprigs of thyme

PLACE THE BONES in a large stock pot, cover with the 8 quarts of water and bring to a boil over high heat. Then lower to a simmer and skim off any fat and foam that has accumulated on the surface. Add the remaining ingredients and simmer, uncovered for 2 hours, skimming scum off of the surface as necessary. Pour the stock through a fine mesh strainer to remove all solids. The stock will keep refrigerated for a week, or freeze for up to 3 months.

Shrimp Stock

MAKES ABOUT 5 CUPS

2 pounds large shrimp, preferably with heads intact

1 large carrot, sliced

1 celery stalk, sliced

¼ fresh fennel bulb, sliced

1 medium yellow onion, chopped

2 cloves garlic, peeled and crushed

1 bay leaf

1 teaspoon whole black peppercorns

2 tablespoons tomato paste

1 cup wine

10 cups water

PEEL THE SHRIMP. Reserve the shrimp meats for another use. Heat the olive oil over high heat in a stock pot. Add the shrimp shells and heads (they contain all the fat, which will impart a rich flavor to the stock) and toast them by drying out their moisture until they begin to crisp, about 8 to 10 minutes, stirring occasionally. Add the vegetables, bay leaf, peppercorns, and tomato paste and cook for a minute or two until the vegetables start to soften. Next, add the wine, stirring and scraping to deglaze the pot, and cook for 2 more minutes.

Add the water, raise the heat, and bring to a low boil, then lower to a simmer until reduced by half, about 45 minutes, skimming the surface as necessary. Remove from the heat and pour through a fine-mesh strainer into a clean container. Use immediately, or cover and store in the refrigerator for up to 3 days, or freeze for up to 2 months.

MAYONNAISE

Once you use your own homemade mayonnaise in dressings and on sandwiches, well, I doubt you'll go back to jarred. Also, the phrase "Hold the mayo" will become completely foreign.

1 whole egg, at room temperature

2 large egg yolks, at room temperature

4 teaspoons freshly squeezed lemon juice

2 teaspoons champagne vinegar

1 teaspoon Dijon mustard

2 teaspoons salt

2 cups canola oil

IN A FOOD PROCESSOR, combine the whole egg, egg yolks, lemon juice, vinegar, mustard, and salt and process for 30 seconds. With the machine running, add the oil in a slow, steady stream, processing until emulsified. Use immediately, or cover and refrigerate. It will keep for up to 3 days.

HARISSA VINAIGRETTE

Traditional *harissa* is a thick and pungent paste of chiles and garlic seasoned with coriander and cumin. It is wonderfully versatile, good in stews and sauces, as a spread for sandwiches, or as a tasty dip for a plate of crudités. You'll find it here spicing up a salad of haricots verts and *serrano* ham (page 45), and adding a jolt to our falafel sandwich (page 100). Our *harissa* features all of the flavors of the classic, but we present it in a more refined way: to spice up a vinaigrette. We use freshly roasted bell pepper and jalapeño chile instead of dried chiles, and we scale back the heat a bit. If you want a more fiery mix, double the amount of chile, or add a hot chile of your choice.

Scant ½ teaspoon coriander seeds

Scant ½ teaspoon cumin seeds

Scant ½ teaspoon fennel seeds

1 red bell pepper

1 small jalapeño chile

Olive oil, for drizzling

1 clove garlic, chopped

3 tablespoons sherry vinegar

1 teaspoons kosher salt

¼ cup canola oil

¼ cup extra-virgin olive oil

IN A SMALL FRYING PAN, toast the coriander, cumin, and fennel seeds over medium heat, shaking the pan often to avoid scorching, for 2 to 3 minutes, or until fragrant and just turning color. Let cool completely, then grind in a spice grinder or in a mortar with a pestle to a medium-fine grind. Set aside.

Place the bell pepper and chile on a small sheet pan, drizzle with a little olive oil, and toss to coat lightly. Place in a 350°F oven and roast for about 30 to 40 minutes, or until the skins blacken and blister and the flesh softens. Transfer to a bowl, cover with plastic wrap, and let stand for 10 minutes. Remove from the bowl and let cool to room temperature. Peel the pepper and chile, discard the seeds, and coarsely chop.

In a blender, combine the chopped pepper and chile, garlic, vinegar, spice mixture, and salt and process until smooth. With the blender on low speed, add the canola oil and then the olive oil in a slow, steady stream, processing until emulsified. Set aside.

COUNTRY BISCUITS

The secret to making the biscuits is to have both the butter and the dough very cold. That way, the heat from your hands won't activate the gluten and you will get a nice, flaky biscuit. This method will give you a biscuit with a texture that is perfect for the ham and pepper jelly on page 65 or the fried chicken breast sandwich on page 117.

MAKES 15 BISCUITS

4 cups all-purpose flour

1¹⁄₂ tablespoons baking powder

1 teaspoon baking soda

2 tablespoons sugar

1 tablespoon salt

¹⁄₂ pound, plus ¹⁄₂ stick butter, frozen, cut into ¹⁄₂-inch cubes

1 cup buttermilk

YOU CAN MAKE THE BISCUIT DOUGH in a stand mixer or by hand. To use the mixer, fit it with the paddle attachment, then whisk together the flour, baking powder, and salt in the bowl. Scatter the butter over the top. On low speed, beat until the butter is about the size of peas. Add the buttermilk and continue to beat until the dough begins to come together. Stop the mixer and scrape down the sides of the bowl and incorporate the dry crumbs at the bottom of the bowl. Then continue to beat until combined and the dough comes together.

To mix by hand, in a bowl, whisk together the dry ingredients. Scatter the butter over the top and, using a pastry blender or 2 knives, cut the butter into the flour mixture until the butter is the size of peas. Add the buttermilk and mix with a wooden spoon until combined and the dough comes together.

Turn the dough out onto a lightly floured work surface. Fold it over onto itself a few times, patting it down after each fold. The dough should be soft and cohesive. Roll out the dough about 1 inch thick and transfer to a sheet pan. Refrigerate for at least 30 minutes or up to a day. (If you need to speed the process, slip the pan into the freezer for 15 minutes.)

Line a sheet pan with parchment paper. Clean the work surface and lightly flour it again. Reroll the dough into a round about 1 inch thick. Shore up edges of the round with your hands as needed to ensure the dough is of uniform thickness. Using a 2-inch round biscuit or cookie cutter, and pushing straight down, cut out as many biscuits as possible. You should have about 15 biscuits. Arrange the biscuits on the prepared sheet pan and place the pan in the refrigerator for 15 minutes. Meanwhile, preheat the oven to 400°F.

Bake the biscuits for about 25 minutes, or until lightly browned on top and baked through.

Town Hall
SPICE MIXTURE

Many chefs have a signature spice mix, a blend that is a kind of trademark. Paul Prudhomme had his spice mixture (now on grocery shelves across the country); and at the Four Seasons, Seppi Renggli's featured many aromatics like mace and star anise, nice complements to fish. This is a mixture I've come up with. You'll note that the main ingredient is cayenne, giving dishes an added jolt of heat, and reflecting what I like to do at Town Hall. But don't feel bound by this mixture, play with the proportions. Consider this Town Hall Spice Mixture a starting point for your own.

MAKES A SCANT ⅓ CUP

2 tablespoons cayenne pepper

1½ teaspoons paprika

1 teaspoon salt

1 teaspoon white pepper

1 teaspoon black pepper

1 teaspoon onion powder

1 teaspoon garlic powder

½ teaspoon dried thyme

½ teaspoon dried oregano

½ teaspoon ground cumin

¼ teaspoon ground coriander

¼ teaspoon dry mustard

⅛ teaspoon celery salt

MIX TOGETHER all the ingredients until well combined. Store in an airtight container in a cool cupboard. The mixture will keep for up to 6 months.

Spicy Bourbon
BARBECUE SAUCE

For smoke flavoring, I like to go to the source. No liquid smoke here. A great way to make this sauce is, if you have room, to put the ketchup in the smoker along with your ribs or pork shoulder (or whatever you happen to be cooking), for the first two hours of a long smoke. Put a drip pan under the meat and substitute a tablespoon of the drippings for the bacon fat below, which adds a nice little extra something.

MAKES 1½ QUARTS

2 (24-ounce) bottles ketchup

2 or 3 handfuls hickory chips, soaked

⅔ cup bourbon

⅔ cup Dijon mustard

⅔ cup dark molasses

½ cup water

⅓ cup Tabasco sauce

¼ cup firmly packed golden brown sugar

2½ tablespoons Worcestershire sauce

4 teaspoons onion powder

4 teaspoons garlic powder

1 tablespoon rendered bacon fat

1 tablespoon salt

PREPARE A BARREL SMOKER with an offset firebox according to the directions on page 126 (or adapt your charcoal or gas grill). You want the temperature to be between 225° and 250°F. Place the ketchup in a large metal bowl, put the bowl in the smoker, add handful the soaked hickory chips to the coals, and smoke for 2 hours, stirring every 30 minutes. Be mindful of the temperature inside the smoker, adding charcoal as needed to keep it in the 225 and 250°F. Also, add more soaked hickory chips as needed to keep the smoke flowing.

continued

When the ketchup has finished smoking, transfer it to a large pot. Add the bourbon, mustard, molasses, water, Tabasco sauce, brown sugar, Worcestershire sauce, onion powder, garlic powder, bacon fat (or drippings), and salt and stir well to combine. Place over low heat and cook, stirring occasionally, for about 30 minutes, or until the sugar has dissolved and the sauce has thickened and darkened slightly.

Use immediately, or let cool, cover, and refrigerate. It will keep for up to 2 weeks.

PRESERVED LEMONS

Plan ahead if you want to use your own preserved lemons with the Sautéed Scallops with Spiced Couscous (page 199). They take three weeks. Worth the wait.

8 to 10 lemons (Meyers are especially fine preserved)

2 to 3 cups kosher salt

6 star anise pods

2 cinnamon sticks

Freshly squeezed lemon juice as needed

CUT A THIN SLICE OFF one end of each lemon. Then make 2 evenly spaced cuts along the length of each lemon, cutting only three-fourths of the way through so that the lemon is divided into quarters and the quarters are still attached at the uncut end. Pull the sections apart to expose the flesh, and pack each lemon with the salt.

Toss 3 star anise pods and 1 cinnamon stick into a sterilized quart jar, then begin packing the salted lemons tightly into the jar. When you have packed in half of the lemons, add the remaining star anise pods and cinnamon stick, and then add the remaining lemons. As you pack in the lemons, they will release their juice. When all of the lemons are in the jar, the lemons should be covered with juice. If not, add lemon juice as need to cover.

Seal the jar and store at room temperature in a cupboard. Shake the jar every few days, and add more lemon juice as needed to cover. The lemons will be soft and ready to use in 3 to 4 weeks.

To prepare the lemons for the Sautéed Scallops with Spiced Couscous , remove them from the jar, rinse off the salt with cold water, and then remove and discard the pulp and finely dice the peel.

HOW TO PEEL *and* SEED
TOMATOES

BRING A POT of water to boil. Meanwhile, cut the stem end out of each tomato, and score the blossom end with an X. Plunge the tomatoes, a few at a time, into the boiling water and leave for 1 minute. Using a slotted spoon, transfer them to a bowl of cold water. Peel them and then let them sit in the cold water for a few minutes. Cut each tomato in half and scrape out and discard the seeds, then cut as directed in individual recipes.

HOW TO MAKE
CLARIFIED BUTTER

1 cup butter

CLARIFY at least 1 cup ($1/2$ pound) butter for the best results. Place the butter in a small pot or frying pan over low heat. Allow the butter to melt slowly, and skim any foam that forms on the surface. The milk solids will sink to the bottom of the pot. Remove the pan from the heat and carefully pour off the golden, clear liquid into a clean container, leaving the milk solids behind in the pan, then discard the solids. Use immediately, or cool, cover, and refrigerate. It will keep for about 2 months; 1 cup unsalted butter yields roughly $3/4$ cup of clarified butter.

HOW TO COOK *and* CLEAN
A LOBSTER

¼ cup sea salt

2 bay leaves

1 tablespoon black peppercorns

2 lemons

3 lobsters

First fill the pot with water, add the salt, bay leaves, and peppercorns. Slice the lemons in half, squeeze the juice into the pot, and toss in the lemon halves. Bring to a boil over high heat. Cut the rubber bands off of the claws of each lobster (be careful!) and plunge the lobster head first into the boiling water. Cover and boil for 12 to 15 minutes, until the shells are bright red and the tail is curled. Remove the lobsters with tongs and allow to cool enough to handle.

TO CLEAN, first pull off the claws and discard the small pincer. Strike the claw with a mallet or nutcracker and remove the meat. It should come out in one piece. Set aside. Next, take the knuckles, and, using kitchen shears, snip along their length and then pry open and extract the meat (you can also use a nutcracker). Separate the tail from the head and discard and tomalley or roe. Bend the flipper back and gently separate it from the tail. Then , using a finger, gently push the meat from opening where the flipper was removed. It should come out easily. If not, make a snip along the underside of the tail with kitchen shears to help things along. When freed, pull off the top, and remove the black digestive vein and discard. Finally, you can remove any meat in the body using a seafood pick.

Freeze the shells for stock.

ACKNOWLEDGMENTS

Although credited to "mitchell rosenthal," this is not just my book. *Cooking My Way Back Home* is a collaborative effort, and I'd like to thank some of the many people who made it possible.

First, to my partners Doug Washington and Steven Rosenthal. Although the text here is in my voice, and tells my story, that story just couldn't be told without Steven and Doug. Our lives in the restaurant business have been intertwined for more than twenty years. We have a history, the three of us, the dynamics of which play out as a sort of marriage. A good one, too. And the fruit of that marriage is four successful restaurants. The process of opening a restaurant is an amazing thing; attending to every detail, nursing it along like a new baby, and proudly watching it grow. There is no one I trust more than these two. Putting this book together required taking a lot of time off, but I never needed to worry. I knew that Steven and Doug were taking care of everything. That's what a good marriage is all about, supporting each other. Now, to send them some flowers.

Doing a book was a new experience for me, and at times a difficult one. However, it could have been worse. Thank goodness for my editor, Jenny Wapner, and the rest of the staff at Ten Speed Press, who gently helped to navigate us through the process and steer us safely into port.

My deep appreciation goes to Kitty Cowles, without whom this book wouldn't be in your hands. Her initial insistence ("Mitch, you *have* to do a book . . . "), as well as the enthusiasm, guidance and critiques that followed were invaluable.

When Kitty put me in the mind of doing this book, my first thought for a writer was my brother-in-law, Jon Pult. He grew up in the Bay Area, but has lived down in New Orleans for more than twenty years. Except, that is, for a six month spell when he lived with us. That half-year in 2002 coincided with the initial phases of our work on Town Hall, and Jonny and I spent many hours talking about my vision for the restaurant. As a result, he has a pretty good understanding of what I'm about and was a natural choice to help me write this book. He also served as a pretty decent sounding board in helping me to find its shape. And while his vocabulary is much more extensive than my own (I studied photography after all, and have never used the word "harbinger"), with some effort he was able to capture my voice and help me to articulate my ideas.

While Jon helped me with the words, it was Paige Green who brought those words to life through her brilliant and beautiful photography. Every photograph in this book—the restaurant shots, the plated food, me in the kitchen, *everything*—was shot 'au natural,' with ambient light. Those artistic choices really helped shape the overall tone of the book. Her photos are real. Paige would let me plate a dish to my exacting specifications. She'd photograph it, then turn to her trusty stylist Bridget Farmer for a whispered consultation. They'd proceed to muss up the plate a bit, but by design, and photograph it again. I'll admit, most of the photos here are that second shot. I could go on lauding Paige and Bridget, but just look at the photos. They speak for them better than I can.

Hearty thanks and utmost appreciation goes to the chefs at our restaurants—Bob Leva at Salt House, Eric Markoff at Anchor, Vernon Morales at Town Hall, and Sarah Schafer up in Portland at Irving Street Kitchen— for sharing their food and ideas with me. Their contributions have made this a better and more interesting cookbook than I could have offered alone. And thanks, too, to the staff at the restaurants, the managers and waiters, barkeeps and cooks, all of whom make going to work seem, well, like not going to work.

Finally, it seems to me that every large and worthwhile undertaking needs that certain someone, an individual who serves as a kind of force, guiding the thing, whatever it may be, to completion. In a kitchen, the chef plays that role, making sure everyone works together to create that perfect plate of food. In the case of this book, it was my wife Mary Pult. The testing for each and every recipe presented here was done at home, in our small kitchen in Mill Valley. Throughout that process Mary, an acclaimed chef in her own right, liked to refer to herself as "head tester," but she is so much more. In creating this cookbook hundreds of decisions, both large and small, were made, from the order of the recipes, to the title. Mary was part of them all.

We spent countless days and nights cooking; testing and re-testing, making sure the recipes were just right. All the while we were dealing with the busy and varied lives of our two young kids, Athena and Eli, not to mention trying to get our house guest, Mary's little brother Jonny, to straighten his room, turn off the internet, and get back to work. What I mean to say is that sometimes it was complicated, you know, dealing with the book and the kids and all of the normal everyday things. But she handled it all like a champion. I don't really know how to thank her for helping me get this done, but now that it finally is, I'll have a lot more time to figure it out.

Thank you, Mary. 1,000,000 times. Love, Mitch.

INDEX

Published in the United States by Ten Speed Press,

an imprint of the Crown Publishing Group, a division of Random House, Inc., New York.

www.crownpublishing.com

www.tenspeed.com

Ten Speed Press and the Ten Speed Press colophon are registered trademarks of Random House, Inc.

Library of Congress Cataloging-in-Publication Data

Rosenthal, Mitchell, 1960-

Cooking my way back home : recipes from San Francisco's

Town Hall, Anchor & Hope, and Salt House / by Mitchell Rosenthal with Jon Pult;

photography by Paige Green.

p. cm.

Includes bibliographical references.

ISBN 978-1-58008-592-2

1. Cooking, American—California style. 2. Cooking, American—Southern style.

3. Town Hall (Restaurant : San Francisco, Calif.)

4. Anchor & Hope (Restaurant) 5. Salt House (Restaurant)

6. Cookbooks. I. Pult, Jon, 1966- II. Title.

TX715.2.C34R67 2011

641.59794—dc22

2011011631

Printed in China

Design by Toni Tajima

10 9 8 7 6 5 4 3 2 1

First Edition